The Destruction of Hitler's U-boats

The Destruction of Hitler's U-boats

The Epic Struggle Against Hitler's Wolfpacks

Jak P. Mallmann Showell

Frontline Books

First published in Great Britain in 2025 by
Frontline Books
An imprint of Pen & Sword Books Limited
Yorkshire – Philadelphia

ISBN 978 1 03612 753 4

A CIP catalogue record for this book is available from the British Library.

Typeset by Mac Style
Printed in the UK by CPI Group (UK) Ltd, Croydon, CR0 4YY.

MIX
Paper | Supporting responsible forestry
FSC® C013604
FSC www.fsc.org

The Publisher's authorised representative in the EU for product safety is Authorised Rep Compliance Ltd., Ground Floor, 71 Lower Baggot Street, Dublin D02 P593, Ireland.
www.arccompliance.com

For a complete list of Pen & Sword titles please contact

PEN & SWORD BOOKS LIMITED
47 Church Street, Barnsley, South Yorkshire, S70 2AS, England
E-mail: enquiries@pen-and-sword.co.uk
Website: www.pen-and-sword.co.uk
or
PEN AND SWORD BOOKS
1950 Lawrence Road, Havertown, PA 19083, USA
E-mail: uspen-and-sword@casematepublishers.com
Website: www.penandswordbooks.com

Contents

Erratum

Page 13. Top image: This shows the later conning tower design for accommodating heavier anti-aircraft guns with two 20mm twins on the upper platform. The single 37mm gun was often substituted with an automatic quadruple 20mm. At the front of the conning tower is a bulge holding a magnetic compass, which could be viewed by the helmsman in the central control room through an illuminated periscope. The conning tower was made from a type of bronze, so as not to interfere with the magnetic compass. The central control room, occupying a large part of the boat, also has several major diving tanks under the deck. The conning tower contained the commander's submerged attack position with the eye piece for the periscope with the small head lens. The eye piece for the sky or navigation periscope terminated in the central control room when raised. On the larger, ocean-going boats there was enough space in the conning tower to raise this periscope higher than in the smaller boats.

On U-boats photo opportunities occurred only when nothing much was going on and serious action pictures are rare. Life was rather boring for much of the time and flying the flag added considerable interest to mundane days.

Introduction

Many uncatalogued papers lie hidden in archives, libraries and other information centres, where they might never see the light of day unless someone stumbles upon them. This book is based on some of those abandoned papers, placed there for safe keeping. No one went looking for them: they were found accidentally while searching for something else. As a result, this book has become a patchwork without a beginning or an end, but with a few interesting snippets in the middle.

Some exciting reminiscences were rejected because they could not be authenticated. Sadly, a lot of eyewitness accounts and historic books, especially those written by the victors, are based on imagination, with an emphasis to make memories politically acceptable. Much of this book is different. It was written by those losers who survived the unnecessary vile killing spree, or holocaust, or genocide (call it what you want) of the Second World War.

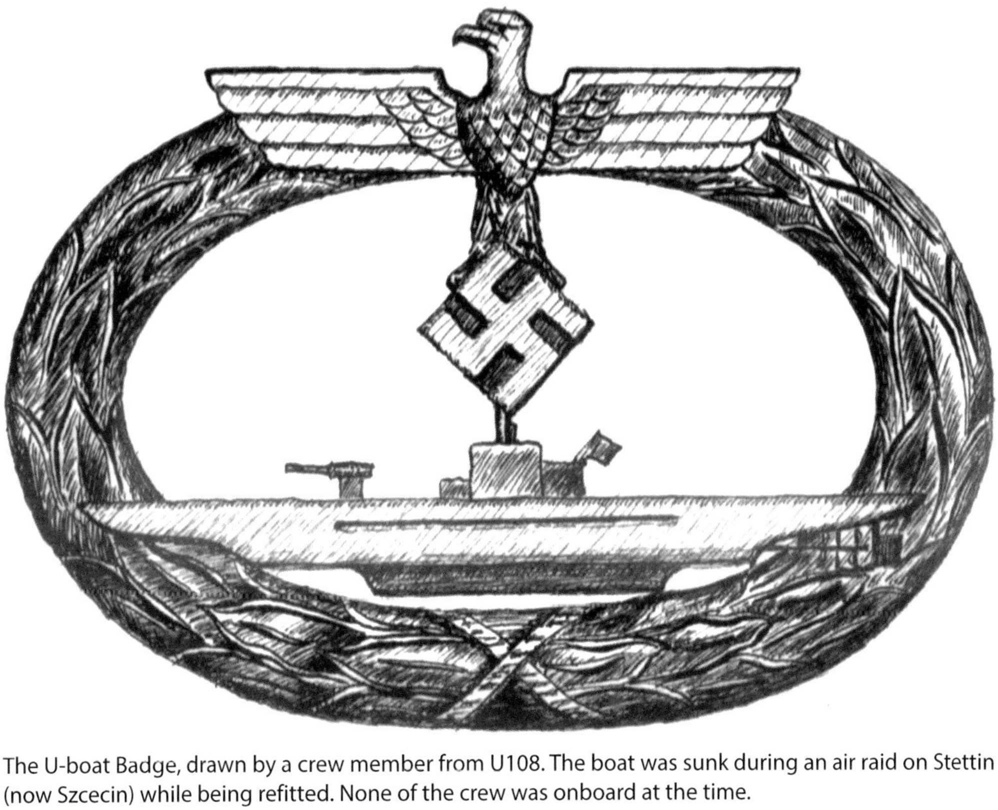

The U-boat Badge, drawn by a crew member from U108. The boat was sunk during an air raid on Stettin (now Szcecin) while being refitted. None of the crew was onboard at the time.

My own casual interest in U-boats was converted into serious research in 1968 by a strong urge to discover how and why my father had died with U377 more than two months before I was born in Hamburg (Germany) on 4 April 1944. My mother had tried before me but failed because too much information was still classified as secret. We were not allowed to know what went on during the war, why my father died or why our family was partly exterminated by western air forces. My own project into my father's death also had a precarious beginning due to the lack of information. Almost everything I wanted to know was still secret and it was not until 1984 that finding information was made easier for me after a meeting with Horst Bredow on the North Frisian Island of Sylt, where he had founded a new private U-boat archive. This was later renamed the U-boat Museum after it moved to Cuxhaven-Altenbruch. It can now be found on the Internet at www.dubm.de.

Horst Bredow, founder and director of the German U-boat Museum in Cuxhaven-Altenbruch, who collected many of the memories related in this book.

On the other side of the water, the Royal Navy Submarine Museum in Gosport, then under the leadership of Commander Richard Compton-Hall, with 'Professor' Gus Britton and Margaret Bidmead, was more than helpful. They also had piles of unusual information and many brilliantly helpful contacts. Later, when Bletchley Park opened, and was at first staffed by genuine codebreakers, this wonderful mine of information provided a mass of interesting material through John Gallehawk. Peter Tamm, whose collection was turned into the International Maritime Museum of Hamburg (Germany) also offered tremendous support. On the other side of the Atlantic there were a vast number of Americans who have helped over the years, too many to list them all. Copies of logbooks came from the National Archives and Records Administration in Washington DC, and I am most grateful for the help provided by the staff there. Dr Timothy Mulligan's friendly directions through some of the more difficult tangles in their vast collection got me off to an easier start.

Despite this help, there were still a good number of problems during those early days. Photocopiers, for example, existed but very few people could use them, and they were expensive. At first, Horst did not even have his own copier. Instead, he drove to a printing shop, usually carrying a wash-basket full of papers for copying. Photography was a problem as well. Very few people had both the cameras with their expensive accessories and the knowledge for such exacting work as copying old pictures. Modern cameras, as used by children these days, digital printing and computers did not appear until much later. At first, the costs of film, developing and printing were exasperatingly expensive. To make matters worse, many public libraries-cum-archives prohibited copying. Some of these establishments still imprison information to this day, allowing people to copy only by writing with a pencil on paper. The better archives, where reasonably charged photocopying was available, were still terribly expensive when one had to travel a long way and pay for a lot of copies. As a result, it was often possible to take away only essentials and now, looking back, one notices many details are missing. Title pages with the names of authors were often not copied because one saved money by writing such details in notebooks, and many of these have since disappeared or no longer make sense. Six house moves over the years did not help in preserving all of them.

My personal research received a terrific boost in 1997 when I gained more time to explore the world. The school where I was teaching science and computing closed and I was forced to take early retirement. This was the second time I had been made redundant by a school closure. The school in Shropshire where I had been teaching before this for fifteen years had also been closed, forcing major life changes. Just to complete the picture, I came to England in 1954 when my mother married a Londoner, and from then on, I was educated in this country.

Photographs used in this book are from the author's collection, from the German U-boat Museum in Cuxhaven-Altenbruch or from the Royal Navy Submarine Museum, unless otherwise indicated.

Most of the books used to help write this book have been mentioned in the text. A few exceedingly helpful books not so mentioned include: Paul Kemp, *U-boat Destroyed*

Karl Dönitz greeting an incoming crew. The U-boat Chief, who became the Supreme Commander-in-Chief of the German Navy in January 1943, was revered by his men, with many saying he always had a fitting word for everyone and would go to considerable lengths to discuss details with low-ranking sailors. Some commanders were moved to other jobs because of comments made by experienced petty officers. Note the man on the right and the third from the right do not have large collars or lapels on their jackets, indicating they were engineers.

(Arms & Armour Press, London, 1997). Since it was written, a lot of new information has been made available and some of this has been published in Axel Niestle's *German U-boat Losses during World War II* (Frontline Books, London, 2014). Paul Kemp used the Royal Navy's secret monthly anti-submarine reports to provide good, detailed information about those boats from which survivors were rescued. Another most useful book is Peter Sharpe's *U-boat Fact File* (Midland Publishing Limited, Leicester, 1998). Sadly, this easy-to-use reference book now needs urgent revision. David Balme, *Enigma: The Untold Story of the Secret Capture* (Whittles Publishing Ltd, 2016) is a most interesting recent edition. There is a lot of information on the publisher's website.

U-boat commander details come from Rainer Busch and Hans-Joachim Röll, *Der U-Boot-Krieg 1939–1945 – Die Deutschen U-Boot-Kommandanten* (Verlag E.S. Mittler & Sohn, Hamburg, Berlin and Bonn, 1996), translated into English as *U-boat Commanders* (Greenhill Publishing, London). Sadly, this English edition did not include the many corrections in the U-boat Museum's working copy, which was used for much of this book. The same authors have also produced another worthwhile volume for Verlag E.S. Mittler & Sohn entitled *Der U-Boot Krieg 1939-1945 – Deutsche U-Boot-Verluste von September 1939 bis Mai 1945*, which could also do with revision. The two-volume work by Kenneth Wynn, *U-boat Operations of the Second World War* (Chatham Publishing, London, 1997) provides a good overview.

Admiral Karl Dönitz with Kpt.z.S. Hans Rösing in the middle. The man on the right is a Maat or petty officer, as indicated by the gold braiding around his collar. His rank and trade badge combined with the chevron indicates he has the higher grade of Ober~torpedo~maat. Dönitz is holding his admiral's baton, which was stolen from him by the British Army after the war and was last known to be on display in the Castle Museum in Shrewsbury (England). Looting became a widespread activity for many Allied soldiers after the war.

Chapter 1

The U-boat War in a Nutshell

THE THREE MAIN TYPES OF ATTACK U-BOAT

For people new to the subject, Germany had three main attack U-boats: Types II, VII and IX. The Type II, a small coastal boat, had room for only three torpedo tubes but despite this a high proportion of them saw serious action. They were highly manoeuvrable and stood up exceptionally well to depth-charging, although their agility also made it difficult to keep them at periscope depth for submerged attacks. Inside they were terribly crowded, and they rolled with vigour. Even seasoned sailors, used to coping with heavy storms, found they were, once again, badly seasick inside them. About forty-four of the variations IIA, IIB, IIC and IID were in service.

The brunt of the conflict in the Atlantic was borne by the sea-going Type VII and the larger ocean-going variety, the Type IX. A modified version of the former, the Type VIIC, first launched during the summer of 1940 as *the* most advanced U-boat, became the largest submarine class ever built. Over 600 were commissioned, and the type was considered important enough for production to continue after it had become obsolete. Shortly after the war, Fregkpt. Günter Hessler, the Supreme Commander-in-Chief's son-in-law, wrote that 'this type proved itself to be very suitable for attacks against convoys'. He considered the larger Type IX to be a more conventional design and more difficult to handle, although it could carry more torpedoes and had a longer range. It also had two torpedo tubes in the stern while the Type VII had only one. About 165 Type IX variations were built, while another thirty or so had longer hulls to make them very-long-range submarines for journeys to the Far East. Before the war, the term 'long-range' meant operating as far as the eastern Mediterranean without sea-going support. One reason for their bigger size was to accommodate a flotilla leader with his staff, a doctor and additional radio facilities. Sailing as far as America was not within ordinary thought lines during those days, despite such journeys having been made during the First World War by specialized submarines.

A GLIMPSE AT THE BATTLE OF THE ATLANTIC

Author's note: Statistics are very variable, depending on how the figures are added up and which sources are used. The following is based on what appear to be reliable figures and should give a fair picture, although the details must still be treated as fluid and changeable.

* * *

The German U-boat Archive (now the U-boat Museum) concluded some 1,171 U-boats were commissioned during the Second World War era, which confirms Allied reports of 'thousands' of U-boats having been pitched against merchant shipping. It was not until 1968, when the first German edition of Professor Dr Jürgen Rohwer's book *Axis Submarine Successes of World War Two* was published, that it was possible to delve deeper into the goings-on of the war. (*A revised English edition was published in 1999 by Greenhill Books, London and Naval Institute Press, Annapolis, Maryland.*) Rohwer's incredible insight produced a totally different picture from what had been recorded so far. Instead of 'thousands' of U-boats, there were only a few, as follows:

Second World War:
25 U-boats attacked and at least damaged 20 or more ships
36 U-boats attacked and at least damaged 11 to 19 ships
70 U-boats attacked and at least damaged 6 to 10 ships
190 U-boats attacked and at least damaged 1 to 5 ships

This adds up to a total of 321 U-boats. A few more might be allowed for possible calculation errors, but this still leaves some 850 U-boats that never made contact with a target.

Many of the basic records have since been checked and modified by Axel Niestlé, Innes McCartney, Derek Waller, Paul Kemp, Peter Sharpe and others, who painstakingly combed through old records, making it possible to conclude 870 U-boats left for operational voyages and 550 of them never sank a ship. In other words, more than half of the U-boats

An early type of sea-going VIIB showing the net-cutter on the bows, the plain conning tower without wind or spray deflectors and the 20mm anti-aircraft gun on the main deck aft of the conning tower. The armament forward of the conning tower were quick firing deck guns, 105mm on the large ocean-going Types IX and 88mm on the medium sea-going Types VII. Small coastal boats were fitted with a 20mm gun mounted on a variety of different supports. (*Drawing: Elaine Womack from Antwerp, Ohio, USA*)

never fired a torpedo in anger. In addition, about 300 U-boats – which adds up to about a quarter of the fleet – were never used operationally. It is likely Britain and the United States were aware of the U-boats' poor performance and therefore never bombed the building yards nor the huge U-boat bunkers to make sure Germany continued to build a relatively ineffective weapon. The major U-boat sites were not seriously bombed until almost the end of the war, and not a single boat was destroyed or even badly damaged by bombs in the building yards until shortly before the end of the war. One wonders what might have happened had Germany abandoned U-boat construction in favour of something more effective, such as long-range heavy bomb-carrying aircraft. So, was the British Prime Minister Winston Churchill correct to say, after the war, that he had feared U-boats the most – or was he merely deliberately propagating propaganda?

The German U-boat Command recorded that some 3,500 ships were sunk by U-boats, but Jürgen Rohwer's figures add up to only 2,450, and the grand total of all shipping lost to all causes comes to about 2,775. This means that during the war Germany overestimated U-boat sinkings by about 30 per cent, or almost a third. These figures also illustrate one other significant misconception. Many U-boat men, including the German High Command, were under the impression that U-boats met so much opposition because British, and later American, forces were patrolling the entire Atlantic. Sadly for the Germans, Britain had increased its Intelligence staff considerably after the beginning of the war and could fairly accurately forecast the movements of the U-boat fleet. Therefore, it was possible to employ its limited forces in the most effective areas. From 1941 onwards this strategy was often highly successful, due to only a small number of astute men who kept tabs on what was happening at sea. The contribution made by these ingenious people has never been explained in detail and much information is still missing, making it a good subject for further study.

Almost 800 of the 2,450 ships mentioned above were sunk by just thirty U-boat commanders, while the total number of qualified commanders was more than 1,400. This means that 2 per cent of Germany's U-boat commanders were responsible for sinking almost 30 per cent of all Allied shipping. Eight of these commanders had joined the navy before 1927, nineteen joined between 1930 and 1934, and three belonged to the 1935 class. This is significant because 1935 was the year when Hitler repudiated the Dictate of Versailles and re-introduced national conscription, very much against the rules imposed by the victorious Allies at the end of the First World War. It was also the year in which the Third Reich started to create a submarine arm. The Dictate of Versailles, signed after the end of the First World War, did not allow Germany to build or own submarines. (To complete the picture, Hitler was made Chancellor of Germany on 30 January 1933.)

Chapter 2

Successes, Disappointments and Distorted History: An Insight into Germany's Options

Author's note: Warning! This chapter could seriously annoy people in the United Kingdom who hold conventional views, but the information is based on recorded facts, and it is necessary to know how the opposition looked upon events at the time.

THE OCCUPATION OF NORWAY AND DENMARK IN APRIL 1940

The British and French declaration of war against Germany on 3 September 1939 came as an incredible shock to many, except extremely rich and powerful members of the British War Lobby, who were eager to collect the profits from such an 'emergency'. On hearing the declaration of war, Grand Admiral Dr Erich Raeder, the Head of the German Navy, told his staff all the small navy could do was to show the world how to die honourably in a civilized manner. Then he ordered 'full engagement and die with dignity'. People in the naval base at Wilhelmshaven were among the first to do this when an air raid wiped out their lives the very next day. Despite the well-known propaganda poured out in the past, up until that time the German naval leaders had never considered another war against Great Britain. A mainly land-bound country in the middle of Europe, Germany had neither the hardware, nor the manpower nor the ability to tackle such a challenge. The bombing of England during the summer of 1940 came about with the hope of getting the British War Lobby to negotiate an end to the fighting through one of several international peace initiatives. Apparently, no one asked anyone to surrender but only to stop fighting for the benefit of everybody in all of Europe, and indeed for the whole world's sake, but profits for the rich were enormous and more important to them than the lives of the poor.

The fighting around Narvik was intense enough for Germany to have instituted a special award, the Narvik Shield, which was worn on the left sleeve.

'Germany invaded Poland' was not how the Germans saw this vital trigger event. It was not seen as an invasion but as an effort to liberate former countrymen from serious ill-treatment. Many people who had been German at the end of First World War vanished in concentration camps, human rights offences were rife and there were enough frontier incursions against Germany to be worrying. In places there were frightening foreign military build-ups by nations created after the end of the First World War and these even went against the rules dictated by the Allies at that time. Sadly, very few people in the West have any knowledge of what went on in those Eastern areas when the First World War came to an end. Even schoolchildren were prevented from learning the details by creating a trend where atlas publishers were put under pressure not to print political maps of Europe, and on no account to show the old pre-1918 national frontiers on highlighted maps. Even today one sees in many television quiz programmes how the media makes it necessary for contestants to know intricate details of the United States and its history, but with barely a mention of the difficulties the Allies created in Eastern Europe when Germany surrendered in 1918.

In 1939 the terrible British and French declaration of war once again cut almost all German overseas supply routes in one blow, and although we are often told Germany sank the first ship of the war, the British Royal Navy had been better prepared to have already laid its hands on several German merchant ships by the time Germany attacked its first target. Following the declaration of war, the only two remaining open sea routes for Germany were of vital importance because much of the country's industry depended on imports of iron ore from Sweden. The mine where this came from was only a short distance south of the Arctic Circle and totally landlocked, about halfway between the Atlantic and the Baltic Sea. The specially built Lapland Railway, which crosses the Arctic Circle, carried the iron ore either west to Narvik in northern Norway or east to Lulea in Sweden, on the cold northern shores of the Gulf of Bothnia, the northern arm of the Baltic. The sea there froze solid for about three months each year, making it impossible for ships to reach the port. Narvik, although further north, remained ice free all year round due to the 'warm' Gulf Stream. Ships therefore continued to sail through Norwegian territorial waters carrying the valuable ore to Germany and to many other customers such as Great Britain, France, the United States and other countries. Narvik was of vital importance because it loaded two-thirds of all Germany's essential iron ore imports, without which Germany could not have survived, even in times of peace.

Without delving too deeply into the political spheres, one needs to consider how Britain's history of foreign bargaining was far superior to Germany's, although several negotiators stated it was not the skill of the British officials but the size of their guns which was the decisive factor in discussions. Despite their inferiority in this field, the German government did give Norway an assurance on the day before war was declared that, whatever happened, Norwegian neutrality would be fully recognized by the Third Reich. On 10 October 1939, when Grand Admiral Erich Raeder raised this Norwegian neutrality conundrum for the first time with Hitler, he was told this question had so far not even featured in the government's thinking. This early discussion with Hitler came about because the Chief of Naval Intelligence, Admiral Wilhelm Canaris, told Raeder there were indications of serious activity aimed at establishing British bases in Norway,

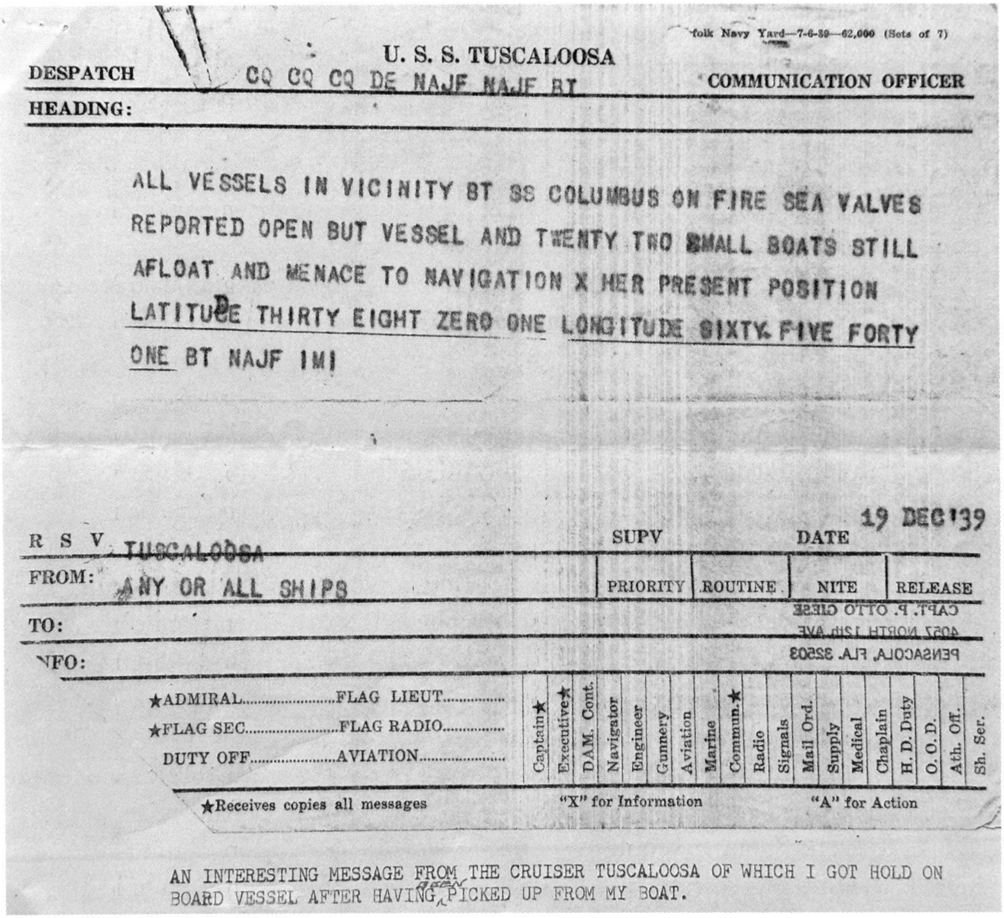

folk Navy Yard—7-6-39—62,000 (Sets of 7)

U. S. S. TUSCALOOSA

DESPATCH CQ CQ CQ DE NAJF NAJF BT COMMUNICATION OFFICER

HEADING:

ALL VESSELS IN VICINITY BT SS COLUMBUS ON FIRE SEA VALVES REPORTED OPEN BUT VESSEL AND TWENTY TWO SMALL BOATS STILL AFLOAT AND MENACE TO NAVIGATION X HER PRESENT POSITION LATITUDE THIRTY EIGHT ZERO ONE LONGITUDE SIXTY FIVE FORTY ONE BT NAJF IMI

R S V TUSCALOOSA SUPV DATE 19 DEC '39

FROM: ANY OR ALL SHIPS PRIORITY ROUTINE NITE RELEASE

TO:

INFO:

★ADMIRAL FLAG LIEUT
★FLAG SEC FLAG RADIO
DUTY OFF AVIATION

Captain★ Executive★ DAM. Cont. Navigator Engineer Gunnery Aviation Marine Commun.★ Radio Signals Mail Ord. Supply Medical Chaplain H. D. Duty O.O.D. Ath. Off. Sh. Ser.

★Receives copies all messages "X" for Information "A" for Action

AN INTERESTING MESSAGE FROM THE CRUISER TUSCALOOSA OF WHICH I GOT HOLD ON BOARD VESSEL AFTER HAVING (been) PICKED UP FROM MY BOAT.

A message stolen from the radio room of USS *Tuscaloosa* by Otto Giese as a souvenir of America's warped neutrality. Otto Giese was an officer aboard the German passenger liner *Columbus* when it tried a home run from Mexico in December 1939. He listened in to the shadowing 'neutral' cruiser sending position reports, calling-in the British destroyer HMS *Hyperion*. In the end, the Germans set their ship on fire rather than surrender it to the Royal Navy. The crew was saved, ending up in American internment rather than going as prisoners of war to Britain. A few men escaped from the USA to make their way back to Germany. Otto Giese eventually came home from the Far East aboard the blockade breaker *Anneliese Essberger* and subsequently served in U-boats. His knowledge of far-off waters was required by the new very-long-range boats sailing into the Indian Ocean. After the war he became an American citizen with a son in the US Air Force. (*Photos: Otto Giese*)

obviously with a view to cutting off all German sea routes. Canaris did not have to tell Raeder this was not just a merchant marine problem because such a move would also make it exceedingly difficult, if not impossible, for the German Navy to put to sea. Germany felt there would be serious repercussions from Russia if Norway were to be occupied by German forces, and it is important to know the First World War was won not by guns on the battlefields but by Britain's sea blockade preventing essential imports from feeding Germany's industrialized population.

Considerations of Norwegian neutrality were thrown into a new light on 30 November 1939 when Russia invaded Finland. This meant there was now a possibility of Britain ignoring both Norwegian and Swedish neutrality to use these countries as a through-route for sending supporting troops to Finland. No one in Germany knew which side they would support. It is more important to know that in September 1939 Russian military forces moved into Poland with Germany, but the British declaration of war was made against Germany but not against Russia. Apparently, both Norway and Sweden refused a British request for its troops to pass through their countries and this northern neutrality was bubbling furiously in both Britain and in Germany when Winston Churchill, then the First Lord of the Admiralty in London, invited the northern neutral countries to join Britain in its war against Germany. His request was rejected almost instantly while neutrality was again emphasized with the desire not to become involved in another war that could easily escalate into a global conflict.

The question of Norwegian neutrality was given a severe jolt only five weeks later when the British destroyer HMS *Cossack* (Captain Philip Vian) sailed into Norwegian territorial waters to attack the German supply ship *Altmark*, which was masquerading as a merchant freighter. The ship was accepted as such by Norwegian forces and given an official naval escort through territorial waters from the north to where it could run through the Baltic to Germany without easy British interference. None of the escorting Norwegian vessels made any attempt to intervene in this blatant violation of their neutrality, suggesting Norwegian 'neutrality' was weighted very much in favour of the British, and this led to Hitler ordering the highly successful occupation of the Norwegian coast with all the German armed forces, army, Luftwaffe and navy, participating in the operation. The navy was too small to have achieved this on its own.

Denmark, also a neutral country, was occupied at the same time to prevent Britain using it to create bases from which to attack Germany. One of the main impetuses here was the Luftwaffe claiming it needed the north Danish airfields for refuelling to maintain a presence in Norway. Flying so far was indeed a serious problem in those days and some U-boats were especially modified to carry highly volatile aviation fuel to north Norway.

The bitter fighting in Norway and the German occupation of this neutral country have been interpreted by historians as a German bid for world domination, but in reality, it was an effort to maintain the only two supply routes for bringing essential iron ore into its industrial heartland. Germany could not have continued to fight if it did not have access to this essential commodity. Of course, this situation changed very rapidly just over a year later, on 22 June 1941, when Germany discovered Russian forces were preparing for an

Grand Admiral Dr Erich Raeder, Supreme Commander-in-Chief of the German Navy from 1928 until January 1943, when he was succeeded by the U-boat Chief, Karl Dönitz. Raeder's predecessors served in this top position for about four years each and it was strange the navy has not created an experienced deputy to take over this top position.

invasion of Western Europe. Britain was, of course, aware of this and was already planning to send Arctic convoys with war goods to northern Russian ports in support of this move, but it came as a horrible surprise to the Germans. The non-aggression pact between Germany and Russia, signed on 24 August, just a week or so before the outbreak of war, resulted in German Intelligence services not even being allowed to intercept Russian radio messages and the unexpected invasion of Russia came about to nip the Russian attack on Western Europe in the bud.

THE GERMAN MOVE INTO FRANCE, BELGIUM AND HOLLAND

Initial planning for an invasion of France hardly involved the navy and the German army obviously ignored the powerful defences of the Maginot Line, built along the French side of their common border. Instead of tackling this formidable obstacle, the German Army entered France through Belgium and Holland, just as it had done during the First World War. No one, not even the German High Military Command, thought this would be an easy offensive and at best hoped to reach a similar defensive line as the trenches of the First World War. Despite a possible bloodbath, the German military move into France was considered necessary because several months earlier Britain had established a military presence along parts of the French–Belgian border. Holland had to be occupied to stop British forces establishing spearhead bases there.

The German offensive to move into France, Belgium and Holland started on 10 May 1940, the same day that Winston Churchill became Prime Minister in London. Ten days later the German Army and Air Force had driven a wedge between French and British military positions and proceeded far beyond the First World War battlefields to reach the Channel near the Somme estuary, some distance east of Dieppe. From there, progress continued at a steady pace to reach Paris and the French Atlantic coast along the Bay of Biscay. Only a few weeks later, on 7 July, the first German U-boat, U30 (Kptlt. Fritz-Julius Lemp), made fast in the French naval base in Lorient for replenishment. This access to French Biscay bases dramatically changed the basic configuration for the Battle of the Atlantic in Germany's favour by making it much easier for U-boats to reach the Allied convoy routes.

In his Memoirs, Grand Admiral Dr Erich Raeder wrote:

> At first glance, the jump across the Channel [to invade England], whose opposite shore could easily be seen from France in good weather, would seem far less dangerous than the Norwegian landings. But any experienced naval leader would know just the opposite was true. A long and careful preparation was absolutely necessary. Such a landing would be extremely difficult, attended with the gravest risks and such an operation should be regarded only as last resort in case England could not be induced to negotiate for peace by any other means. A U-boat campaign would in all cases be far more practical.

In the middle, wearing a leather coat, is Grand Admiral Erich Raeder, supreme Commander-in-Chief of the navy from October 1928 until he was succeeded by the U-boat chief, Karl Dönitz (*left*) in January 1943.

Having gained access to the French Atlantic harbours, the German Navy found itself in a most advantageous position, being able to easily reach British convoy routes without having to pass through the dangerous blockades in the German Bight. Instead of planning an invasion of England, Germany poured more effort and resources into the Atlantic War. The niceties of Prize Ordinance Regulations were abandoned, and unrestricted sea warfare in the Atlantic became a dangerous and largely pointless undertaking. It consumed vast resources, cost many lives and created untold misery for those who suffered there. For almost all the time the U-boat war was led by optimistic ignorance, which could only flinch and react to technological advances introduced by the Allied opposition. There are two interesting points to note. First, Admiral Dönitz considered the Battle of the Atlantic to have started in July 1940, not in 1939, and secondly, there are no significant German records for the now well-known Battle of Britain. The details for this battle were written after the war in English while the original German texts, which were translated into English before 1948, were still not available some fifty years after the war.

In the middle is Kptlt. Herbert Sohler, Chief of the 7th U-boat Flotilla in St Nazaire, France; to his right is Herbert Kuppisch, who was awarded the Knight's Cross in August 1941 when he commanded U94.

Kptlt. Herbert Sohler talking to Udo Heilmann, commander of U97, in St Nazaire, France. Several officers who travelled without escorts carried pistols due to a few almost childish strikes against Germans.

Chapter 3

Built-in Handicaps: Features U-boats Did Not Have

A GLIMPSE INSIDE THE MAIN U-BOAT TYPE

The inside of a sea-going Type VIIC U-boat. This model of U995 was photographed in the International Maritime Museum of Hamburg; the real, full-size boat is a museum next to the Naval Memorial in Laboe near Kiel.

The front section:
The bows are towards the left.
The ends of the torpedo tubes (1) are visible on the left side of the cut-out, and a reload torpedo (2) can be seen hanging from the ceiling. The black cylinders (3), fixed below it, are steel bottles for storing compressed air. Below the deck are several tanks for holding air or water (4) and there was a pit with manual controls and a set of necessary gauges including a depth indicator for the hydroplanes or depth rudders. There are also folding bunks (5) in this compartment which served as seats during the day. The rectangular vents in the casing at the top allow seawater to flood into the space between the upper (outside) deck and the pressure hull. The second compartment, towards the right, was shut off from the bow torpedo room by a heavy metal door (coloured white, to the left of 8). This accommodation section contained a vast array of batteries (7) below deck level (6). Immediately above the number (6) was a lavatory. The area around (8) was the warrant officer accommodation, with the commissioned officers' mess towards the right (9). (10) shows the sound detection room towards the left and the radio room on the right. The commander's quarters were on the other side of a central corridor, opposite the radio and sound rooms. Under the radio room was a magazine for ammunition and side arms. This space was accessed through a hatch in the corridor without interfering with the radio operator. Towards the beginning of the war each boat had an 88mm quick firing deck gun forward of the conning tower. Ammunition for this gun had to be carried through the central control room, up the inside of the conning tower to the main hatch and then back down on the outside towards the rear of the conning tower, to eventually reach the gun on the front. The deck was made either with iron or teak struts, never oak, as some have claimed, and was usually rather slippery.

The centre section (see page vii for caption).

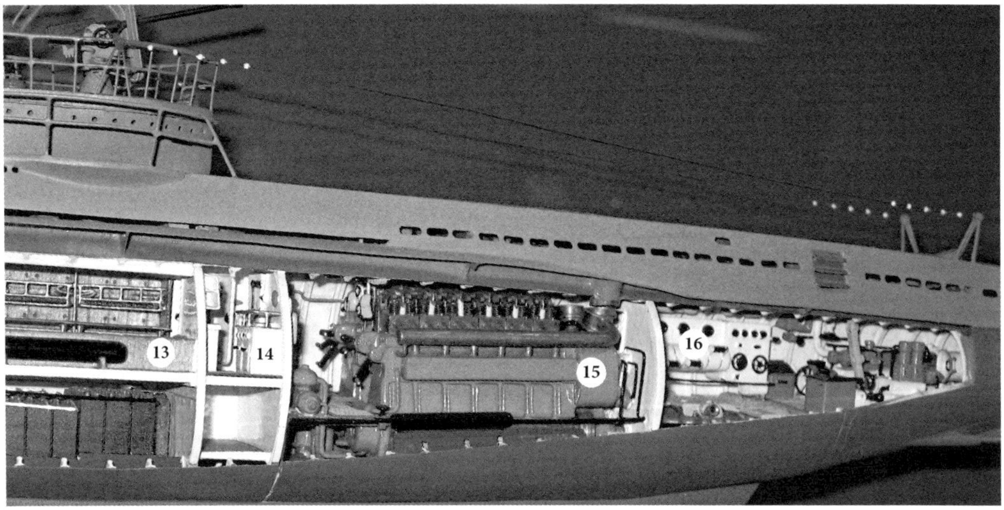

The stern section:
Immediately aft of the central control room is an accommodation section for petty officers (13), where the upper bunks folded away to provide seating on the lower bunks with folding tables occupying the central corridor. There were also several black storage bottles for compressed air and at the bottom was another large section holding batteries. Batteries could be accessed through a small hatch in the main deck with just enough space for a man in a lying position to crawl over them for maintenance. The galley or kitchen (14) is between this accommodation area and the diesel engine compartment (15), and below it are several water tanks. The galley had four water taps, labelled drinking water, filtered drinking water, washing water and warm seawater. The hatch in the ceiling was locked tight once at sea but served as front door when the boat was in port.

There is also another lavatory on the starboard side, but this was often used as a larder, making it impossible to access it for its designed purpose. The engine compartment has two diesels with identical controls and there is another set of controls for the electric motors on each side, aft of this engine room. This stern compartment also has a single torpedo tube and there is a compressor for making compressed air, a tube for ejecting an Asdic foxer, a manual emergency steering wheel and compressed air bottles. Below the deck are several tanks and, as in the bows, there is a pit with manual hydroplane controls together with a set of necessary gauges.

FEATURES MISSING FROM GERMAN U-BOATS

Since many books have been written about the specifications and achievements of these boats, this chapter will concentrate on those features they did NOT have, to show how they also came to be the biggest contributors to Germany's defeat in the Atlantic.

- Each boat had four bow torpedo tubes, while many British submarines were already fitted with eight tubes. This was significant because the general doctrine was to shoot a salvo of three in the hope one might hit. So why were there only four torpedo tubes in German U-boats? The Royal Navy submarine HMS *Tuna* (Lieutenant D.S.R. Martin) shot a salvo of five torpedoes to sink U644 (Oblt.z.S. Kurt Jensen). *Tuna* had six internal bow torpedo tubes with six reload torpedoes and four external tubes.
- Torpedoes had to be man-handled when reloading. This took a minimum of half an hour per tube when conditions were good and often considerably longer. None of the three attack types had mechanical reloading systems.
- Reload torpedoes were winched up with chains from their floor-level storage positions, making reloading difficult in stormy conditions.
- At the beginning of the war there was a major crisis with torpedoes not functioning properly and Germany experienced another catastrophe towards the end of the war when only one in ten of the new anti-destroyer cum anti-convoy torpedoes worked.
- Once dived, U-boats became almost stationary. The top submerged speed of 7.6 knots could be maintained for only very short periods when evading attacks. Submerged cruising speed is often given as 4 knots, but neither the Type VIIC nor the IXC had the battery capacity to maintain such a speed for any significant length of time. Except for dire emergencies, the submerged speed was slower than an average walker. (Faster underwater speeds were later achieved by adding more batteries to new U-boat types; Hitler's high-submerged-speed U-boats could have been built as early

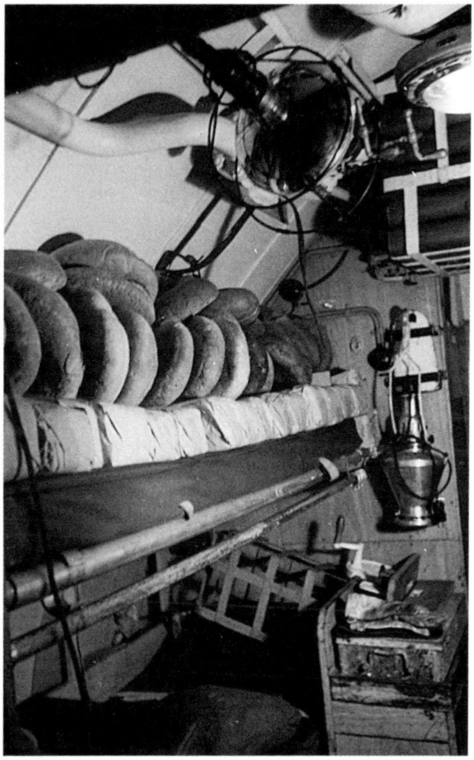

Fresh bread was often stored on bunks because these were in the driest parts of the boat, but the air was always humid, meaning bread would develop serious mould. U-boats were also supplied with tinned bread, and if the modern version is anything to go by then this tasted not at all bad. Note there was only a little space for a man in this bunk.

as 1935, but hardly any saw active service before the end of the war.)

- There were only two lavatories for more than forty-four or more men. One was often filled with provisions and could, therefore, not be used for its designed purpose.
- Towards the beginning of the war lavatories could only be used when the boat was near the surface. Men used buckets when the boat dived deep. This makes one wonder why they never had sewage tanks, allowing men to use the heads at any time and at any depth. Later toilets had a complicated operating system where it was possible to accidentally flood the boat if the controls were not worked in the correct order. Reports about a U-boat sunk by its own lavatory are not true.
- There were hardly any washing facilities and often not enough non-salty water for washing bodies. Fresh (non-salty) water for washing bodies was often rationed on longer voyages.

Claus Korth (*right*) of U57 and U93 and Herbert Kuppisch of U58 and U94 (later he commanded U516 and U847). Both are wearing U-boat overalls, derived from British army battledress captured in France after Germany's occupation in 1940.

- Only the higher ranks had bunks, many of which were in the main corridor where there were frequent disturbances. Sleeping was often a serious problem because on-duty men worked in the same spaces where men slept.
- There were no proper facilities for storing fresh provisions and not many boats had large fridges or cool compartments. The few boats fitted with freezers towards the end of the war had crews who were not instructed in their use. As a result, packets containing frozen food collected moisture on the outside while waiting to be taken onboard and the food then froze into one huge lump, making removal of individual packages almost impossible.
- Batteries giving off an explosive mixture of oxygen and hydrogen vented into accommodation areas, meaning naked lights were not allowed. This gas mixture was already known to be unhealthy for people.
- There was no ventilation system other than fresh air blowers, which could only be used when the boat was on the surface. Even then, fresh air did not always penetrate into the stern and bows properly. Makeshift ventilation systems were not fitted to boats until long after the start of the war. At first, men had to wear cumbersome breathing apparatus when submerged for long periods.

- The incredibly noisy engines required constant maintenance. The noise was deafening, making it impossible to have even a shouting match in the engine room. The engine noise was too loud for the bridge telegraph to be heard, so lights flashed when the engineers had to look at telegraph indicators for making speed adjustments.
- Later in the war, when U-boats remained submerged for long periods and charged their batteries via a schnorkel or breathing pipe, there was no efficient way of ejecting garbage, meaning rotting food created an offensive stench.
- Using the schnorkel was painful for the crew or at best very uncomfortable.
- Solid-bottomed small boats for transferring goods between two U-boats at sea were not generally issued, despite life rafts with soft bottoms being most unsuitable when it came to replenishing from supply submarines on the high seas.
- Early boats did not have spray or wave deflectors, meaning lookouts were often exceedingly wet. Water washing over the conning tower made it difficult or impossible for them to see in rough weather.

An interesting group of U-boat commanders. In the middle is Claus Korth of U93, with Hans Pauckstadt on the right. He later became a staff officer with the U-boat Command and for three months stood in for the leader of the 5th U-boat Flotilla. The man wearing a white commander's cap and U-boat leathers is Herbert Wilk, the actor who played the commander in the UFA film 'U-Boote Westwärts'. There never were any hard rules about who should wear a white cap but once the war started a fad developed that these were worn only by commanders.

- The anti-aircraft armament was inadequate.
- Mechanical failures, some of them serious enough to warrant returning to a shipyard, were significantly frequent and almost certainly appeared in all boats. Some attacks were abandoned because the periscopes did not allow the target to be seen. These mechanical shortcomings were significant.
- An underwater sound detection room was provided next to the radio compartment but a ranging device, like the British Asdic, was not fitted to operational boats and the space was instead used for food storage. Passive sound detectors for picking up noises were fitted but these could not determine the distance to the target.
- For most of the time U-boats operated on their own without very-long-range reconnaissance aircraft directing them towards convoys.
- U-boats usually did not coordinate their attacks to make the best use of group tactics.
- Although Germany built huge bunkers to protect U-boats from air attacks, there was hardly any support to help them in and out of these bases. As a result, many submarines were sunk or damaged close to their own ports.

In addition to these shortcomings, there were other significant defects, some with roots dating back to the First World War when good sturdy workmanship was seriously rattled

This iconic photo of U47 (Kptlt. Günther Prien) was taken by a press officer in Kiel shortly after the famous raid into the Royal Navy's anchorage at Scapa Flow in the Orkney Islands. The ship in the background appears to be the heavy cruiser *Admiral Hipper*, then still on training schedules following a serious refit. This shows the early type of conning tower with a very small rear platform or 'conservatory' and with the 20mm anti-aircraft gun mount on the so-called 'upper deck' (seen here without the gun in position). Just left of the four men by its side is the open galley hatch cover and aft of that is a 'T' Spanner for dealing with outside deck fittings. The lower hatches into the interior would have been closed before the boat moved from a pier to stop water washing into them. Some attempt has been made to provide these early boats with a wind deflector at the top and a spray deflector halfway up the front of the conning tower, but they were highly ineffective.

by depth charges causing both machinery and joints to break because they were too rigid. This was rectified by replacing solid fittings with flexible connections, leaving individual components free to vibrate. By the beginning of the Second World War this essential built-in elasticity had gone too far in the other direction. Engines, pumps and compressors were no longer capable of running at fast speeds without wobbling out of position. Thus, serious emergency remedial work was more than necessary, putting considerable strain on the already overworked shipyards. Despite these corrective measures, not all faults could be cured, meaning it was necessary to place significant limitations on some machinery and many early boats could not be driven to the extremities of their designed performance. Naval experts have said this could well have contributed to the loss of several boats.

THE TORPEDO CRISIS

The smooth-running success of the Norwegian Campaign in April 1940 made it blatantly obvious there was a definite and major problem with U-boat torpedoes. On the 20th of that month, Grand Admiral Dr Erich Raeder (Commander-in-Chief of the Navy) set up a Board of Inquiry to investigate the many torpedo failures. Some of the early mishaps, where these led to the sinking of a U-boat, would not have been known to the Naval High Command and the first failure reports from irate U-boat commanders were put down to war nerves. Thus, it took a while before action was taken. The following are extracts from reports in U-boat logbooks from two high-achieving commanders. U48, a Type VIIB under Kptlt. Herbert Schultze, had become the most successful U-boat of the whole war as early as June 1941 when it was withdrawn from active service to join training establishments. The other boat included here, U93 (Kptlt. Claus Korth), was the first Type VIIC, which left for its first operational cruise on 5 October 1940.

Herbert Schultze wrote a most favourable report on the first few months of the war. He told the Commander-in-Chief of the U-boat Arm the performance of both boat and crew was better than expected from earlier exercises:

> Experience had shown the pressure hull to be excellent and only a few minor problems had occurred. The torpedo tubes worked well, but the attack periscope was awful enough to make submerged attacks impossible. Both the magnification and the clarity, especially towards the rim, were nowhere near good enough. Condensation inside the tube was by far the greatest problem. One attack was abandoned because it was impossible to see the near-by target.

Schultze suggested it should be possible to double the diameter of the head lens to provide a better performance. He also complained that 'the speed indicator and navigation equipment were prone to too many breakdowns, making the calculation of exact positions exceedingly difficult'. The Navy's system proved to be totally useless and fishing charts with accurate depths, combined with the echo sounder, provided the best aids for finding the way back home from the west of Ireland. He also said the magnetic compass and the

Obviously the first watch officer but not many had their position so clearly defined.

Loading ammunition for the deck guns. The cartridges were stored in metal containers and modern divers have reported that the brass inside these tubes was still shiny after having laid for such a long time inside a wreck.

Harvesting crops was a major problem when most people were away from home fighting the war and many naval men were given the option of helping on farms for this vitally important work. It may be surprising, but many U-boats had a good number of men who had the knowledge and experience to harness horses and work with them. Even men from towns had used horses for many types of work.

This shows a similar conning tower after modification to hold the single 20mm anti-aircraft gun on a slightly enlarged platform. The partly raised attack periscope with the small head lens is also visible.

gyrocompass had to be checked against each other at least once every four hours. Especially large variations occurred after torpedoes had been discharged and this difference should not be left for boats to discover for themselves but must be included in training schedules.

It was possible to use the 88mm deck gun if the sea was not too rough, but this was hardly advisable since it produced such insignificant results. The deck was usually slippery and therefore the pitching and rolling made aiming extremely difficult, if not impossible. For most of the time it would have been criminal to order the gun crew into action because the resulting injuries would have been too severe. Men were often washed off their feet to crash into hard protrusions, making the transfer of ammunition, the loading and the aiming too risky. The anti-aircraft gun, attached to the upper deck aft of the conning tower, was virtually useless as well. Shortly after the start of the war this 20mm gun was moved onto a newly built platform at the top of the conning tower. During the first months of the war this weapon was used only for stopping ships and occasionally to prevent them from illuminating the U-boat with searchlights.

The upper deck torpedo storage containers proved useful. Moving the 1.5-ton 'eels' down into the boat was not too difficult, despite the cold winter weather making this process hazardous and highly unpleasant. However, the torpedoes themselves had given Schultze great cause for concern. There were far too many failures, and he emphasized most strongly that not all of these could be put down to the aimer having missed the target. Many torpedoes simply did not explode, while others detonated long before they reached the target or shortly after having missed it. There had to be a major fault with the torpedo mechanism.

Schultze's report, written shortly after the start of the war, went on to say:

The tactics of sending lone boats to operational areas at sea, which have been used since the beginning of the war, are only good as long as there is an abundance of independently sailing merchant ships. The fact that many of these move at a slow speed has been an added advantage. Yet, attacking convoys is somewhat different to what we had imagined at the beginning of the hostilities. The first detonation causes merchant ships to scatter in all directions over a much wider area, making it difficult to get into a favourable position for a second attack. This problem is made considerably worse by the presence of destroyers, which keep us down long enough for the opposition to get a good head start, forcing us into another lengthy chase. Consequently, it is difficult to catch another target for a second attack.

Operations in shallow coastal waters are also becoming noticeably more difficult as time goes on. Aircraft are the main nuisance here and the close proximity to land means they can quickly call-in support. Attempting to attack convoys with a group of U-boats in shallow coastal waters appears to be pointless because the opposition reacts too fast. In view of this, it is necessary to develop a submarine capable of attacking surface craft while deeply submerged. I think some type of rising mine or a torpedo

The wind deflector at the top of the conning tower and the spray deflector halfway up were drastically improved after the start of the war, as can be seen here. The boat in the foreground is U130 (Korvkpt. Ernst Kals) with U502 (Kptlt. Jürgen von Rosenstiel) behind, both photographed during 1941 around the time of the *Bismarck* sinking. The difference in ranks of the two commanders is almost ten years. Kals joined the navy in 1924 and Rosenstiel in 1933.The badges painted on the conning towers, exceedingly useful for identification, were used in Britain to help with U-boat intelligence. The wooden planking is part of the camouflage to make moored boats difficult to spot from the air.

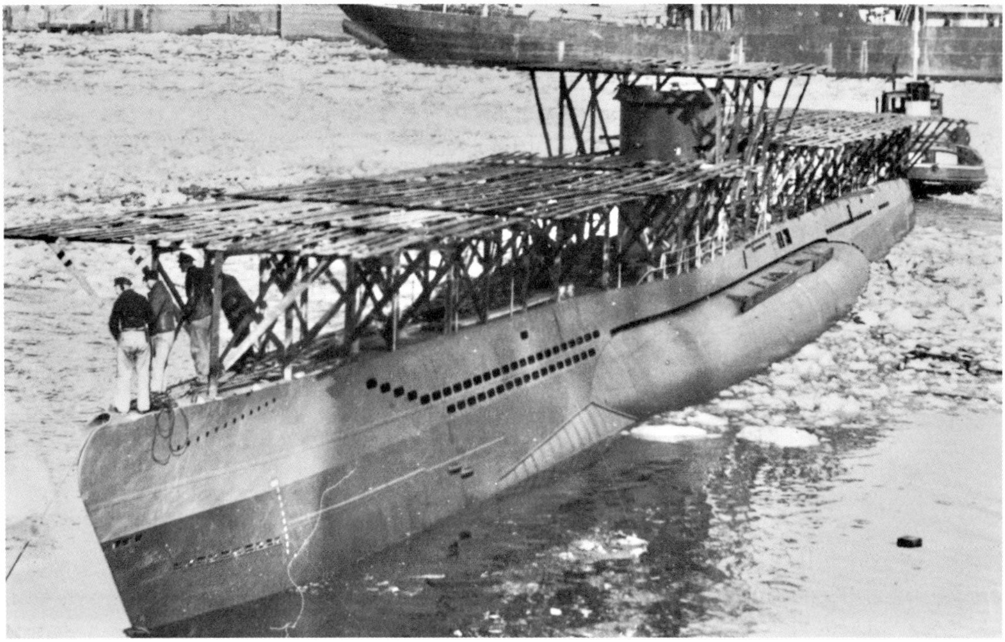

U221, a Type VIIC, immediately after launching at Germania Works in Kiel on 14 March 1942, with anti-aircraft camouflage planking to hide the typical submarine shape from the air. The steps on top of the saddle tank will be removed before the boat is commissioned.

with a sound detector should meet such requirements. This needs to be considered as a necessity and introduced as soon as possible, to enable a 'blind' submarine to shoot from depths of 20–25 metres. Our own realization of a surfaced submarine being virtually impossible to spot in poor light has come slowly into our minds through our own experience. At night submarines are invisible, and we must use this advantage to attack the opposition. Convoys, and those ships which Prize Ordinance Regulations allow us to attack without warning, are definitely the best targets. Our night binoculars appear to be much superior to those used by the enemy. It often seems to be a case of us being able to see surface ships very clearly, while their inferior optics make it impossible for them to see us. Even after a submarine is spotted head on, it still offers only a tiny target which gives us ample opportunities for a successful attack before the merchant ship can take evasive action. It is important to use the large deck gun only when the opposition is unarmed or has clearly demonstrated their shooting to be considerably inferior to our own. At times, when the artillery officer gets it right and does not forget important parts of the routine, then the 88mm gun can have a significant uplifting effect on the morale of all of our crew. Using the big gun aways exposes the boat to additional dangers, meaning it is important to keep a strict eye on the apparently uninteresting parts of the horizon while such fascinating bombardment is taking place.

PROBLEMS WITH NEW U-BOATS

U93, under Kptlt. Claus Korth, was chosen for the following account not only because it was the first Type VIIC but also because it was commissioned by an experienced commander. Korth had been second and first watch officer in U31 (Type VIIA, under Johannes Habekost) for almost a year before taking command of U57, a small cramped coastal boat of Type IIC, with which he undertook ten voyages. So, he and some of his men had often been up to their knees in muck, water and bullets. They had also 'drowned' on wet conning towers often enough to know the limitations of both men and machinery and were unlikely to make greenhorn mistakes. This section is based both on the log from U93 and on discussions with Claus Korth and with Maria von Tiesenhausen, whose husband had been watch officer in U93.

* * *

The boat was still fitting out, training and dealing with necessary essentials before going to war, when something significant happened. Korth was avidly following the goings-on with his old boat, U57, now commanded by a newcomer, Oblt.z.S. Erich Topp. A couple of diving tanks had been modified to also hold fuel, allowing this small North Sea Duck with only three bow torpedo tubes to travel as far as the French Biscay ports. From there, Topp became the first person to succeed in doing what many had been talking about for some time. Men knew U-boats had accidentally ended up close to the enemy without serious repercussions. It was almost impossible to spot them at night among the turbulence

U-boat building yard camouflage as seen from above.

of the waves. So, in the middle of August 1940, while some distance west of Scotland and to the north of Ireland, he headed straight into the columns of Convoy OB202, shooting all three torpedoes one after the other with a minute or so gaps between each. This short-range surface attack at night was a brilliant success. Two ships went down while the third was damaged: an outstanding achievement for such a tiny 'canoe'. Topp had confirmed suspicions. The escorts were not there to protect the convoy from U-boats, but to prevent neutral ships escaping from the closed formation, to prevent them attempting home runs back to their own country.

It was the middle of October 1940, only two months later, when the much superior U93 was in the area where Topp had completed the first short-range surface attack at night and where merchant traffic funnelled into the narrow Western Approaches leading to important ports such as Glasgow and Liverpool. Avoiding the escorts of Convoy OB227, Korth ordered the first watch officer, who aimed torpedoes during surface attacks, to shoot at a 6,000-ton freighter. U93 was now well on the way to beating Topp by hitting four or even five ships instead of only three. But nothing happened. The electric drive 'eel' did not leave a wake or give any indication it was running, so lookouts could not see it approach, meaning the target was in no position to take evasive action. Yet instead of exploding, the torpedo merely disappeared into the blackness of the night. Korth waited anxiously with stopwatch in hand for eight minutes before ordering von Tiesenhausen, the 1WO, to discharge another torpedo against the same ship. Again, nothing happened, other than a long wait while stop watches ticked. The expensive torpedo also disappeared into the darkness of the night. Five minutes later the shipping positions had changed to make this giant no longer accessible,

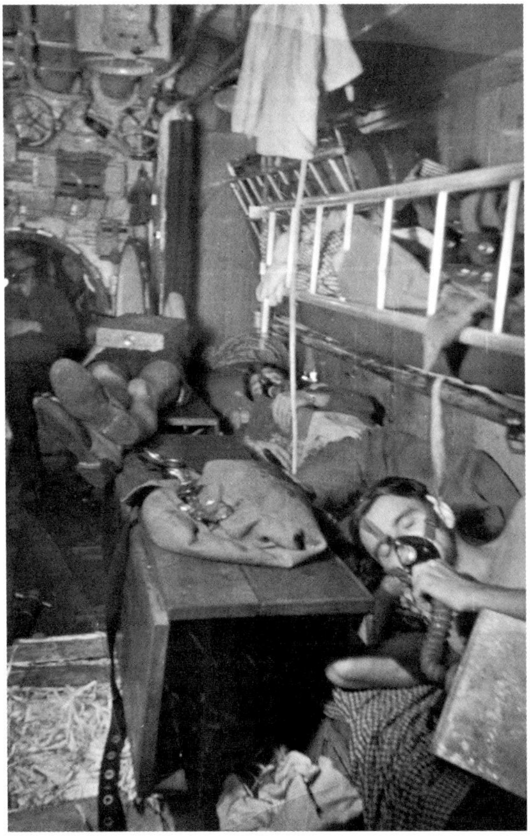

A posed photo taken aboard U73, a Type VIIB, showing men wearing personal breathing apparatus. This allowed them to breathe in air from their surroundings, but exhaled breath passed through the box containing a chemical for absorbing carbon dioxide. These devices, although effective, were most cumbersome for working in or when having to move about. It is unlikely a man would have chosen to sleep on top of a table where he could easily fall off, and if the men were short of air, they would also not have had enough electricity for the lighting to be on full power. The crew cannot have been ordered to rest to conserve power and air because one of the upper bunks have not been folded down. If the situation had been real, then the men would have been left in almost total darkness. (*Photo: Karl Keller*)

U57, a Type IIC commanded by Claus Korth, showing the early plain conning towers without wind or spray deflectors. In the foreground is the mount for a 20mm anti-aircraft gun without the gun in position. The bulge at the base of the conning tower contained a magnetic compass, which could be viewed by the helmsman through an illuminated periscope. A horseshoe-shaped lifebelt can be seen hanging on the side of the tower by the navigation light. Identification marks and brass eagles were removed shortly after Britain declared war on Germany.

so Korth gave instructions to aim at a slightly smaller ship less than half a kilometre away. Again, the torpedo disappeared without saying goodbye. The next torpedo hit the 9,331-ton freighter *Hurunui* towards the back of the convoy, but the ship showed no signs of sinking, and then U93 fired the last torpedo from the rear tube. This behaved the same way as the first three. It was an exciting but rather disappointing attack, sparking off a lot of cursing and foul language. Incidentally, the first watch officer at this time was Hans-Diedrich Freiherr von Tiesenhausen, who later became commander of U331, which sank the battleship HMS *Barham* in the Mediterranean. This most dramatic explosion was caught on film from other British ships and has since appeared in many books and films.

The sad point for the men in U93 was that this was not the end of the story, nor the end of passing convoys. Targets continued to gate-crash without being invited. Another torpedo just disappeared during another dark night. Then there was another. And another. And then another. And to keep the pot boiling, another torpedo went adrift. This last one was a bit more exciting than the rest. It missed the target and exploded very dramatically when it hit a ship on the other side of the convoy and created some noteworthy commotion. U93 was later approached by aircraft, shot at with large guns and had depth charges dropped too close for comfort. One of these was close enough to rattle a torpedo heavily enough for it swim away all on its own without the trigger having been pressed. Fifty-seven days after having left Germany, U93 put into St Nazaire in France without having achieved a great deal other than to annoy everybody on board.

Korth wrote the top of the conning tower was constantly awash with too much water. As a result, the lookouts could hardly see, frequently putting U93 into impossible situations.

This small coastal submarine of Type IIC had hardly any wind or spray deflectors on the conning tower. The loop above the men's heads is a radio direction finder. It rotated and indicated the direction from which radio signals were coming. Above the painting of the clenched fist is a foghorn and an intake from the forward 'jumping wire', which served both as a radio aerial and as a holdfast for safety harnesses for men working on the outside deck.

(Lookouts usually worked a duty spell of four hours but in action areas commanders were often on the bridge for two or more of such periods.) Korth suggested the spray and water deflectors should be modified, as had already been advised some time ago by Korvkpt. Ernst Sobe (Head of the command for testing boats and men before they went on their first operational tour). Korth also stuck his neck out by asking for the designers of this new miracle VIIC boat to be allowed to sail with U93, to stand on the wet conning tower for eight hours and feel the incredible discomfort of cold water crashing over them. And please remember, he was referring to *the* most important U-boat type in the German armoury, at a time when the war had been raging for almost one and a half years.

The following year Royal Navy experts made some astonishing discoveries after U570 (Kptlt. Hans-Joachim Rahmlow) was captured by a Coastal Command aircraft. They reported the defects that had led the crew to surrender were easily rectified, as many were due to fuses falling out of their fittings and to poor-quality switches turning themselves off. Once replaced, the machinery worked again. This could perhaps explain how U93 came to lose a torpedo during an earlier depth charge attack. Of course, other boats found themselves in similar predicaments and there was one incident in U377 (Kptlt. Otto Köhler) where the torpedo mechanic accidentally tested the trigger without first switching it off.

U457 (Korvkpt. Karl Brandenburg) showing the enlarged wind and spray deflectors on the conning tower. This boat undertook six war voyages from the end of May until 16 September 1942 when it was attacked and sunk by HMS *Impulsive* in the Arctic Seas while attacking Convoy PQ18. There were no survivors.

Taking pity on the man, the commander later fired a salvo of three when he knew there were only two, but this saved him having to appear as witness at a court martial. The men in U93 coped with parts of the machinery not just dropping out but hurtling through crowded spaces to end up in impossible hiding places. Having so many men squeezed into such confined spaces meant people were often hit by bits of machinery. Sometimes, they could catch the objectionable parts again, or someone saw where they landed. To cope with such difficulties, one needs the right type of leadership with an adequate supply of carrots to make men react quickly and efficiently. The magic words 'experienced leadership' appear to have been missing in many U-boats. Enthusiasm created on land by a powerful propaganda system and the camaraderie of being members of an elite quickly wears thin if the leaders are without the experience to cope with such dreadful disappointments as U93 had to endure.

* * *

Logbooks can be difficult to understand. There have been incidents of former U-boat commanders visiting the German U-boat Museum in Cuxhaven-Altenbruch having to ask the meaning of what they themselves had written during the war. In addition to this, logs were written by people who very rarely saw those written by others. This meant that at the beginning of the war there was no standard way of recording information, and some pages look like extracts from romance novels, while others are curt to the point of not revealing what was going on. Korth had the terrific advantage of having had more war experience than the three main leaders of the U-boat Arm and, on top of this, he had enjoyed a most varied career before taking command. He also had the courage to tell his superiors politely what was wrong with the U-boats. The following are significant points mentioned in his logs early in 1941 while in command of U93, after the war had been raging for fourteen months.

The gun crew of U124 in action? No. Actors from the UFA film 'U-boote Westwärts' being filmed, but without a queue of men carrying ammunition; the absence of ammunition carriers was probably done on purpose to prevent the enemy from discovering how these guns operated. The inside scenes of this film were also especially modified by fitting First World War instruments, where, for example, the maximum diving depth was much shallower than in the Second World War. The man leading the gunners is on the left. His shoulder straps indicate he is a warrant officer, probably the Ober~steuer~mann or navigator. Usually, an officer would have been on deck to give orders to the gun crew. The snag was, he did not do this terribly often and created some harrowing incidents when he forgot the correct procedure.

Seawater crashing over the top of the conning tower was heavy enough to prevent lookouts facing into the wind from seeing anything. The windward lookouts were therefore totally 'blind'. All Korth could do was to hold on for dear life and 'we were definitely in the wrong position when it came to attacking. The sharpness of the water beating into our faces made the aiming of torpedoes impossible.' Weather reports from British ships during that 1940/1941 winter were bad enough for land-based desk warriors of the Royal Navy not to believe their sea-going counterparts, who therefore ordered a full enquiry into the natural conditions in the Atlantic. This then confirmed the severity of the storms. On U93 the waves were too bad for evaluating the new spray deflectors at the top of the conning tower. These had been modified in St Nazaire towards the end of 1940 but during their first test there was no spray being blown 'up' the tower. Instead, huge deluges crashed 'down' over the top. The situation was hopeless.

The middle of January 1941 saw a considerable change. Half of the crew were promoted to other positions and then, to top it all, an experienced petty officer was replaced shortly before going to sea. Korth was furious enough not to sail to his allotted area by the usual shortest route; instead, he made a detour, away from the action, to train the new men. That

Stopwatches had already been an essential part of submarine life during the First World War. They were used to keep tab on torpedoes after they had been discharged. Knowing the adjusted speed, it was possible to work out when they should hit the target.

he had made the right decision was confirmed a few days later when the last man down from the top of the conning tower (the duty officer, a new one) failed to notice the prongs for locking the hatch had been closed before they gripped the collar and therefore left a 4cm-wide gap for water to pour in. All U-boats had two circular hatches in the conning tower, one on the top and another at the bottom, and there was always more than one man standing-by to close this lower hatch if there was an accident. The commander's position for submerged attacks was inside the conning tower by the eyepiece of the raised attack periscope, the one with the small head lens. The engineer officer with the helmsman and two hydroplane operators, plus several others, were positioned in the central control room, immediately below the conning tower compartment.

This whole process of water flooding through the upper hatch lasted for only a short time. The engineer officer was ready for such mishaps. Standing at the bottom of the ladder, he could keep an eye on the instruments and look up to see what was going on at the front door. Immediately, he ordered an emergency surface or an alarm dive in reverse. Despite his quick reaction, the ballast pump had to work fast to remove some 10 tons of exceedingly wet intrusion before Korth launched an enquiry to find out what had gone wrong. In doing so, he was astounded to learn the mistake came because the U-boat school had not taught the correct procedure for closing the hatch. One wonders

A posed picture of men looking at watches in the bow torpedo room. They would not have been so neat-and-tidy had they been shooting for real. The chief torpedo mechanic was the only warrant officer to have had a bunk in the bow torpedo compartment but without responsibility over the men. A Maat or petty officer would have overseen the crew in this area.

how many other U-boats went down as a result of something similar. Korth was the type of commander who did not blame men for their shortcomings. Instead, he made a determined effort to find out why a mistake had been made, to prevent it happening a second time.

There was still one more day in January 1941 when the bad weather subsided enough to provide brilliant conditions for shooting the evening sun. It was also peaceful enough for several people to take calm readings with more than one sextant. Now, suddenly, Korth found there was a difference of 70 nautical miles between their calculated position and that determined by measuring the angle of the sun. Mathematics were done in the head or on scraps of paper or even on a slate. Portable calculators had not yet been invented. None of these figures remained, meaning there was no way of checking how this incredible difference came about. Again, this may sound insignificant when comparing it with the vastness of the Atlantic, but such mistakes were far more common than might be imagined and men often had means of hiding their mistakes. In the case of U377 (Kptlt. Otto Köhler), such a navigation error helped the boat to survive the incredible sinkings of May 1943. Broadcasting the wrong positions back to base meant British codebreakers could not identify the position of the boat.

Towards the end of April 1941, U93 went into the repair yard in Lorient for the removal of the 88mm quick firing gun in front of the conning tower. There were now too few

Taking a reading with a sextant from a constantly moving platform demanded considerable skill and many commanders insisted on several men practising this when conditions allowed. Merchant Marine officers owned their own sextants. In the Kriegsmarine they belonged to the boat or ship rather than to the men.

opportunities for this most cumbersome weapon. Retaliation from the opposition had become too aggressive. The rear torpedo tube, which had been welded shut after the previous voyage, also needed further attention to prevent it from leaking. This especially long refit was necessary due to severe damage caused by attacking aircraft, and Korth remarked some faults were due to mistakes made by dockyard workers. This is an interesting comment because generally the French workers turned U-boats around faster than their German counterparts, but it would appear they were lacking some basic engineering skills. Or was it deliberate sabotage?

Not all the mechanical deficiencies were noticed straight away. The diesel engines' unusually high fuel consumption was not noticed until the boat had been cruising for several days and by then it was far enough away from land to make a return impractical. All the men could do was adjust their endurance calculations to match the newly discovered figures. Korth insisted on meticulous checking of everything, but one wonders how many inexperienced crews might not have noticed such an unexpected error.

At the beginning of June 1941, the U-boat Command was fully aware that things were not as sweet as they had been only eight months earlier, during the previous autumn. The 'Happy Time' – the sinking of masses of shipping in Britain's Western Approaches – would never take centre stage again. Things had changed at sea. The big question was, 'What had changed?' While making every effort to find the reason, U-boat Command reacted by reducing the headquarters staff. The thinking behind this was to have fewer

The result of a magnetic torpedo having exploded under the target to break the hull and keel. Bulkheads are preventing water from reaching the extremities, thus keeping the ship afloat.

people around who could inadvertently pass on vital clues about what was going on. In Britain, exactly the opposite happened. Land-based Intelligence officers were increased to deal with the ever-increasing flow of data and in this respect U93 can also be used to illustrate one of the many shortcomings at the German headquarters, which will feature in a later chapter.

U995 now a museum next to the Naval Memorial in Laboe near Kiel.

Chapter 4

In the Beginning

THE FIRST AND ONLY MAJOR PRE-WAR U-BOAT EXERCISE

In 1935, when the Third Reich's first U-boat flotilla was commissioned, the initial objective was to get inexperienced young volunteers acquainted with their new weapons – a task that proved nowhere near as easy as has been made out by many post-war historians. The 'modern' boats may all have been launched shortly before men clambered inside them, but the crews quickly discovered the machinery was far from functioning properly, meaning the boats were not new marvels. Many needed urgent modifications, returning to the building yards for serious remedial work. Once the war started, these procedures had to be escalated, with a good number of boats being subjected to major limitations to prevent them from being driven to their maximum until they had been modified. Some of the earlier boats were moved to training establishments in the eastern Baltic because they were no longer capable of meeting the demands made on them.

Otto Köhler (left) while commanding the minesweeper M18. He was an artillery officer aboard the light cruiser *Königsberg* before the war where he had the opportunity to become closely involved with early radar, which created a significant brush with the U-boat Chief. He commanded U377 without having been a U-boat watch officer, and in 1943 was put in charge of the instruction processes for shooting the new acoustic torpedoes. The words on the binoculars indicate the person on right is M18's Obersteuermann.

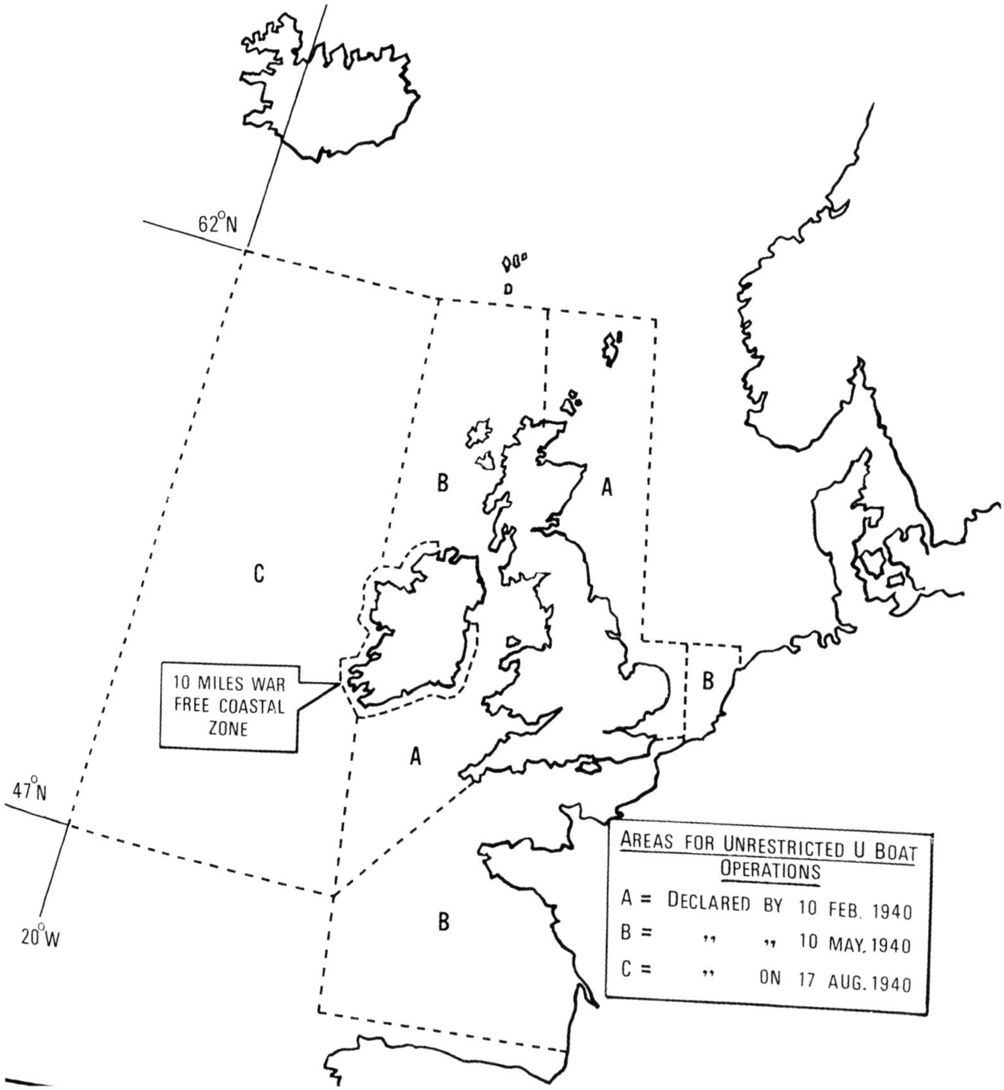

Unrestricted sea warfare operations areas in 1940.

The Third Reich's first U-boats were launched at a time when the victors of the First World War had prohibited Germany from building and owning submarines. At that time, the National Socialists did not yet have a majority within the country, meaning they were still standing on shaky foundations, lacking support from the majority of voters. On top of this, there was a good chance of Western nations sending another military occupation force into Germany to requisition the new submarines. Therefore, the first ones did not have all the new modern features which had been patented since the First World War. The reappearance of U-boats, together with the government's reintroduction of national conscription in March 1935, was a wonderful opportunity for the National Socialists to end up in an 'all-win and no-lose' situation – something which is pretty rare in politics. If the foreign powers who imposed so many harsh restrictions on Germany at the end of the

First World War now crossed the frontiers to enter the country, then the National Socialists would no doubt have won a voters' majority by launching a verbal attack to throw them out again. By this time there were a considerable number of radios in Germany, meaning there was no need for anyone to stand on a soapbox to talk to the masses. There had been armies of occupation in Germany until the early 1930s, with foreign troops ensuring Germany was paying its war reparations. Armed soldiers shot a good number of starving Germans who were watching foreigners taking away their meagre supplies of food and coal. The National Socialists did not have any official standing when this happened and therefore could not cash-in on these events. But now, in March 1935, this major violation of the post Great War rules resulted in nothing untoward happening. Instead of enforcing their own regulations, the Allied Powers applauded Hitler's bold move and thereby placed him on an incredibly powerful pedestal, leaving the navy free to acquire the previously prohibited weapons and making it possible for the government to create the previously prohibited Air Arm or Luftwaffe.

Right from the start, U-boat training was highly concentrated and vigorous enough to drive commanders to the limits of their mental and physical capabilities. Heinrich (but better known as Ajax) Bleichrodt (U48, U67 and U109, also a Knight of the Iron Cross with Oakleaves) told me: 'By the time the war started almost all commanders' nerves were totally burnt out by the intensity of the training. You only have to look at how many were taken off their command or their boats were sunk because they could no longer

In Atlantic waves U-boats were exceedingly difficult to spot at night and filming such situations in the Baltic was difficult because the sea lacked huge waves most of the time. This scene of U124 (Kptlt. Karl-Heinz Moehle) was especially filmed in a safe Baltic area for the UFA film 'U-boote Westwärts'. Both the attack periscope with the small head lens and the larger sky or navigation periscope can be seen above the wave.

cope with the pressures upon them. There were times when they went for days on end without proper sleep.'

Bleichrodt also pointed out how some technical investigations were not covered at all by any training. This produced a significantly positive crunch early in 1942, shortly after the United States had joined in the war. At that crucial period and so late in the war, no one knew for certain how far the various U-boat types could travel with a full load of fuel. Several engineering officers had devised their own methods for achieving the most economical progress and these methods were discussed in the mess with men from other boats over a glass of wine or beer but none of the leaders ever went in for experiments to see which was the best. Reinhard Hardegen (U147 and U123, Knight of the Iron Cross with Oakleaves and the first commander to attack the United States) said: 'When we attacked the United States, we were pleasantly surprised to find our boats, especially the smaller sea-going types VII, could go a considerable distance further than what we had expected. Of course, towards the beginning of the war, there was no great need to be too economical with fuel because we operated not far from our French bases.'

Although early U-boats were constantly training, three years passed before they took part in their first large-scale war exercise against a small, simulated convoy made up of several ships instead of just one target. The light cruiser and artillery training ship *Königsberg* was used as a floating convoy headquarters for the higher leaders to test whether their attack plans were at all feasible. Group attacks had failed during the First World War because radio had not advanced far enough to get the boats to the right place at the right time. This first and highly successful experimental manoeuvre took place during the autumn of 1938, less than a year before the Second World War started. The mock-up convoy, protected by anti-submarine hunters, was decimated and the small boats retrieving spent torpedoes worked overtime. Lights were located in the 'warheads' of practice torpedoes to allow observers to see them at night. The success of the attacks gave the U-boat staff good reasons for their high spirits as they returned to base.

Despite the obvious success, however, not everyone shared the newfound enthusiasm for submarines. Among the sceptics was *Königsberg*'s radio officer, Otto Köhler, a young lieutenant of 29, who had joined the navy direct from university and had been selected to act as liaison officer between *Königsberg* and the U-boat guests. He pointed to an invention on top of the forward gun turret, which later became known as radar. This device could detect ships around the *Königsberg* during dark nights and in the thickest of fogs, enabling the ship to slip in and out of harbours in thick fog when it was impossible to see the tiny buoys marking each side of the deep-water channel. This device would also show up every submarine as it closed on its targets. Hiding under cover of darkness was no longer an option since the radar would still 'see' all, even during the darkest nights and in the thickest fogs. Köhler told the U-boat officers that had this device been switched on, the approaching submarines would have been 'seen' long before they came close enough to fire their illuminated torpedoes.

The German naval leadership also showed little enthusiasm for this new radar, largely because they considered it detrimental to the tiny German Navy's main advantage: its

U124 (Kptlt. Karl-Heinz Moehle) during the UFA filming for 'U-boote Westwärts', when especially good weather conditions allowed for some clear photography.

ability to remain hidden from potential attackers. Radar signals travelled considerably further than the distances over which targets could be detected. Therefore, it was possible for an enemy ship to detect the presence of a submarine's radar set without the radar operators being aware of it. In view of this, Germany set about developing the system as an additional rangefinder to be used after a target had been visually sighted. This would have been most useful when targets were hiding behind artificial fog, in gun smoke or in patches of bad weather. The other major snag with this invention was that only a few people understood its intricacies. It was called Dezi~meter~telefonie~gerät, abbreviated to DT Gerät, which the uninitiated thought meant Dreh~turm~gerät or Revolving Turret Apparatus. Its location on top of the forward gun turret was far from ideal because its delicate glass valves, forerunners of modern transistors, were shattered by vibrations every time a salvo was fired. This weakness was exploited by die-hard conventionalists to emphasize the advantages of optical rangefinders. The officer commanding operational

U-boats, Kpt.z.S. and Kommodore Karl Dönitz, apparently did not even examine this new equipment, possibly because he had already been influenced by the negative gossip. A year later, when the war started, Germany lost its supreme advantage with radar because the government dictated all research should be abandoned, unless it could be completed within one year. So instead of using this invention to their advantage, U-boats found it became a powerful tool for their opposition to whip them away from their targets.

It is quite likely the U-boat Chief's mind had already been filled with a far more intimidating threat, created by newly developed underwater sound detectors. Everybody had heard Britain boasting loudly about the new 'pinger' for finding submerged submarines. Called Asdic, after the Allied Submarine Detection Investigation Committee, it was said to render future submarine attacks impossible. The experts announced, rather publicly, how this invention would prevent similar disasters to those which had occurred during the U-boat blockade of the First World War. U-boats would never again be able to attack and decimate merchant shipping. Even submerged submarines would be detected as they approached their quarry.

Germany also produced some similar high-quality sound detection gear but only as a passive listening device. It could hear ships too far away for lookouts to see but lacked the facility of determining the distance to the target. Yet this follow-on step had already been foreseen. The early large U-boats already had a special sound room forward of the radio room built in to accommodate such apparatus for when it was mass produced. Unfortunately, it was never developed, and the tiny room was used instead for storing provisions rather than helping with attacks.

This iconic photo from the First World War with Heligoland in the background gives a good impression of what submarines looked like in stormy weather. One of the most significant remarks recorded in a logbook during such conditions must be a comment by Heinrich Lehmann-Willenbrock, who wrote the war correspondent Lothar-Günther Buchheim was on the bridge of U96 taking photographs when he should be in his bunk concentrating on being seasick.

THE THREE-FRONT-WAR PROGRAMME AND PRIZE ORDINANCE REGULATIONS

Emergency war plans, to cope with several possible political situations, had been updated by the Naval High Command around the time when Hitler became Chancellor of Germany at the end of January 1933. The most comprehensive of these was the so-called Three-Front-War Programme intended to react to tension in the Baltic, the North Sea and the Atlantic, all at the same time. The high-ranking officers who devised these defence plans had grown up with a profound fear of having their entire fleet incarcerated inside their own bases because powerful warships, lurking just out of sight, prevented them from leaving. This anxiety went back to the middle of the nineteenth century, when the first German submarine, *Brandtaucher*, was built by a Bavarian artillery officer, Wilhelm Bauer, to help break such a blockade in Kiel. Much later, the First World War started with a similar situation. A few British submarines in the German Bight near Heligoland prevented the entire German fleet from leaving their North Sea estuaries. To get over this problem, the high admirals created orders for all ships to be sent to sea before any conflict could stop them from leaving their bases. This was at a time when the higher admirals looked upon U-boats as 'servants' for the fleet rather than autonomous units operating under their own leadership. The Naval War Staff within the High Naval Command in Berlin allocated each U-boat a specific operations area, where commanders were told to take up waiting positions while remaining undetected, and a good number of boats were dispatched to such positions during the second half of August 1939. When the war started, they were almost ready to come home again to refuel. By this time U-boats had their own autonomous command under a naval captain, Karl Dönitz, who also held the position of commodore to put him slightly higher in rank than captains of light cruisers and bigger ships. Dönitz had served in U-boats shortly before the end of the First World War, but hardly long enough for him to feel he was a true submariner. His reaction to the declaration of war was to ask the Naval War Staff for a recall of all boats, saying Britain and France would have withdrawn vulnerable shipping before declaring war and so it was important to have the U-boats freshly kitted out and refuelled, to be ready for when British and French traffic re-emerged.

The initial hesitation to tackle merchant shipping was due to Hitler's insistence for U-boats to adhere to the internationally agreed Prize Ordinance Regulations. These strict rules consisted of more than fifty complicated pages of which each unit at sea had least one copy; furthermore, the navy had provided commanders with a German-made circular slide rule listing the main war contraband and indicating the action to be taken if such material was found on board a stopped ship. This process of stopping and inspecting ships became a significant part of the pre-war training schedules and remained in operation until aggressive action by Britain made it necessary to lift the rules, piece by piece. The final restrictions were not lifted until August 1940, when the war had been raging for one year.

The general frustration at the beginning of the war, when U-boats were ordered to obey Prize Ordinance Regulations, is summed up by Kptlt. Heinrich Schuch in U37's log. He questioned various orders that U37 had been given. The position he was allocated before

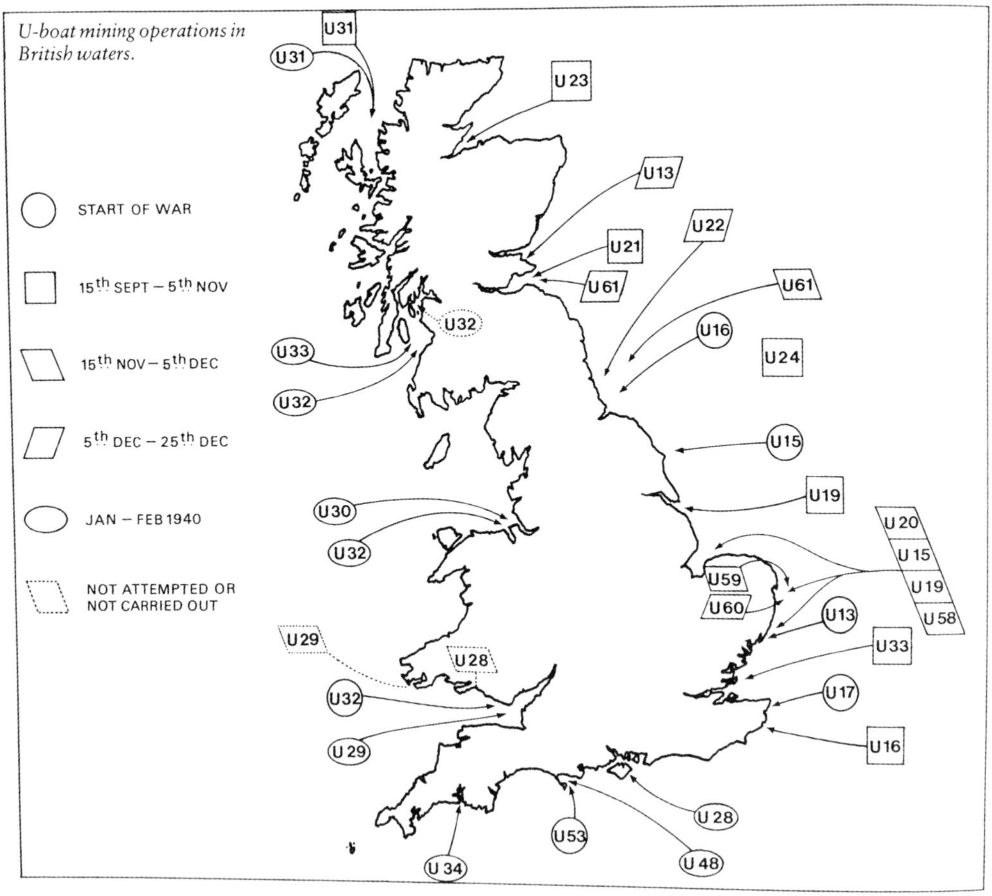

Inshore mining operations in British coastal waters during the first winter of war.

the outbreak of war was some 400km (250 miles) from the nearest coast and there were a good number of U-boats much further away to the west. He wrote:

> Orders and instructions received at home made it clear any future conflict was to be conducted according to Prize Ordinance Regulations. This meant stopping ships and inspecting their loading papers before sinking them and these rules applied both to enemy ships and those from neutral countries who were sailing from or to a British port. These instructions from the political leadership suggested they did not have an overall view of the rules. The regulations regarding lifeboats being inadequate for merchant crews unless they were close to the shore made life rather difficult for U-boat commanders who were far away from coasts where lifeboats were regarded to be unsuitable for accommodating merchant seamen. We certainly could not take any more men into an already crowded U-boat.

One wonders how such contradictory instructions could have been given by the high and mighty, and it suggests there were people in higher leadership roles who did not understand the essential basics. What was the point of sending U-boats to areas where rules prohibited them from attacking?

Prize Ordinance Regulations did not apply to warships or to merchant ships sailing in convoys. These did not have to be stopped but could be attacked without warning. Hitler's desire to keep to the spirit of the Regulations meant German surface ships at sea were not given permission to start aggressive action until the end of September, almost a whole month after the beginning of the war. Unfortunately, this goodwill was blown out of the water on the first day of the conflict by an over-aggressive submarine commander, Kptlt. Fritz-Julius Lemp (U30), who became the first German to sink a ship while ignoring the Regulations. His target, the passenger ship *Athenia*, was carrying a good number of American civilians, and her sinking created a terrific furore, which was fully exploited by every propaganda system against Germany. The situation was made considerably worse for Germany by its own national propaganda department. Many of the early books written about U-boats focused on these dramatic circumstances and therefore the attack will not be detailed in this book. However, it is worth emphasizing a statement made by Professor Dr Jürgen Rohwer, a respected authority on naval warfare. In his classic book *Axis Submarine Successes in World War Two*, hc pointed out how the Supreme Naval Command ordered U30's logbook to be altered to delete the *Athenia* sinking. Rohwer commented 'This was not the only case where the logbook of a U-boat was changed after an event.' British, American and German historians have found profound evidence of the Allies also having changed records and logbooks after the war. America, and possibly Britain as well, employed well established historians to remove papers detrimental to the Allies or showed Germany in a positive light. Wars are not only dangerous but also filthy, and the rich, who benefit from such action, do not go to the front line themselves. They also have a powerful escort when taking their rich profits from the war to a safe bank.

HOW U-BOATS WERE TRAINED TO ATTACK

How U-boats attacked during this first year of war was summarized by Germany's most successful U-boat commander, Flottillen~admiral (Federal German Navy) Otto Kretschmer, in a letter to the author.

> Before the war U-boat training concentrated on submerged daylight attacks from ranges of about 600 metres. Sea and ocean-going U-boats already had an Asdic (later known as Sonar) Compartment but the equipment to go inside had not yet been made operational. So, this tiny 'hole', immediately forward of the radio room, was used mainly as a storeroom, leaving enough space for the passive sound detector, the so-called Group Listening Apparatus. This could pick up sounds but not send out 'pings' like Asdic and could not determine the exact position nor the distance to a target. The underwater microphones or hydrophones were originally situated in a rotating 'T' shaped stalk on the bows but later they were incorporated into a specially

built bulbous dome below the bows with several receivers pointing in different directions, whence the word 'Group'.

Surface attacks were only practised occasionally. These followed a similar pattern to the techniques developed by small motor torpedo boats [MTBs]. The main problem was the speed of U-boats was considerably less than torpedo boats, meaning it was more difficult to get away after an attack. [*MTBs of about 100 tons were capable of reaching over 35 knots, while a 1000-ton U-boat could only manage about 17 knots for short periods when the best conditions prevailed.*] Of course, the tiny silhouette of the U-boat made it easier to get closer to the target before being spotted. If there were submarine hunters in the attack area, it was necessary to dive in absolute silence rather than run away. If submarine hunters were spotted, then it was usual for the U-boat to dive on the way into the attack, which then made it possible for the opposition to hear the U-boat with their Asdic. As a countermeasure, the U-boat should then have gone into silent creeping mode to attack or to escape. For shooting during night attacks, it was suggested U-boats should discharge a double or treble torpedo spread from outside the convoy's protective ring to achieve one hit. If attacking in bright moonlight the tactical rules recommended to do this from periscope depth to get nearer to the target without being observed.

Trying this out during naval exercises in the Baltic, U-boats discovered they would often have to remain in contact with their target for more than a day before reaching an attacking position, which meant they would lose even a slow-moving target if they dived. Therefore, to remain mobile, they had to stay on the surface. There were no rules about what to do if approached by a destroyer. The U-boat commander knew it was necessary to remain undetected, but no one told him how to do this and he was left to his own devices to find his own solution. During the night he had the choice of either diving when approached by a hunter or to run away by exposing his smallest possible silhouette and in both cases he was free to aim torpedoes at any attacker rather than concentrate on merchant ships.

Once the war had started, we all collected more experience, and it was not long before we realized it was possible to remain on the surface for far longer than had previously been thought possible. Moving on the surface became a pure case of keeping one's nerve and I found it was possible to break through a convoy's defensive escort ring without diving and then shooting torpedoes on the surface within the columns of the merchant ships. At first, escorts expected attacking U-boats to be some distance away and a detonation usually resulted in them searching the area by the sides of the convoy. The group attack or wolf pack idea had already been introduced by the U-boat Leadership under Karl Dönitz before the war, but commanders were never given any detailed advice how to react when close to the opposition. Once the war started each commander was interviewed when he returned from patrol and his experiences and opinions were shared with everybody else. Even after the initial skirmishes, there were never any hard and fast rules about how to behave and every commander was left free to do what he thought was best.

U32, a Type VIIA, loading torpedo mines of Type B. These were often referred to as TMB. Note the early conning tower does not have any spray or wind deflectors, meaning lookouts were often blinded by spray, rain and wind.

It is important to emphasize the Royal Navy's shortage of escorts during this period of the war. Escorts formed a ring around the convoy, which they were not allowed to leave for long. All they could do was to put an approaching U-boat down before returning to their allocated position. Later in the war, the opposition had enough small warships to create not only a security ring around each convoy but also to have another hunter group at hand to concentrate on killing U-boats. This meant people like Captain Johnnie Walker, Britain's most successful U-boat hunter with his *Starling* type sloops, could easily spend more time away from the convoy to chase U-boats until their batteries were exhausted, which then forced the U-boats to the surface. In 1941 convoy escorts hardly ever had the opportunity to be away from their protective position for such a long time.

THE INSHORE MINING OFFENSIVE DURING THE FIRST WINTER OF WAR

U-boats had a 'secret' and well functioning weapon and used it with a high success rate during the first war winter. This was the magnetic mine. The only two U-boat types capable of carrying the ordinary moored mines were the huge minelayers of Type XB and Type VIID but these did not come into service until later in the war. Only eight minelayers of Type XB and six of Type VIID were commissioned. The rest of this chapter deals mainly with the smaller torpedo mines, so called because they could be ejected through torpedo tubes. The boat needed a special modification to do this, and the commander and torpedo mechanic also needed special training. Later boats could eject one mine at a time from the surface or from a submerged position, but it is believed the older Type VIIA could do this only when submerged.

Three 'Torpedo Mines of Type A' (TMAs) and three TMBs could be placed at the same time into one torpedo tube to be jettisoned one at a time. When this basic mine design was later enlarged to create the TMC, only two fitted into one torpedo tube. There was another small mine for laying into rivers, but these were not carried by U-boats. Magnetic torpedo mines were highly effective because they could not be cleared by normal minesweepers. They remained lying on the bottom until a ship passed overhead and set off the detonator. Their great advantage over conventional moored mines was their ability to explode under

The Thames Estuary looking south from high over Essex (England). This is Shoeburyness, where the first German magnetic mine was captured. A mass of military islands can be seen at (1), while the Isle of Sheppey and the Swale Channel, separating it from the County of Kent, is visible on the other side of the river at (2). To the right of (3) are several water-filled gravel pits and the huge airfield at Manston is to the left. From here the Thames Estuary looks to be as wide as the English Channel. During the war a German pilot, Heinz Ehrhardt, returning from a raid over Essex, landed by accident at this airfield, thinking he had crossed the Channel and was landing on a German airfield. Sadly for him, he became a prisoner of war.

the passing ship, breaking the keel and hull to make it sink quickly. Mines with spikes or contact detonators had the disadvantage of often making only a comparatively small hole, and watertight bulkheads allowed the victim to limp on and a good number reached their destination, despite the damage.

Magnetic mines were not a naval prerogative. The Luftwaffe had a special aerial version for dropping from aircraft. The person doing so had to know the exact position of the deep-water channel, and aircraft navigation was, at that time, not up to much. Training concentrated on dropping mines at low tide, when it was sometimes possible to see the deep-water channels leading into ports. Britain's discovery of how this highly sophisticated weapon worked must rank as one of the most significant achievements of the war. It is also one of the U-boats' most noteworthy defeats. What is more, many people in Germany realized this magnetic mine would remain as a 'wonder weapon' for only a short time – until Britain found an unexploded one and worked out how to neutralize it. Sweeping it away was easy: in many ways easier than removing moored mines, and apparently even low-flying aircraft could do it. Therefore, U-boat commanders were warned not to drop the mines anywhere where they could be observed, and not to place them in positions where the mines might be washed ashore. But magnetic mines had to be used in comparatively shallow coastal waters, and ideally in narrow channels of harbour approaches. During the first two months of the war Britain lost two small warships and more than twenty merchantmen in inshore waters close to harbours, and the newly commissioned cruiser HMS *Belfast* was also put out of action by a magnetic mine. The damage was severe enough to put *Belfast* out of service with a broken keel and split deck for two years before she was recommissioned. These mines were far more worrying than U47's (Kptlt. Günther Prien) attack on Scapa Flow, where the battleship HMS *Royal Oak* was sunk inside the British anchorage, yet this dramatic incident received far more coverage than the dreaded magnetic mines.

The most painful part of these mercantile losses was that no one in Britain had the faintest idea how they happened or what had been responsible, and nobody was able to do anything to curb the disasters, other than to switch off essential navigation lights near vulnerable harbours. It was not difficult to guess U-boats must have been responsible. Switching off navigation lights was indeed a significantly difficult decision. The war had not removed merchant shipping from coastal waters. Instead, this traffic had increased to meet new demands and with many experienced seafarers being called up to serve in the Navy, this meant there was a strong likelihood of more inexperienced men having to cope with naturally difficult harbours which were now plunged into darkness. Three months earlier, when the war started and everything in the country was blacked out, it was thought to be important for maritime navigation lights to remain visible, albeit on reduced power.

This new situation of total darkness had hardly been implemented when coastguards at Shoeburyness in Essex spotted an aircraft dropping what looked like a kitbag with a parachute. By taking a bearing on where this hit the water, the observers confirmed it had landed not in the deep-water channel but on either a sandbank or mudflats along the side.

The name Shoeburyness requires some digestion. It is the eastern extremity of Southend, where the railway line from London ends. Beyond it is nothing more than a mass of fascinating islands and saltmarshes, still used by the military for highly secret undertakings. During the war this mishmash of saltmarshes was used for testing and modifying weapons, and during the First World War the first prototype tanks were put through their paces in those barren locations. Since the place had excellent mechanical, workshop and communication facilities, the Germans could not have found a better place for presenting Britain with one of their most successful and highly secret new weapons. The men who went out to defuse the magnetic mine would not necessarily have agreed with this statement, pointing to Southend's pier. At over 2km in length, it still is the longest pleasure pier in the world and even has its own little railway for carrying passengers to and from the coastal steamers that used to make fast in the deep-water channel. The mud there is deep, wet, uncomfortable, and covers a vast area; the local rescue services use special equipment for pulling out those unfortunate enough to get stuck in the 'magnetic' mud. The rescue services do not have to train for this very often because there are enough real incidents to keep them well practised. Locals avoid the hazards but the good rail connection to London brings people who venture far out to wallow in the mud. This is said to be good for cooling the blood, but this works only in summer – cold winds will do the same job for the rest of the year. The investigation team walked out to investigate their first magnetic mine in November – not a good time of year to be exploring wet mud in the northern hemisphere.

The three men who ventured out onto the mudflats at low tide with 42-year-old Lieutenant Commander John Ouvry were Lieutenant Commander Roger Lewis, Chief Petty Officer Charles Baldwin and Able Seaman Archibald Vearncombe. The two officers came from HMS *Vernon* in Portsmouth, a training centre for sailors going on to work with torpedoes and mines, and it could well be the other two were recruited locally in Shoeburyness. The *Independent* newspaper's obituary quotes Ouvry as having said he was not pretty, intelligent or brave, just blessed with steady nerves and strong hands. The author, A.B. Sainsbury, added, 'This self-assessment was typical of the man, but nerves and hands however strong are not much use unless they are controlled by a brave mind.' Having negotiated several miles of sandbanks interlaced with soft mud, the men were surprised to find the monster embedded in firm sand, which made working on it considerably easier than had it been lying in a softer patch.

Ouvry had obviously been in such unusual situations before. He came prepared, with large sheets of paper and crayons to take rubbings of the external fittings, and he double-checked that no one was carrying any iron objects. Magnetism was the prime suspect for detonating the mine, although acoustics had not yet been ruled out. The detonator's cover happened to be at the bottom, firmly embedded in the sand, and the mine was too heavy for one man to turn over. All four were required for this incredibly heavy muscle work. These mines weighed between 800 and 1,115kg, of which at least 215kg was high explosives. Had it been hollow, it would have been big enough for a man, and perhaps a child as well, to hide inside it. An especially adapted tractor, able to cope with the hostile location, was required to eventually bring the mine onto firm land. The men's only consolation while they heaved it over was they would neither hear nor feel an explosion. Death would be instantaneous, and without pain. The country had already lost several bomb disposal experts and the men out on those desolate mudflats were aware of the delicacy of the situation. One wonders what went through their minds at the critical moment where they first moved the mine. Less than a year later, men from another team were killed when their captured mine exploded.

Back on land in Shoeburyness there were no significant problems in assembling a team of highly skilled engineers, although some of them must have uttered strong words at being woken in the middle of the night. Making the necessary tools was quite some undertaking. Iron was no use. A non-magnetic metal was required, and then the finished products required a bag of considerable size because one man had to muster all his strength to undo some of the screws. The spanners had to be of considerable size. Yet despite this mammoth undertaking, by the following low tide Ouvry's team had a complete set of tools for taking the mine to pieces, to hopefully defuse the detonators. For much of the time Ouvry worked on his own with Charles Baldwin helping, while the other two watched from a safe distance, holding a camera and making detailed notes about what the two operators were doing. This was necessary in case the mine exploded and someone else might have to tackle the same job at some other time. Lying on its side, the device was not a great deal higher than a man's knees, so it was necessary to wallow in the wet sand without allowing it into the interior of the mine or into one's boots. Everybody who has been out to those flats at low tide will know both mud and sand have an ability to get everywhere, even into sandwiches. The best defence is to wear swimming trunks, which was not terribly practical at the time of year when Ouvry's team was out there. To keep out the cold weather they needed warm jumpers, heavy coats and big boots without hobnails.

As a result of the effort put in by these men, Britain was able to neutralize this incredible weapon, and one wonders how many seamen's lives were saved as a result. What is more, all this activity took place in the highest secrecy. Germany never realized the magnetic mine could now be swept away like all other moored mines. All Britain needed was a new type of minesweeping device.

What is difficult to understand here is the thinking of British officialdom. A soldier doing something brave while being shot at by an enemy who cannot shoot straight would have been eligible for a Victoria Cross, but these men, who must have said their last prayers more than once, were considered not to have been in the face of the enemy. That huge pack of explosives, which no one in Britain had seen before, did not count as facing the enemy and therefore the men were not eligible to receive Victoria Crosses. If officialdom were to rethink this, and make posthumous awards, then no doubt there would be masses of children, whose fathers survived because of this team's bravery, who would volunteer to place such decorations on the graves of the people whose courage has been largely forgotten by time. These four men, later accompanied by Dr Wood (Chief Scientist of the Mine Design Department at HMS *Vernon*), surely made one of the most significant contributions to winning the war. King George VI, the father of the late queen, was so concerned that he not only visited HMS *Vernon*, the Torpedo and Mining School in Portsmouth, but also instituted a medal, the George Cross, to be awarded for acts of outstanding bravery which were not eligible for the Victoria Cross.

A class in a German boys' school. The walls were bare, windows were generally high up to prevent pupils from being distracted by looking out and there was little to inspire them. Even the best teachers were supported only by dreary books, almost all without illustrations and often printed in German script. Yet youngsters were encouraged to take part in non-curricular activities, and sport was considered important enough for the government to have introduced a National Sports Badge. Many naval officers spent years in rooms like this before going to naval college for a short time and then being sent out in ships to face a determined enemy. Almost all grammar schools of the time spent more time teaching classics rather than science, technology and engineering.

As an interesting side-line deviation for the eagle-eyed: try counting the pupils. Note, there are two adults. One of them is probably the class teacher and the other the headmaster.

By the end of November 1939 there had been thirty mining incursions into British waters, and from early December until the beginning of March 1940 there followed another eleven similar undertakings. The first wave of mines hit twenty-one ships, while twenty-nine from the second hit ships. Following this, there was a dramatic tail-off in successes and for the rest of the war magnetic mines were used only in areas where there were no clearing facilities.

THE NORTH CHANNEL BETWEEN SCOTLAND AND IRELAND

This section is based on several reports from the German Federal Navy's Fregkpt. Rudi Conrad, who was a submariner during the war. They could have been written by him or by Robert Gysae, commander of U98 and U177.

> One wonders how locals cope with the weather in the sea area between Scotland and Ireland. For much of the autumn, when we were there, it was always milky with fog banks drifting slowly at leisure, making it virtually impossible to get a bearing on stars

or the sun. Navigation had to be done by dead reckoning, which is not terribly accurate, especially in such a relatively confined space so close to land. When a gap appears in the low clouds, one can rest assured a coastal reconnaissance plane will also appear through it and then it will not be long before all hell breaks loose, and we are chased by submarine hunters and destroyers. Annoyingly, these always come out of an area of bad visibility where you cannot see them approach. We never seem to see them first. You can guarantee it will not long before the alarm bells ring to interrupt our smoothly running routine. This emergency diving works well. The tanks are almost flooded by the time the last man, the officer on duty, drops down into the central control room. Often our men are sharp enough to spot approaching aircraft before they have seen us and then this whole procedure runs quite peacefully, but it does prevent us from being on the surface. The trouble is the peace does not always last and even conversations with experienced men, who said the aircraft cannot have seen us, were interrupted by a dose of depth-charging. Those blokes up there in the sky are fully awake. They are quick and accurate. It is necessary to remain down in the cellar until the aircraft has, hopefully, lost interest and we can continue charging our batteries. We stick up the asparagus for a quick look and then go slowly to the surface. The lookouts will often be in position for only a short while before more aircraft appear. This time they come with the miraculous ability to increase in size and numbers. Instead of one small plane there are now two huge monsters and all we can do is to return to the depths. When we do eventually get back to the surface the whole sequence repeats itself. Fogbanks are replaced by rain banks; visibility always remains poor, making it possible for expected convoys to roll past without us seeing them.

The only real variation in this is rain. It rains often, soaking everybody on the bridge with cold water, which is not as bad as not being able to see anything during the heavy downpours. Then, when the weather improves, we get another alarm. You cannot even rest quietly in your bunk without being disturbed by something. It is not always aircraft, sometimes the lookouts spot small fast warships on the horizon and even when these are far away, they somehow seem to know where we are and come running towards us at fast speed. The astonishing thing is, they often come without their reading glasses, sailing past us while we make best use of patches of poor visibility. Some of these hunting groups also have the irritating habit of sailing past us at considerable speed while we are down below. One of them stops, shuts down its engines, making it exceedingly difficult to hear the ship, and then it just sits up there waiting for us to surface. Such tormenting situations are difficult to get away from and impose considerable hardships on us.

Eventually, when we do see some merchant ships, we are all surprised to the point of shaking nervously. Imagine it yourself. There are definite columns of about thirty merchant ships sailing in a straight line. These big ships are much easier to see than our small submarine and, theoretically, it looks good for us, until we make a mental note of the escorts around our quarry. There is nothing we can do. Our orders are to sink merchant ships. Action stations. Bearing in mind the men have not done much during the past few weeks, they are now keen to have a quick go at any action. The boat is ready before we have decided on the best approach. The 'attack in ten seconds' mentality, which every commander must have, does not always help because the general conditions are so variable. There might be hardly any darkness left before dawn, and it might be better to trail the convoy with a view of going in early the following night. This old method of attacking does not work anymore for all of the time because tomorrow the ships will be too close to the coast. So, to hell with it, we go in now for a quick attack, even if we get at only one or two ships. Brilliant. It worked. Four torpedoes were fired by the first watch officer, one after the other, each one aimed at a different target. He does the shooting while the commander keeps an eye on what is happening and tells him which ship to aim at. The American account of our commanders noodling a torpedo calculator inside the conning tower during action is a load of nonsense. The commander is the bloke who tells everybody what to do and when to do it. We would be lost without him. No one else in the U-boat has been trained to attack shipping.

Then, while concentrating on this action, a lookout reports an escort turning towards us and increasing speed while doing so. When the commander takes a quick look in the direction the lookout is pointing, all he sees is a mass of white water being thrown up by the bows. His instant reaction is to leave the other, stern, torpedo where it is and run the diesels to a fast speed. Sometimes this works very well. We seem to vanish into the waves to lose sight of all the action until some huge explosion reminds us about the convoy. Our torpedoes have hit something and there is nothing further we can do. We must now dive to reload the four bow torpedoes and by the time that has been done, we will have lost the convoy. Being so close to land there is hardly any point in chasing it. It is going to be a case of waiting for the next convoy and enjoying the coffee which the cook has made. He had plenty of electricity for boiling water while the diesels were running, although goodness knows how he juggled all his pots in such a small, confined space without spilling the contents. Yes, the cook is the vital part of this equation. We could not manage without him and the goodies he supplies when enthusiasm runs low.

U995 a museum by the Naval Memorial at Laboe near Kiel.

Chapter 5

U-boats Bite Without Wolfpacks – Autumn 1940

SHORT-RANGE, SINGLE SHOT, SURFACE ATTACKS AT NIGHT, DURING THE FIRST FIFTEEN MONTHS OF WAR

The first U-boat group attack was due to take place just five weeks after the British and French declaration of war, with newly provisioned boats sent to the south-west of Ireland. The plan was to sweep seven boats towards Spain along a busy shipping lane. This made it necessary to replace the commander of U37, Kptlt. Heinrich Schuch, with a more senior flotilla chief, Werner Hartmann, who was the leader of the 6th U-boat Flotilla. He was to act as on-the-spot pack leader and, at the same time, control the boat. This was not a demotion for Schuch, who had been in command for one year, and went on to command U38, U105 and U154, but Dönitz wanted a man with more experience in overall charge. U37, an ocean-going Type IXA, was chosen as lead boat because it was large enough to accommodate the flotilla commander's additional staff, including a doctor and extra radio equipment to prevent interference with the boat's communication system.

Despite detailed planning, the whole proposition collapsed before it could be implemented. One of the allocated boats, U47 (Kptlt. Günther Prien), was withdrawn almost immediately for the special raid on Scapa Flow, while another two needed essential repairs. Dockyard space for U25 (Kptlt. Viktor Schütze) and U34 (Kptlt. Wilhelm Rollmann) had been booked but then postponed before the start of the Norwegian Campaign. Three of the other boats were sunk on their way out. (U42 under Kptlt. Rolf Dau left Wilhelmshaven on 5 October 1939 and was sunk south-west of Ireland on 13 October; U45 (Kptlt. Alexander Gelhaar) left Kiel on 5 October, only to be sunk south-west of Ireland on the 14th; U40 (Kptlt. Wolfgang Barten) left Wilhelmshaven on 10 October with orders to catch up by sailing along a shorter route through the Pas de Calais side of the English Channel, where it was sunk by a mine near Dover on the 13th.) This left only U46 (Kptlt. Herbert Sohler) and U48 (Kptlt. Herbert Schultze) to continue with U37 under Werner Hartmann. Despite the difficulties, these three achieved noteworthy successes by attacking and at least damaging thirteen ships, while another twenty-five ships were sunk by other U-boats in other areas.

This activity took place under the tightest Prize Ordinance Regulations, particularly emphasized by the Naval War Staff and by Hitler himself. Both were deeply embarrassed by the first U-boat sinking on the first day of the war, when U30 (Fritz-Julius Lemp) sank the British freighter *Athenia* with many American passengers on board. The events which followed during the next few months clearly showed the situation at sea was very different from what Karl Dönitz had expected. In fact, most of these events were different from how both sides had imagined them before the fighting started, meaning everybody had to adjust according to a new and dramatic learning curve.

The U-boat war continued to roll on slowly, negotiating the mass of Prize Ordinance restrictions imposed in the hope of paving the way for meaningful peace negotiations, and these Regulations dominated the scene until the late summer of 1940. Damage to U-boats incurred during the bitter fighting during the occupation of Norway added to long shipyard queues, meaning it was a while before the Atlantic war got into full swing, from May 1940 onwards. Unfortunately for Germany, the radio waves were instantly filled with more torpedo failures and almost every returning U-boat came home with a list of such disasters. Had these torpedo frustrations not dominated successes during those early days, then the sinkings would have been more than double the recorded results.

U-boats carried two different types of torpedo, known as G7a and G7e. 'G' stood for Gerade~auslauf (running straight on), an old fashioned codeword for torpedoes, and signified the diameter of 53.3cm. The '7' stood for the length in metres, while the 'a' indicated it was the first type. It did not, repeat NOT, stand for 'air', as has been claimed by some non-German authors. The G7a torpedo was not propelled by compressed air. Instead, it had an internal combustion engine where steam from distilled water was injected into the engine by compressed air. The 'e' stood for electric propulsion, or 'Elektro~antrieb'. These torpedoes needed to have their batteries charged twice a week and were slower than

The result of the first wolfpack falling flat meant only two of the originally planned boats got into the Atlantic to have successful cruises. These were U37 (Korvkpt. Werner Hartmann) and U46 (Kptlt. Herbert Sohler). It seems likely this photo was taken around the time Werner Hartmann was leaving U37. The Knight's Cross he is wearing around his neck was awarded on 9 May 1940. On the left is engineer officer Wessels and on the right, the boat's doctor.

Herbert Sohler commanded U46 around the time plans were made for the first wolfpack attack. He is wearing black U-boat leathers with the lapels buttoned up to the top for keeping out the incessant weather. In September 1940 he became the Chief of the 7th U-Flotilla in St Nazaire and after the war compiled a detailed history of this Flotilla. What is probably the only copy can now be found in the U-boat Museum in Cuxhaven-Altenbruch (Germany).

the other type. The explosives in both could be detonated either by a contact pistol when it hit something solid or by a magnet when it passed under an iron ship. Contact detonation did not necessarily sink a ship because internal bulkheads could contain in-rushing water in just one compartment. There were cases where holes punched in oil tankers rose above the sea level due to the oil pouring out and thus making the ships lighter. An explosion under a ship could crack both keel and ship, making it go down much more quickly. The adjustments for all this, and for setting the torpedo depth, could be made shortly before discharge, while it was already inside the torpedo tube, ready for shooting. The torpedo failures were initially 'cured' by using the contact pistol instead of the magnetic detonator. The G7e was used in daylight, when the bubbles and oil trail on the surface from the G7a's engine would be visible to ships' lookouts.

Victor Oehrn in U37, who had left Wilhelmshaven on 15 May to take up position off Cape Finisterre, dominated the air waves with news of four more catastrophic failures. Dönitz cursed everything and everybody, while his staff wished he would tone down his aggressive onslaught on the higher admirals. His second-in-command, Korvkpt. Eberhard Godt, could see his boss being shunted sideways into a position where he was less of a nuisance. Grand Admiral Erich Raeder, the Head of the Navy, had already sent a terse memorandum saying the Commander for U-boats should concentrate on fighting the war at sea and not concern himself with technical matters, so the chop might not be long in coming. Adding to the depression was an almost total absence of significant successes to boost flagging morale. Yet suddenly these appeared, as if by magic.

Early in June Oehrn in U37 returned with a good number of success pennants flying from the extended periscope. Torpedo failures still dominated the conversation, but the bogeyman had partly been tamed with special handling and particular care. Oehrn also reported how the attack process had become considerably easier since many of the Prize Ordinance Restrictions had been lifted. Passenger ships were still not legitimate targets but all other traffic in the exclusion zone around the British Isles had become fair game, making it unnecessary to stop ships to examine their papers, and without having to decide whether these papers were genuine or forgeries. U37 was still at sea when the German occupation of Holland, Belgium and France got under way and by the time it got back to Wilhelmshaven, the first U-boat had already entered the French naval base in Lorient for replenishment. This was U30 under Kptlt. Fritz-Julius Lemp, who called there on 6 June. Placing new U-boat bases close to British shipping lanes made it unnecessary for U-boats to travel along the long, and by now somewhat dangerous, sea route from Germany, and through the British blockade of German ports. Britain responded to the new situation by routing convoys further north and closing many of its Channel ports. This put additional pressure on the west coast and led to the use of several smaller ports, which had previously been too awkward for heavy international commercial traffic.

Despite the precautions taken by Britain to create convoys, the men involved with them were surprised by the new surface attacks at night, when U-boats closed in and fired torpedoes from only about 500m from their target. Much of pre-war submarine doctrine was based on three torpedoes being fired from 3km to hit one target. At first, no one on the British side knew what was happening and wild guesses included the suggestion the Germans had developed a new high-underwater-speed submarine that could come in at periscope depth and then make its getaway under water without being seen. It was thought Asdic could not detect such boats because they were within the surface turbulence of the waves. On 21 September 1940, when Convoy HX72 was hit hard, with the most severe loss of eleven merchant ships, the Royal Navy guessed they were faced with more than one attacker and all of them had attacked from the surface. The men in convoys also guessed torpedoes were being fired from exceedingly close quarters, so that the U-boat needed only a single shot to get a hit.

The first of the new multi-shot surface attacks had taken place shortly after midnight on 24 August when U57 (Oblt.z.S. Erich Topp) fired his three torpedoes in a matter of minutes at ships in Convoy OB202. It was not long before the British anti-submarine reports published fairly accurate accounts of these unexpected attack techniques. Yet they still underestimated the number of attacking U-boats, saying there were one, two or sometimes three when in fact five had been involved. The Germans had already discovered observers within the convoy could not spot surfaced submarines at night, especially when they took best advantage of the natural conditions before starting their attacks.

There must have been a grimmer side to these losses as well. It seems likely the British War Lobby was keen on passing on the dreadful news of the submarine pirates attacking aggressively, to make it look as if the country were under threat from bloodthirsty invaders. This can perhaps be gauged from the secret anti-submarine reports. These could only be read by officers hunting U-boats, and they explained how the high death rate was due to merchant ships not having been fitted with adequate lifesaving aids. A good number of merchant ships were fitted only with defensive guns. So far, there had been what the propaganda system called the Phoney War, where very little was happening, and the British War Lobby desperately needed to convince the majority at home, who did not

Korvkpt. Werner Hartmann and his engineer officer Wessels on U37.

want to continue with the war, of the ruthlessness with which the enemy was hitting them.

The first specially converted convoy rescue ship did not come into service until January 1941, sixteen months after the start of the war; even then, such specialized vessels were not always available and makeshift alternatives had to be used. Throughout the war these saved the lives of more than four thousand people. The initial organization for rescue ships was also fraught with red tape limitations and many of the men manning them refused to be incorporated under the Royal Navy, despite having been offered generous new ranks. William Hartley, a Master Mariner in the British Merchant Navy, who became captain of two rescue ships, *Copeland* and *Goodwin*, told his higher authorities as a Royal Navy officer he would have to ask permission before changing position within a convoy and in the event of an attack he needed to act fast to get to sinking positions. Any delay would result in the rescue ship finding only dead people in cold water. As a result of this argument, almost all the Masters of rescue ships remained in the Merchant Navy in order to be able to react immediately to any threat. One wonders whether they had iron nerves for volunteering for such dangerous duties. Imagine yourself in a stationary ship, picking up survivors, while you knew there was someone nearby who could sink you at any moment.

Throughout the autumn of 1940 an exceedingly high number of wives and mothers cried and grieved for the dead aboard the merchant ships. Many of these were not British but far-off foreign nationals. The first lists of ships sunk, which I saw way back in the early 1960s, were in books listing British and Commonwealth shipping losses, with no mention of the foreign nationalities included in Table 1. These details were extracted from Professor Dr Jürgen Rohwer's *Axis Submarine Successes of World War Two*. These details were published for the first time in Germany in 1968, more than twenty years after the war had ended.

The nationality of merchant ships sunk by U-boats during the first sixteen months of war.

Month	Total ships sunk	British ships	Foreign ships	Foreign ships as a percentage of total ships sunk (%)
1939				
Sept.	52	38	14	27
Oct.	40	25	15	38
Nov.	35	22	13	37
Dec.	45	20	25	56
1940				
Jan.	52	13	39	75
Feb.	50	18	32	64
Mar.	28	11	17	71
Apr.	10	5	5*	50
May	19	10	9*	47
Jun.	70	33	37	53
Jul.	44	25	19	43
Aug.	70	45	25	36
Sep.	69	54	15	22
Oct.	85	57	28	33
Nov.	40	27	13	33
Dec.	64	47	17	27

Notes: British ships listed here include French and USA ships; foreign ships were: Argentinian, Belgian, Danish, Dutch, Estonian, Finnish, Greek, Lithuanian, Norwegian, Panamanian, Russian, Spanish, Swedish and Yugoslavian. The majority of foreign ships were on course to or from British ports or were sailing in a British convoy.

* Low numbers were due to U-boats being used for other duties during the occupation of Norway and Denmark.

Despite Germany making an all-out effort to hit the convoys, there were two major reasons for not forming wolfpacks. First, there were not enough U-boats, and secondly, there were too many targets, meaning it would have been necessary to avoid good ships to reach the action area to which the U-boats were being directed. Several historians have written the most absurd comments on how these success during the autumn of 1940 almost resulted in Germany winning the Battle of the Atlantic. Britain was being 'battered' by hardly more than twelve U-boats at any time. One third of these would have been travelling towards the action area and another third returning from it, so the numbers mounting attacks were incredibly small and their opposition from the British Royal Navy combined with the Merchant Navy was almost as big as the rest of the world's fleets put together. Surely it must be foolish to suggest Germany was near to winning the war at sea? U-boat commanders had learned their trade well in peacetime and their successes were substantial, with each U-boat at sea easily sinking around six ships each month.

U-boats had the great advantage of the Royal Navy having too few escorts to hunt them to extinction. Instead, all the escorts were allowed to do was to put the attacker 'down' to make him immobile, thus giving the merchant ships time to escape. It was essential for escorts to return immediately to their protective position around the convoy, otherwise another U-boat could slip through the gap.

It seems likely those early convoys were protected by warships to prevent foreign ships from attempting home runs rather than bringing their cargoes to British ports. The British War Lobby, of course, needed victims to make the nation realize they were under attack from a ruthless and intolerant enemy.

The successes of the short-range surface attack at night came to an abrupt halt by appalling winter weather that made the Atlantic untenable for small U-boats. Not much more than a year later, in early 1942, they once again achieved considerable successes in American waters but none of these ever came anywhere near the high sinking figures of the late summer and autumn of 1940.

Having a makeshift bath inside the storage spaces on the upper (outside) deck while in warmer areas.

Chapter 6

Harder Times Biting Harder: 1941 and 1942

The high successes of autumn 1940, when each U-boat at sea was sinking up to six ships per month, was brought to an abrupt halt by the arrival of harsh winter weather. This instantly halved the success rate before the decline continued to slide down the slippery path of no recovery. It is likely the U-boat Command, overestimating successes by at least a third, was not conscious of this downward trend until March 1941, when the crunch was announced by a succession of impressive sinkholes, indicating the downhill slide was due to more than just short periodic spells of bad luck brought on by stormy weather.

People searching through original wartime records must also have noticed how new words started appearing regularly in everyday speech and in casual writings. The words 'Termin ist Termin', meaning 'Schedule is Schedule' or 'Target Date is Target Date', featured strongly from 1941 onwards. Keeping to target dates was becoming more important than anything else, even when it meant shortening the training period or doing without it.

PAINFUL LOSSES – RADAR'S FIRST SINKING

The first pronounced big bang came in March 1941 when three of what the British called 'Star Turn Commanders' with Knight's Crosses did not come home: Günther Prien in U47, Otto Kretschmer in U99 and Joachim Schepke in U100. In addition to this, March also saw the loss of U70 (Kptlt. Joachim Matz) and U551 (Kptlt. Karl Schrott), both sunk on their first war cruise. On 5 April U76 (Kptlt. Friedrich von Hippel) was lost, also on the boat's first cruise, and on 28 April U65 (Kptlt. Joachim Hoppe) was lost on its seventh cruise.

During the bitter fighting of the First Happy Time, in the autumn of 1940, there had never been more than two U-boat sinkings per month and there were none at all in January and February of 1941, so these losses came as an especially hard blow. As a consolation prize, on 18 March 1941 the experienced Kptlt. Hans Eckermann in UA limped into Lorient with serious damage. (UA had been built before the war for Turkey as *Batiray* but was not handed over, whence the letter 'A' instead of a number after the 'U'.) The action against this boat was initially recorded as a kill for HMS *Wolverine,* who was assumed to have sunk U47 on 7 March.

* * *

U99 with the most successful commander of the Second World War, Kptlt. Otto Kretschmer, showing his full face towards the camera. His left hand is gripping the pit for the radio direction finder aerial, and sighting binoculars are clipped in position on the top of the torpedo aimer. The long pennant flying from the detachable commander's flagpole can be seen next to it. The large black 'horseshoe' is a lifebelt and at the front of the handrails is a real horseshoe painted a gold colour. Two of these were pulled up by the anchor chain and attached to the conning tower as a good luck symbol. The superstition of luck falling out when hung this way was not known in Germany. The man on the right is holding a 'whisper tube' or megaphone, which was merely a hollow metal cone for shouting through.

The following is based on a letter from Otto Kretschmer (U99) written in February 1977, while he was working as a retired Federal Navy Flottillen~admiral with Thyssen Nord~see~werke in Emden, and later with clarification from Volkmar König (U99).

> Each U-boat commander was free to issue his own rules to his crew on how they should react to any situation. My watch officers, one of whom was positioned on the bridge when I was down below, consisted of the 1WO and 2WO, both commissioned officers, and they were supplemented by the Ober~steuer~mann (navigator), a warrant officer, as 3WO.

Although not commissioned, the Ober~steuer~mann often had more seagoing experience than all the higher officers put together. In peace time, he would have joined the navy after having graduated from a technical apprenticeship and he would not have been admitted to a Warrant Officer School until he had several years of seagoing experience. Claims by American authors that warrant officer schools were abolished by the Third Reich are not true.

My watch officers were given the following instructions for when we were on the surface without myself on the bridge:

1. Aircraft in sight: Dive immediately.
2. Merchant ship in sight: Remain as far away as possible without losing sight.
3. Destroyer in sight during daylight with only mast tips visible and the opposition's lookouts still beyond the horizon: call commander to the bridge.
4. Destroyer in sight at night: run away with smallest possible silhouette and call commander to the bridge.

The decisive issue for a U-boat was its ability to remain hidden on the surface among waves, making it most difficult to spot, and from there it could quickly be driven to a fast speed. Once dived, it became almost stationary and could then be detected by Asdic and easily attacked. [Asdic could not detect a surfaced submarine.] The surface speed of U-boats depended a great deal on the state of the sea. There was a time when I tried to run away from two corvettes on the surface in the North Atlantic but found both ships were slowly getting closer on the other side of the horizon. More and more of their superstructure was coming into sight, meaning our only alternative to remain hidden was to dive and remain almost stationary with just enough silent drive speed to keep the hydroplanes or depth rudders effective. Attacking these ships was out of the question because the torpedoes with which we entered the war would hardly have hurt them, something both we and the opposition learned very quickly. This situation of attacking small escorts changed only when the next generation of torpedoes was introduced in the autumn of 1943.

In March 1941 HMS *Walker* (Commander Donald Macintyre) and HMS *Vanoc* (Lieutenant Commander J.G.W. Deneys) were searching for survivors from U100 (Kptlt. Joachim Schepke) when they stumbled across U99. One our own lookouts had carelessly failed to report the presence of a small warship and then, when it was spotted by others, the duty officer ordered the boat to dive instead of turning away while exposing our smallest silhouette. As a result, we were detected by *Walker*'s Asdic, seriously depth charged and only just managed to get back to the surface, despite the interior rapidly filling with water. Strangely, once back on the surface the sinking process seemed to stop and the engineer officer, Kptlt.Ing. Schroeder, climbed back down to make sure the boat was going to sink without men from the Royal Navy getting inside. Sadly, this delay meant he and two others were not rescued with the rest of the crew. [Ing. is short for Ingenieur, meaning Engineer.]

The sinking of U100 was significant because, although we did not know it at the time, this was the first success of the Type 236 Radar aboard HMS *Vanoc*, which made it possible to 'see' even such small objects as a surfaced U-boat during the darkest night and in the poorest visibility. The other major aid for hunting U-boats, the High Frequency Direction Finder, or H/F D/F (known as Huff Duff), which could determine the direction from which even short U-boat messages were coming, was not introduced until later in 1941 and only started playing a significant role towards the end of the year.

British radar had been in use since the last few months of 1940, but it did not achieve a great deal when it was first introduced. Set to detect surfaced submarines at 10 miles or so, it managed this quite well, but the nearness of the convoy produced masses of echoes from merchant ships, bouncing off the wave tops, making it difficult to identify whether a dot on the screen came from a submarine or whether it was one of these reflections. The problem was overcome by first making the equipment less sensitive and thereby significantly reducing the number echoes. Although this helped, it was still a while before the apparatus could be calmed down enough to eradicate the distraction.

Much of what has been written about the loss of U47 (Kptlt. Günther Prien) has not stood the test of time. U47 was the boat that penetrated the defences of Scapa Flow in the Orkney Islands to sink the battleship HMS *Royal Oak* inside the British naval anchorage. The fires of war were still burning when Britain instructed two committees, the Chief of Naval Operations Committee on Assessment of Damage to Enemy Submarines and the British Admiralty Assessment Committee, to investigate what had happened to all the U-boats. Among other things, these committees were later instrumental in supplying information about losses to enquiries by next-of-kin of lost soldiers. They created detailed lists of what had happened to each U-boat by comparing mainly German, American and British records. Once the war had finished, it would appear many people were keener on leaving the armed forces than staying in what had suddenly become a shrinking or stale occupation. There were masses of good jobs to be had for civilians. As a result, there must have been a shortage of staff, allowing several boats, including U47, to slip through the net. The probable reason for U47's loss has been put down to either human error or mechanical failure. All boats of this type (VIIB) were no longer in the best of mechanical condition, and in addition to this their experienced men were being withdrawn to boost crews in new boats.

The general situation of the war in 1941 can be best appreciated when one remembers the most successful commander of the war, Kptlt. Otto Kretschmer, was sunk during the war's nineteenth month and the fighting continued for another fifty months. Similarly, three months later the most successful boat of the war (U48, under three ace commanders) shot its last torpedoes in anger, to be withdrawn from active service due to its poor mechanical condition. Technically speaking, there were no successful boats at all. The success came from the crews inside them, not from the machinery.

TWO MAJOR ENIGMA CONTRIBUTIONS

The following is partly based on information from George Högel (radio operator in U110 and in U30) and the French historian Albert Lebasch, with considerable help from Gus Britton and Commander Richard Compton-Hall of the Royal Navy Submarine Museum. John Gallehawk provided access to GCHQ papers at Bletchley Park and helped with other information.

One of the most significant 'key books' for the naval side of Enigma is Patrick Beesly's *Very Special Intelligence*, which originally came out before the code-breaking story was published. Therefore, it is essential to find an edition published in the year 2000 or later by Greenhill Books in London or Stackpole Books in Pennsylvania. This later edition has an introduction by Lieutenant Commander W.J.R. Gardener (Royal Navy Historical Branch) and an afterword by the code-breaking expert Ralph Erskine, all in most readable English and with more details than in earlier publications. Beesly worked in London's Submarine Tracking Room, making him a valuable source. Another interesting new source is the book by David Balme, *Enigma: The Untold Story of the Secret Capture* (Whittles Publishing, Caithness, 2016), which gives a detailed history of the period leading to this most significant event. Many of these details are now available online from various sources, but not all the online material is true.

* * *

On 9 May 1941 Fritz-Julius Lemp (U30 and later U110), a Knight of the Iron Cross, who torpedoed the first non-German ship of the war, went down under incredible circumstances

A three-wheel Enigma machine. The naval version had a plugboard at the front.

The later four-wheel Enigma machine was introduced on 1 February 1942. This introduction blacked out the codebreakers at Bletchley Park until such a device was captured towards the end of the year.

wherein the Royal Navy captured the entire contents of his radio room, including the Enigma code machine with its manuals.

The year 1941 was a bad one for Germany, with the navy wandering from one failure into another, without knowing what was hitting them. One of the main culprits for causing this downturn of events was thought to have been radio. Although still very much in its infancy, radio was already a feared aid when the war started, with many people shying away from using it because the sender's position could be determined by radio direction finders. The most successful U-boat commander of the war, Otto Kretschmer, was nicknamed 'Silent Otto' because he refused to transmit radio messages unless his position was known to the opposition. He was not the only one. Many others did not use their radios either. The German Navy overcame this dread by creating a Short Signal Code Book, where long phrases were condensed into a few letters of Morse code, all of them too short for conventional direction finders.

This fear of the transmitter's position being detected led the German Navy to create powerful land-based radio stations. The naval version of the Enigma code was considered to be 'unbreakable'; therefore, it was thought, there would be no danger of sending long messages from known fixed locations. Should the enemy ever manage to capture an Enigma machine with the correct settings, then they could only use it until the starting positions were changed at the end of each day. For the human mind, Enigma settings were endless, and the machine was easy to use, although for speed two people were needed to code or decode one message. The Enigma code may have been 'unbreakable' but a small number of astute people from Poland and Great Britain managed it. Their brilliance can be all the more appreciated when one knows the machine had one major fault: it would never code a letter as itself, so each letter had to be one from the alphabet but not the one shown in

In U-boats one man usually worked the Enigma machine while another wrote down the illuminated letters, but on busy land stations there was a device for printing the result directly onto a strip of paper. These were then glued onto telegraph or information sheets. Hanging on the back towards the left is an original form for writing coding messages by hand. (*Photo: taken in the Aeronauticum Museum in Nordholz near Cuxhaven*)

the code. This weak point was used by code breakers to crack Enigma. The story of how they did this is fantastically complicated and incredibly exciting, and of course none of the codebreakers had ever seen a computer. After the war, when Alan Turing was looking for finance to build the first commercial machine, the 'experts' told him it would be a waste of money because the whole of the country would NEVER need more than three such digital machines. How the code was cracked is well worth further study, although do start such a project with the knowledge that many original materials have been destroyed.

German advances with radio started before the First World War with the purpose of making itself independent from the British and American worldwide telegraph-cum-telephone network. This progress paid dividends during the First World War, when radio made it possible for ships at sea, like the light cruiser SMS *Emden*, to contact supply ships to enable a successful cruiser war campaign in the Asian and Indian Oceans. This single cruiser had about eighty ships at sea hunting it – an incredibly smart way of drawing vital firepower away from the action areas.

The breaking of Enigma remained a dark secret for many years after the war because some of Britain's Cold War opponents continued to use similar machines until digitization replaced mechanical instruments. Enigma is not the exact word, but it helps to keep things non-technical. The Navy, for example, called its especially modified machine Schlüssel~maschine M (Code Machine M) where 'M' stood for Marine. (The German Navy often called itself Marine, not Kriegsmarine.) The change from a three to a four-wheel machine took place on 1 February 1942 and successfully locked out British codebreakers until one of the new devices was captured towards the end of the year. These new machines were used mainly by U-boats, while the rest of the navy continued with the three-wheel versions. The naval version of Enigma was made more difficult by adding a plug board to the front, giving an incredible number of additional variations, and thus making it impossible for anyone with an army or air force model to read its messages.

At an International Submariners meeting in Portsmouth (England) long after the war. Georg Högel (*right*), an artist and historian, wrote the book about U-boat Emblems (*Embleme Wappen Malings deutscher U-boote 1939–1945*, Koehlers Verlag). He was the radio operator in U30 and later in U110, both under Fritz Julius Lemp. U30 was the first U-boat to sink a ship during the war and U110 was captured by the Royal Navy. With him is the French historian, Albert Lebasch. Both provided material for this book.

The serious beginning of the U-boats' Enigma story came in silence, without a big bang and without many people knowing what had happened, while Kptlt. Fritz-Julius Lemp in U110 was attacking Convoy OB318 on 9 May 1941. This time, he was not terribly lucky. U110's periscope was spotted, and three escorts, *Bulldog* (Commander Joe Baker-Cresswell), with *Aubretia* (Lieutenant Commander V.F. Smith) and *Broadway* (Lieutenant Commander T. Taylor), launched an attack. They plastered the ocean-going submarine cruiser with depth charges accurately enough to smash the stern, causing a total loss of power and leaving Lemp lying on the control room floor in semi-consciousness with a bleeding head. It seems likely all he managed after that was to be helped up to the bridge, where U110's position was seen to be obviously hopeless. The three escorts were nearby, with one of them heading straight towards U110. Without power, all the men could

Admiral Karl Dönitz, the U-boat Chief, welcoming U93 (Kptlt. Claus Korth) with survivors from the supply ship *Belchen*.

do was abandon the U-boat. None of the attackers knew the seriousness of the damage and Commander Baker-Cresswell took this opportunity to send his target to the bottom by ramming it. While approaching at fast speed he became aware it was considerably higher in the water than usual, making him think there might be an opportunity to get on board. The diving tanks had obviously been fully blown to surface and men were seen to be jumping into the water, so he changed course. The Royal Navy had been desperate to get its hands on an Enigma machine with its rotors, and the documentation to operate it. In view of this, many first officers had been primed about what to do if they managed to get aboard a U-boat. On this occasion this rather suicidal move fell to 20-year-old Sublieutenant David Balme. Together with his boarding party, armed with only First World War revolvers, they managed to retrieve almost everything from the radio room: a wonderful haul. All this happened almost within sight of Greenland, not a salubriously warm area in which to be out rowing a small boat, while the Germans in the water had drawn an even shorter straw by jumping into an icy cooler. It may have been May, but all this was happening near the southern tip of Greenland, not an area well known for its sunny delights or warm beaches. To make matters worse, the papers retrieved from the U-boat could not be prevented from getting wet and had to be hung up in the destroyer to dry out again. None of the boarding party had practised such an escapade with their rowing whaler, nor had they been inside a German U-boat; worse, none of them knew exactly which items were the important ones. As a result, they brought back anything portable, including Lemp's Knight's Cross and his hat.

Long after the war, when this story emerged from the secrets list, tales started to germinate about how Lemp got back on board to sink his boat and how he was shot in cold blood, none of which can be supported by anyone, not even his own crew. The wind was strong enough to blow U110 away from the survivors. Some, having rushed up without life jackets, were struggling desperately in the cold water. It is unlikely Lemp could have reached his boat, even if he had not been injured. The other story of Balme having shot Lemp is even more absurd and all the skulduggery which has found its way into print can be ignored. The important point is U110 remained afloat long enough for the boarding party to strip much of the interior of its portable secrets. This material got back to London exceedingly fast, and no one on the German side knew anything about their boat having been captured and boarded. One of the escorts was positioned between the U-boat and the men in the water, who thought it had gone down. These details came back to the U-boat Command when U110's first watch officer, Kptlt. Dietrich Loewe, became part of a prisoner exchange. He was Lemp's cousin and highly unpopular with the crew, who regarded him as a brainless bully. Fellow crew members he met again later as a prisoner of war told him how they had seen men aboard the U-boat with a towrope, but this effort did not come off and others claimed they saw the boat drop below the waves.

A German fuse-box as used in ships and in homes. One ceramic fuse fitted behind each of the white caps and the tiny window made it possible to view an indicator showing whether the fuse was 'alive' or had blown. If broken, a new fuse of the correct value could be quickly screwed into position without having to fit a new wire, as in British fuses. This photo was taken in the radio room of U564 (Kptlt. Reinhard Suhren, and from October 1942 Oblt.z.S. Hans Fiedler). The radio operator wore headphones all the time while on duty unless the commander had ordered the radio to be shut down.

It seems likely this is the exceptionally dramatic end of U575 (Oblt.z.S. Wolfgang Boehmer), the second front boat to have been fitted with a schnorkel.

Everyone thought the Royal Navy could not have got inside their boat. Recent research seems to show U110 could have been towed to Iceland but instead there was a definite decision to 'let her go' in order to get the Enigma material to Britain as quickly as possible. This is pure speculation. We do know for certain the haul arrived at Hvalford in Iceland at one o'clock in the morning of 11 May and from there was taken via Reykjavik to Britain at a rate of 25 knots. It is important to emphasize this was not the only occasion when the British navy got hold of a German coding machine, but having the machine was of little use unless you also had the codebooks to operate it and the instructions of how to set up the daily settings. The astonishing point here is Britain had managed to work out a way of finding the basic settings for the machine without needing this vital information from Germany. This is a fantastic story of one of the greatest achievements of all times, and a brilliant subject for further study.

The machine brought out of U110 in May 1941 was a three-wheel version. This became obsolete in the Atlantic eight months later, on 1 February 1942, when the four-wheel version became operational. As a result, Bletchley Park could not read the U-boat codes until the end of that year, when one of these was captured in the eastern Mediterranean from U559 (Kptlt. Hans Heidtmann) on 30 October 1942. On this occasion, the U-boat was boarded by Lieutenant Anthony Fasson and Able Seaman Colin Grazier from HMS *Petard*. They were helped by 15-year-old canteen assistant Tommy Brown, who had swum over to the submarine. Their haul was enormous and enabled Bletchley Park to get back into reading the German code, called 'Shark' in England and 'Triton' in Germany. The interesting point about this sinking is how the accounts are most variable because many authors made up their own stories. The basic facts centred around a Sunderland aircraft

sighting a U-boat at five o'clock in the morning. The nearest warship was the destroyer *Hero* (Lieutenant W. Scott), sailing to Haifa, now in Israel but in those days in Palestine, changed course while the escorts *Pakenham* (Captain E.B. Stevens), *Petard* (Lieutenant Commander M. Thornton), *Dulverton* (Lieutenant Commander W.N. Petch) and *Hurworth* (Lieutenant Commander D.A. Shaw) left Port Said in Egypt to help. *Pakenham* made contact with the submerged submarine at around lunch time, assisted by another aircraft, Wellesley 'N' (Flight Sergeant R.J. Moore) from

U123 with Kptlt. Karl-Heinz Moehle, who later became the Commander of the 5th U-boat Flotilla, wearing a black naval jacket. Behind him one can see a sighting compass. The three men on the right are part of the UFA film team.

the RAF's 47 Squadron. The aircraft which originally spotted the U-boat had come from the Naval Cooperation Group and had by this time moved on. This capture, in many ways, was one of the war's most important events, having consumed more than 300 depth charges, and the story is exciting enough not to need any input from fiction writers. Sadly, both Fasson and Grazier went down with U559, and Tommy Brown died a short time later in a house fire. Another interesting point is how Bletchley Park used this machine to decode signals on 13 December, but no one seems to have recorded how the captured material got from the eastern Mediterranean back to England.

THE BATTLESHIP *BISMARCK* AND NINE SUPPLY SHIPS SUNK IN TWENTY-EIGHT DAYS

The battleship *Bismarck* (Kpt.z.S. Ernst Lindemann, with the Fleet Commander, Admiral Günther Lütjens, on board) was sunk on 27 May 1941. An interesting and coincidental point is that U110 (Kptlt. Fritz-Julius Lemp) was captured at the southern end of the Denmark Strait between Greenland and Iceland in position 60-22N 23-12W on 9 May of the same year, not far from where *Bismarck* ran into British ships to sink the battlecruiser *Hood* at 63-20N 31-50W.

Bismarck and its consort, the heavy cruiser *Prinz Eugen*, left Germany early in May 1941 and soon after this people in the British Empire were delighted by a newspaper photo with the caption 'The Picture that Sank the Bismarck'. The story attached to it told readers how the German battleship had been sunk in the North Atlantic after it had been spotted in a Norwegian fiord by the photo-reconnaissance pilot Michael Suckling. Bletchley Park in England already had several working Enigma machines by this time, although the cryptanalysts were not yet able to work out for themselves how to set them up at the beginning of each day, but it seems highly likely they discovered *Bismarck*'s presence in Norway. Unfortunately, the English leadership could not act upon this highly secret information for fear of giving away their 'golden egg' source to the Germans. Thus, two experienced

Kptlt. Karl-Heinz Moehle of U123 shortly after having received his Knight's Cross.

Scheerstrasse in the Kiel naval base, with typical military barrack-type buildings.

pilots from the Photo Reconnaissance Unit were dispatched to fly over the area and make it look as if they were there for some purpose other than photographing the German ships. The two men chosen for the job were Flying Officer Cedric Greenhill, a holder of the Distinguished Flying Cross, and slightly his junior, Pilot Officer Michael Suckling. Determining which published version of this incredible achievement is true is now difficult because many slightly different stories have appeared in print, with each author obviously copying from another and adding a bit of their own imagination. This event could well do with more detailed study because it is a brilliant example of well coordinated success by the Photo Reconnaissance Unit. To make it look like an accidental sighting, both aircraft flew over major towns in appalling weather with long routes along the coast to make sure they were seen, and it was the junior of the two who was sent to where *Bismarck* was known to be anchored. Of course, neither Suckling nor Greenhill knew anything about code-breaking, nor were they told the identity of the big ships. They went out looking for two large German warships, one of which 'could be' *Bismarck*. Sadly, the heroic Michael Suckling was to die on active service only two months later and Greenhill was shot down to become a prisoner of war in August 1941. Their mission to find *Bismarck* became an inspiration for many and the Photo Reconnaissance Unit went on to make an enormously big contribution to Britain's war effort. Sadly, much of this has been forgotten, although many of the Photo Reconnaissance Unit's adventures are even more exacting and exciting than the dramatic fighting.

The final word in this dramatic sinking saga must go to the most senior surviving officer of *Bismarck*, the artillery officer Baron Burkhard von Müllenheim-Rechberg. He and others were astonished to find it had been impossible to throw off two shadowing cruisers while

Part of the Kiel naval base after a bombing raid in August 1944 which destroyed part of Haus Atlantik, where the 5th U-boat Flotilla had rooms.

zigzagging for many hours through thick fog, indicating Britain must have efficient radar sets. In his book *Battleship Bismarck*, he wrote 'this had thrown conventional sea warfare into a totally new era'. What is strange and makes one wonder why Germany was hit so hard with radar, is that the Baron was not the only person to have realized something totally new must be happening. And, unlike the Baron, who became a prisoner of war, others returned home to report the matter. On 30 May 1941 (that is, less than three days after *Bismarck*'s sinking) Kptlt. Engelbert Endrass in U46 was having a right old set-to with a tanker, which managed to evade several of his attacks. Endrass, who had been the first watch officer in U47 under Günther Prien and fired the torpedoes that sank HMS *Royal Oak* in Scapa Flow, was definitely no beginner. At 0400 hours, while south of Greenland, he wrote in his log: 'This incident confirms, once again, how lone ships have been equipped with a good search device which can detect U-boats on the surface and when they are submerged. In addition to this, these ships must also have a sound detector capable of hearing approaching torpedoes.' Such warnings can be seen in other logs as well. Only a few months later, in January 1943, people who had worked with German radar were not believed when they claimed to have identified radio signals from such search devices.

The sinking of Germany's battleship on 27 May 1941 hit the world news with a significant punch. Britain made sure every ounce of propaganda was squeezed out of the event, and even after the war continued to cash in on the incident. The film industry produced a convincing film entitled '*Sink the Bismarck*', but this was based on a novel rather than hard facts. Pity. This film also failed to take advantage of another chain of further disasters which were arguably even more depressing than the loss of the battleship. Some experts in both Britain and Germany had partly predicted the *Bismarck* disaster before it happened, but none of them had foreseen the loss of the battle squadron's nine supply ships in a period shorter than one month.

This supply ship catastrophe started with U-boat Command asking whether U-boats could take advantage of the ten ships sent out to support *Bismarck* and *Prinz Eugen*. The idea was to break an incredible stalemate in the submarine war by sending U-boats further afield into areas they could not reach on their own. The Naval High Command agreed for secret refuelling positions to be sent to these ships for supplying the U-boats in what was

Keeping a special lookout for aircraft became more important as the war progressed and later boats were fitted with radar detectors. The man on the left is holding onto such an aerial. Improvised weapons were added as well. This shows a 9mm machine gun. These fitted into brackets in the conning tower wall and were taken below every time the boat dived.

thought to be this wonderful unbreakable Enigma code. The result was shattering. *Prinz Eugen* (Kpt.z.S. Helmuth Brinckmann) managed to get into its new base in Brest (France) despite engine trouble after having been refuelled by the tanker *Spichern* (formerly the Norwegian prize *Krossfonn*, captured by the auxiliary cruiser *Widder* (Korvkpt. Hellmuth von Ruckteschell) a year earlier in June 1940). Now, by June 1941, when *Bismarck* was no more, all was quiet on the Atlantic front. The hubbub of sinking the huge battleship in the North Atlantic had started to quieten considerably when the radio waves suddenly got rather hot again from 5 June onwards. Several other supply ships used their last bits of energy to

Lookouts were among the most important men in submarines. The heavy gloves suggest hard work, or this photo was taken in winter or in the cold north.

send messages they were being approached by the Royal Navy. These horror signals then continued to flood in at an alarming rate until the end of the month, when radio silence ruled once again because none of the supply ships was left at sea. Only *Spichern* slipped through the hunters' nets to run into France. This made it more than obvious German supply ships could no longer operate in the nautical graveyard of the North Atlantic.

The following supply ships were caught after this massive *Bismarck* operation:

3 June	*Belchen*	Scuttled during gunfire from the cruisers *Aurora* and *Kenya*. Ex Norwegian *Sysla*.
4 June	*Esso Hamburg*	Scuttled when HMS *London* approached. Ex US *Esso Colon*.
4 June	*Gedania*	Captured by HMS *Marsdale*.
4 June	*Gonzenheim*	Scuttled after discovery by aircraft from Royal Navy ships *Victorious, Nelson* and *Neptune*. The wreck, still afloat, was sunk by HMS *Esperance Bay*. Ex Norwegian *Kongsfjord*.
5 June	*Egerland*	Sunk by HMS *London* and HMS *Brilliant*. Ex Norwegian *North America*.
12 June	*Friedrich Breme*	Sunk by HMS *Sheffield*.
15 June	*Lothringen*	Intercepted by HMS *Dunedin* and later renamed *Empire Salvage*. Ex Dutch *Papendrecht*.
21 June	*Babitonga*	Scuttled when HMS *London* approached.
23 June	*Alstertor*	Scuttled during an attack by HMS *Marsdale*.

This list needs a serious overhaul. Originally, these were all merchant ships and were manned with a high proportion of merchant seamen, who had gone through a short period of special training for their new role.

Towards the beginning of June 1941, the U-boat Command was fully aware things were not as sweet as they had been only eight months earlier. The 'Happy Time' of sinking masses of shipping in Britain's Western Approaches would never take centre stage again. Things had changed at sea. The big question was 'What?' While making every effort to find the reason for the changes, the U-boat Command reacted by reducing the headquarters staff, the thinking being that the fewer people who knew about what was going on, the less information might inadvertently leak out. In Britain exactly the opposite happened. There, land-based Intelligence officers were increased to deal with the greater inflow of data, and in this field U93 can be used to illustrate one of the many shortcomings on the German side, as follows.

THE SAGA OF THE SUPPLY SHIP *BELCHEN* AND U93

The badge at the end of Admiral Dönitz's baton, which was stolen from his personal luggage by British soldiers. This is a true copy of the original given to the U-boat Museum in Cuxhaven-Altenbruch by Professor Peter Tamm (Founder of the International Maritime Museum in Hamburg).

U93 (Kptlt. Claus Korth), the first operational VIIC boat, did not have an altogether smooth beginning in 1941. The large 88mm quick firing gun in front of the conning tower had been removed because the opposition had grown too fierce, the conning tower was modified, and other repairs were made when it arrived in France. The U-boat patrol line formed when *Bismarck* was known to be in serious trouble had already been disbanded two days after the battleship's sinking. During the new uneasy calmness aboard U93, Korth, sitting in the cramped officers' mess, became aware there was something going on around him, but he could not fathom out what the men were up to. Already slightly annoyed by their behaviour, he was hit by the utter insolence of the radio room making an announcement without his permission. The radio operator had picked up a signal saying Korth had been awarded the Knight's Cross. Mimicking a national news broadcast, he announced the fact while a celebration was hurriedly arranged. Korth's rage was calmed as everybody who could fit in the mess with a glass of something congratulated him. All this was going on while U93 was refuelling from the supply ship *Belchen*. The high spirits, both in the air and in the cups (because U93 did not have many glasses) was halted rather suddenly by the appearance of two cruisers which instantly attacked and sank the surface ship without coming into U93's torpedo range. What followed can only described as an incredible rescue operation.

The tiny U-boat rescued the survivors from the water to end up with an additional forty-nine men on board, more than the entire boat's complement of about forty-four. Conditions were very cramped. Men had to take it in turns to sit or stand. Many of the survivors were in intense pain and having been in the cold waters to the south of Greenland were literally frozen stiff. To make matters worse, Korth knew there was no help nearby. He was definitely on his own. He also knew the boat could not withstand an attack. Everything had to remain calm while U93 broke off its engagement to head back to the nearest French port. Like so many other U-boat men, Korth guessed radio was playing a significant role in the recent punishment. So, without further ado, he shut down the radio transmitter to return in silence, thinking this would be better than giving away his position

German lookout binoculars were NOT fitted with sun filters. Instead, to prevent a momentary loss of sight due to different light intensities, the men wore special sunglasses for butting onto their binoculars.

to enemy direction finders. The experienced radiomen from *Belchen* agreed. The sinking took place on 3 June 1941 and the men on board U93 put up with the most appallingly cramped conditions until 10 June, when the boat put into St Nazaire on the French Biscay coast. Korth said this undertaking was made possible by having no 'passengers' on board, only experienced seamen who all contributed to the welfare of this incredible occasion. 'It was like having two efficient crews on board,' he said.

At his debriefing, Korth was severely reprimanded for having passed close to several convoys without reporting their positions, speed and course. To do so had crossed his mind, but conditions were so exceedingly cramped that any slight disturbance from the opposition could easily have sent his boat crashing down for its last deep dive. Korth, together with other experienced men on board, decided not to risk anything that might upset this delicate balance by attracting hunters with depth charges. Korth may have had nine years' experience as a commander, but with him now he had much older men with a lifetime of seagoing experience and he was grateful for their help and advice. Some even baked fresh bread rolls for everybody on board. Once back in base, he was told U-boats stretched out as far as Greenland had failed to find targets while U93 had ignored the lushest of opportunities. Korth was told in no uncertain terms he should at least have reported the passing convoys. One wonders what might have happened to a lesser commander who had so disobeyed standing orders. Korth had just been awarded the Knight's Cross and so became a notable celebrity. Forty years later, after his retirement, he was still troubled by this most severe reprimand and he spent several days in the U-boat Archive, then in

Kptlt. Reinhard Suhren, a Knight of the Iron Cross, visiting shipyard workers at Blohm und Voss in Hamburg, who built U564. In his hand he is holding a welding rod.

Westerland on the Frisian Island of Sylt, to establish exactly what had happened during this fateful voyage and to establish whether he had made the correct decision or not.

The interesting point here is U93 was not the only boat to have abandoned its ordered objective, creeping home with serious damage or with some other handicap, although the others did not have to endure such incredibly crowded conditions. Those who avoided their planned action often came across an unusually high number of targets, while those on action stations did not meet anything. It is weird how this did not ring any alarm bells with Intelligence staff at the time. It is also strange no one from the German side noticed the new and rather impressive H/F D/F aerials on the highest masts of the ships hunting them. Frgkpt. Hans Meckel, who commanded U3 and U19, and then became a Staff Officer with the U-boat Command, explained how the intercepted technical details of radar ended up on his desk, but he was inundated with too much material to read all of it. The Allies must have been pleased Meckel's office never had enough people to read all the new reports.

Given the appalling situation in the North Atlantic, with the loss of so many supply ships, the German Naval High Command and U-boat Command immediately nominated southern waters as a new and safer refuelling area. A few months later the auxiliary cruiser *Atlantis* (Kpt.z.S. Bernhard Rogge), returning home from far-off waters, was ordered not to attack shipping in the Atlantic but to remain south of the Equator to act as a supply ship for U-boats. A group of submarines, both German and Italian, were due to go south with a newly fitted out supply ship, *Python*, following on behind. Bletchley Park could not read the auxiliary cruiser code because with radio silence being part of everyday operations, there were too few signals for decoding. But now, secret supply positions were broadcast to U-boats in the code which was being cracked quite quickly in England. As a result, *Atlantis* was sunk 4 degrees south of the Equator on 22 November on its 622nd day at sea without having put into a port: an incredible achievement of endurance. U68 (Korvkpt. Karl-Friedrich Merten) had been resupplied a few days earlier and U126 (Kptlt. Ernst Bauer) had dived away from the cruiser's side when a light aircraft from the cruiser HMS *Devonshire* was spotted. The following heavy gunfire was quick and to the point, and *Atlantis* went down. The few U-boats in the area then mounted a most dramatic rescue operation. *Devonshire*'s aircraft had obviously seen at least one U-boat, but the cruiser was not going to close to within torpedo range for a rescue attempt. It was war and times were cruel. The commander of U126 was aboard *Atlantis*, enjoying a welcome bath, when the small reconnaissance aircraft appeared; he was the only person in the U-boat trained in attacking techniques, but the Royal Navy was not to know that. The survivors from *Atlantis* were later handed over to the recently fitted-out *Python* and shortly after this the county class cruiser HMS *Dorsetshire* appeared to sink the supply ship as well. Once again, the southern U-boats and several Italian submarines came to the rescue to bring survivors back to France, with some getting home in time for Christmas and others only a short while later. Incidentally, *Atlantis* did not go down with her guns blazing as has been reported by several non-German authors. The commander, Bernhard Rogge, said he never gave permission to uncover the ship's hidden armament because he thought it would be better for the opposition to believe they had sunk a merchant ship, perhaps a blockade breaker, in order to keep their warships in far-off waters, searching for the elusive ghost cruiser.

The guard by the entrance to the 5th U-boat Flotilla offices in the laid-up liner *St Louis*, with the flotilla emblem above the doorway. Several passenger liners laid up in a variety of ports were used for accommodation, offices and small workshops.

The news of *Bismarck*'s sinking was still percolating with considerable force when on 22 June 1941 came the news of German armed forces having moved east to destroy a huge build-up of arms being assembled for a Russian invasion of West Europe. Since this build-up contained a considerable proportion of modern weapons from Great Britain and the United States, it would suggest both these countries were in cahoots with the Soviet Union, but that is a story for another book. Anyone thinking of writing it should consider whether the flight of Rudolf Hess, the deputy Führer, to Scotland was to bring to the attention of the British government the decoded papers dealing with Russia's invasion of western Europe.

CAPTURING AND SINKING U-BOATS

The following comes from original documents collected by Gerry Raffe, a member and voluntary historian of the RAF's 269 Squadron, which captured U570 on 27 August 1941. The capture of U570 was significant but wartime secrecy made it necessary to play down its valuable benefits to discourage the Germans from modifying their ineffective technology. For example, the navy learned U-boats could dive deeper than the settings on British depth charges. Royal Navy experts also reported the defects leading the crew's surrender were easily rectified because many of them were due to fuses falling out or switches turning themselves off. Once replaced, the machinery worked again. In addition to this, all manner of other important technicalities were drained out of the boat, making it much easier to develop new weapons and techniques.

* * *

The complement of U570 consisted of 4 officers, 3 warrant officers with swordknot (chief petty officers), 11 petty officers and 25 ratings. The inexperience of these men was most striking; the engineer officer, a couple of petty officers and one rating were the only ones to have taken part in a war cruise before joining U570. Only one rating had been in the navy for more than eighteen months. The commander, Hans-Joachim Rahmlow, joined the navy in 1928 to become a land-based naval artillery officer.

The liner *St Louis* in Kiel, seen from a distance. The word 'Brücke' in this case translates as 'pier' rather than the more common 'bridge'. The notice on the left post says 'Photographing, painting and sketching as well as entry with motorized vehicles is prohibited'.

> Starting his U-boat training in April 1940, he went to sea as a trainee commander with the most successful U-boat of the Second World War, U48. Following this, he commanded U58, a small Type IIC training boat, in the Baltic for just over four months before setting out on his first and only mission with the new U570. Most of his technical ratings had done only three to six months' U-boat training, the seamen even less.
>
> The chief petty officers and petty officers expressed considerable concern about the inadequacy of the training and the lack of experience of most men and officers. None of them made any attempt to disguise the incompetence of the crew and officers. The prisoners said the morale of the ratings was high at first when they arrived. They had been filled with propaganda about the glamour of belonging to a U-boat crew, but they had little or no knowledge of active service conditions. Many of them were seriously seasick and at the first sign of trouble they tended to panic to become useless. Many of the men admitted they were glad to be out of the war. The chief quartermaster (Ober~steuer~mann), by far the most competent member of the crew, complained he had only once been on home leave since the outbreak of the war, during a period of two years. The engineer officer, Lt.z.S. Erich Menzel, had been promoted from the lower deck on the first day of 1940, having been in the navy since 1924 and having served in several other U-boats; making him by far the most experienced member of the crew.

To this it might be interesting to add a sentence from the British Secret Submarine Reports, which states: 'The evidence of prisoners confirms that, whatever degree of efficiency may exist in the crew, the success or failure of a U-boat depends in the personality of one individual – the captain.'

THE 5TH U-BOAT FLOTILLA, REFOUNDED IN JUNE 1941

How U-boats at sea were going to be controlled had not yet been decided by the time the war started, but it did not take long to conclude this should be done from land rather than at sea. Even the pre-war headquarters aboard the tender *Weichsel* were too cramped. What was more, many people thought anything floating in a harbour was likely to make too attractive a target for the enemy's air force. A secret location on land was far more appealing. In any case, before the war U-boats never gathered as fighting groups and the idea of using them in a similar manner to motor torpedo boats, where several went into action together, evaporated because submarine technology contributed too many impracticalities. The pre-war U-boat flotilla system was built up to be especially top heavy, to ensure there were enough skilled people at the top. Things had to change when the war started to produce a more streamlined organization. Thus, the flotillas were made into purely administrative units to turn boats around in port as quickly as possible by providing them with operational necessities. The flotilla leaders were ex-U-boat commanders, supported by teams of specialists to deal with every contingency. They would, for example,

The ferry port near *St Louis* in Kiel. Regular passenger ferries or water buses ran throughout the war and the navy also had its own fleet of small boats to get over to the other side. The direct distance across the water is about 3km, but going by road meant covering 10km over cobblestone roads, so the small ferries were more than just convenient.

have had a senior engineer to determine whether any reported faults were to be ignored, repaired or replaced, and there were medical staff to see to the men. They also secured the supplies necessary for operational boats, others who moved the crew's personal luggage, and pen-pushers dealing with the masses of reports, forms and official documentation. The controlling body for operational boats at sea, which later became known as just 'U-boat

The Tirpitz Mole or Quay and many of the loading piers, where ships made fast for longer periods, were covered with camouflage planking to make them less obvious to bombers flying overhead.

Command', did delegate some of its responsibilities to specialist authorities away from the main fighting areas. For example, the Black Sea, the Mediterranean, the Far East in monsoon Asia and the Arctic were often overseen by specially appointed leaders.

This administrative work came to a head early in 1940, when it became apparent the increase in war production would soon swamp the capabilities of the existing U-flotilla system. Thus, the 5th U-boat Flotilla, disbanded after the start of the war, was recreated in June 1941 to kit out only boats going on their first tour. From that date on, almost every operational U-boat passed through it. The commander was Kptlt. Karl-Heinz Moehle, who also became the Senior Officer for U-boats in Kiel and was promoted to Korvetten~kapitän in April 1943. He had considerable experience aboard several boats as watch officer and he had commanded U20 and U123. The latter was a successful ocean-going U-cruiser, which Moehle handed over to Kptlt. Reinhard Hardegen. Six months later this boat became the first to lead the attack against the United States. Long after the war, one of Moehle's female secretaries described him as an easy person to work for. He never seemed to get into a flap or go into panic mode and never gave the impression of being in a hurry. He was always kind and would stop to talk to anyone who had something to say. He was a nice person to work with, she said.

The 5th U-boat Flotilla had several dedicated mooring places in Kiel with huge notices on the quayside to direct the new boats to the right location for loading. There were also offices in the naval base and the flotilla used the passenger ship *St Louis*, moored far out at the end of a long pier, together with four more redundant passenger ships. Walking there in rain was not ideal, but it did mean the location was hopefully far enough away from the main buildings to perhaps escape bombs dropped on the base. Moehle, as senior U-boat Officer in Kiel, had to deal with a lot of visitors, many of whom had never been there before. This meant many people got lost when searching for his offices. Maps showing the layout of ports were prohibited during the war to prevent spies and undesirables from taking advantage of naval facilities. As a result, Moehle was instrumental in producing the U-boats' own map of the naval base. These included the places visitors often had to visit but avoided sensitive information about luggage depots, ammunition depositaries, fuel depots and such like. Some of these maps were taken away and survived the war and now provide useful details of what was going on in Kiel. Moehle also made another piece of interesting history by getting the officers of boats passing through the flotilla to sign a Visitors' Book and perhaps produce some illustration to go with their signatures. This quickly ran into several volumes. These colourful books survived the war and ended up at first in the German U-boat Museum in Cuxhaven-Altenbruch; they give a good insight into the mentality and ability of the men who were still so vibrantly alive before they died. The 5th U-boat Flotilla became a rather intricate and important part of the seagoing experience, providing each boat with not only a huge load of consumables but also the basic portable equipment they might require. It remained as an operational unit until the very end of the war.

SEQUESTERED EVENTS OF 1941 AND 1942

Long ago, respected Allied historians told us how in 1942 the high admirals of the British Empire were quivering every time they went to bed for fear of U-boats cutting their vital supply routes during the night. Some have said this period was the grimmest of the war while they were waiting for the expected total collapse of the war in Germany's favour. What these authors failed to explain is why and how a huge number of U-boats at sea for most of the year never managed to set up a single major convoy battle. Where were the fantastic successes? Although there were many U-boats at sea, the performance of each one was desperately poor. Even the terrific successes in American waters never came up to half of the totals from the autumn of 1940. So, what was going on in the Atlantic? Why were U-boats failing so miserably in finding convoys? Bear in mind that in 1942 Bletchley Park could not decrypt the new four-wheel Enigma code.

First, and most obviously, in 1940 the dozen or so U-boats at sea each day were away from their French bases on average for about three weeks. One-third of this total were in the operations area, while the other two-thirds were either on their way out or going back home. In early 1942, just after Germany had declared war on the USA, each boat was away for a *minimum* of eight weeks yet achieved less than half of what they had managed only a few months earlier. The incredible successes they reaped in American waters were initially due to the United States not fighting back. Unescorted merchant ships continued sailing along the American coast, where illuminated settlements provided ideal background lighting for U-boats known to be lurking on the dark eastern horizon. The

The Iltis Pier on the western side of the military harbour. The box on the right contained grit for when the surface was icy. During the First World War the navy had an auxiliary cruiser with this name, which was also used by a gunboat. Note the names of the U-boat commanders Kptlt. Otto Ites and Oblt.z.S. Rudolf Ites did not have the 'I'.

resulting bonanza was incredible. To stop the ordinary people from being overwhelmed by grief at the seriousness of their losses, the American media referred to these merchant seamen as draft dodgers. Many of them were on fuel tankers and they died horrible deaths in huge fires while doing their duty for their country. Long after the war, around 1980, a post-war youngster, Ian Millar, founded the American group 'The Sons and Daughters of US Merchant Seamen of World War Two' to collect information to put the records straight and to achieve some recognition for their parents' contribution to the war. This recognition came sometime later when the men from the merchant marine were, at last, awarded veteran status, something they should have had right from the beginning.

Moving to American waters was easy for the Germans because their 'Happy Hunting Grounds' of 1940 had vanished. They were no longer there. Aircraft had driven the U-boats away and, to make matters even worse, aircraft had also started to make life hell for boats crossing what had become known as the Black Pit of Biscay, the sea area in front of their French bases. Not knowing whether U-boats made it through this fire and death zone or not, U-boat Command introduced a system for them to phone home once they were well clear of the coast. By doing this, Germany unwittingly presented Britain with a terrific advantage. Radio direction finders could determine the latitude from where these signals were sent, and from that make a good, educated guess as to where they were going. After all, they knew where the boats had come from, so all they needed to do was draw a 'straight line' on the curved surface of a globe, the so-called Great Circle. In addition, knowing

The 5th U-boat Flotilla had around twenty-five main departments, all requiring not only storage space but also offices. Several of the buildings were wooden huts where sea-going men could store their personal belongings when not in port. These were sent on automatically to the boat's next permanent base.

the cruising speed of U-boats, it was not too difficult to work out when they were likely to arrive to be ready for a magnificent ambush. Sadly, for the Allies, they still did not have enough ships to hunt U-boats to destruction, and therefore not many U-boats were sunk. The German lookouts often spotted aircraft a long way off, and many airmen saw U-boats vanishing beneath the waves before they could get close enough to drop depth

An excerpt from an article written in 1986.

When next you go to the seashore son –
Look way beyond the setting sun –
Beyond where the sky and oceans meet –
To where forgotten heroes sleep.

Ian A. Millar

Founder of The Sons and Daughters of United States Merchant Mariners of World War Two

The Sons and Daughters of United States Merchant Mariners of World War Two is a group concerned with the lack of recognition given by the United States to the men of her Merchant Marine during the war. We are also most interested in sharing our knowledge with maritime historians so that we can remove the mythology that is very often regurgitated in history books about the US Merchant Marine and American merchant seamen during the war. We welcome everyone of all nations to our group. Our only request would be that if you are going to write about our American merchant seamen, please seek the truth through facts or write nothing at all.

Several photos here were taken at the ship builder Deschimag AG Weser in Bremen where long and very-long range boats were produced. (Type IXA – IXC and the very long-range modifications of Type IXD1 and IXD2.)
Once training was complete the 'Frontreif' badge was painted on the side of the conning tower.

This must be a complete (or nearly complete) crew for one of the larger, long-range boats with men wearing their everyday going-out uniforms. It is interesting to note a good number are wearing U-boat badges to indicate they have been on at least two operational voyages. Exceptionally good performance could have resulted in men gaining this badge during their first voyage, but such cases were rare. The commissioned officers are wearing silver brocade belts, whose only function seems to have been to make them look more important. There was nothing attached to this belt, and it did not keep their trousers up. The men with peaked caps but without these belts are warrant officers with swordknots. Petty officers can be identified by their caps without a peak and by the elaborate gold braid around the collars of their jackets. Ordinary seamen looked similar but without the braid.

Officers in their ordinary walking-out uniforms. The silver brocade belts were worn only on official occasions. The ribbons through the top buttonhole of two men indicate they hold the Iron Cross Second Class and the commander in the middle also has the Iron Cross First Class. The other Oberleutnant zur See with a cog wheel above his two sleeve rings must be the engineer officer. Two of these men also have U-boat badges. The badge clearly visible on the engineer officer second from right is the Minesweeper Badge, which also seems to sit under the belt of the man on the right. The river Weser is tidal in Bremen and the men are standing on a floating pontoon with steps leading up to the shore.

charges. But, near convoys, these very-long-range aircraft did put U-boats down, keeping them away from the ships and preventing attacks: a fantastic advantage for the Allies.

By the time America came into the war, early in December 1941, it was already plainly obvious the German Navy could no longer send surface supply ships into the North Atlantic. The first submarine supply tanker had been laid down at Deutsche Werke in Kiel as late as 23 November 1940, while another supply aid, Germany's biggest U-boat, a specialized minelayer, had been laid down some months earlier on 15 January 1940. This makes one think that at that time moored mines looked to be more attractive for production priority than supply U-boats. Shortly after the start of the war, the Commander in Chief of the Navy made the decision for all new U-boat types to be determined by the U-boat Chief, and now it is difficult to work out who made this choice of priorities. Was it the Berlin U-boat Office, which had been responsible for construction before the war, or the U-boat Command, located in Paris and later in Lorient? Whatever, when America joined the war, there were

While the British Royal Navy issued its sea-going men with duffle coats, similar in quality to garments worn by commuters in big towns, the German Navy provided sailors with superior leather clothing. There were different colours and different designs. The standing men here are all wearing walking-out coats and would have donned jackets when working inside their boat. Engineers would have had jackets without lapels to prevent these from hanging down when they were dealing with oily machinery. Petty officers wore gold braiding on the edge of their collars, while officers were distinguished by their shoulder straps. The dog kennel-type hut on the top is a shelter for a guard.

no submarine supply tankers and America was a long way away for small submarines. The first of these specialised Type XIV supply submarines, U459, had only been commissioned three weeks or so earlier by Korvkpt. Georg von Wilamowitz-Moellendorf, and it was going to be a while before the crew was ready to take it to sea. But help was at hand. The first minelayer, U116, had been commissioned four months earlier, on 26 July 1941, by Korvkpt. Werner von Schmidt. As a result, U116 sailed from Kiel to Bergen and from there on to Lorient to be kitted out for its first supply mission eleven days later. The first purpose-built supply submarine sailed direct from Kiel on 23 March 1942.

Whilst these new submarine supply ships may have sounded good for the Germans, there was a deeply hidden snag. At first, they battled only against the Atlantic, the weather, their crews' inexperience and poor transfer equipment. There was comparatively little interference from British or American forces once U-boats had cleared the Black Pit of Biscay, but this pyrrhic peace did not last. Less than half a year later Bletchley Park was once again decoding U-boat messages. The results were shattering and primarily made worse by the lack of adequate refuelling aids and highly inexperienced crews. Sadly for German mothers, many lost their sons very quickly. The huge minelayers of Type XB made ideal supply boats. They had several mineshafts in the bows as well as a row on each side, and these free-flooding spaces were ideal for storing sea-resisting cargo containers. The big problem came when transferring items from one wet submarine to another in conditions up to quite unpleasant seas of state six. During such weather, modern cross-Channel ferries between England and France, even with special wave stabilizers, have staff with sick bags standing by to help those passengers who find the motion too challenging.

Even the big U-boats could carry only one or at best two wooden dinghies, and soft-bottomed inflatables had to be used instead. But their soft bottoms were designed to hold shipwrecked men, not wooden boxes with sharp edges; to make them even more objectionable, they were exceedingly difficult to row or paddle. Since there were no specialized craft for transferring goods from one U-boat to another, and paddling inflatables was so difficult, the men themselves solved the problem by pulling each dinghy with long ropes from one submarine to another. The navy had special outboard engines for such purposes, but these

There were no hard and fast rules about how a commissioning ceremony should be conducted and men followed general military etiquette. In this case, the men are wearing their everyday working gear without badges. Metal badges were most awkward in confined spaces and the small size of the crew made it unnecessary for submariners to wear identification marks. Only the commissioned officers are wearing peaked caps while the rest, including the warrant officers with swordknot, are wearing the so-called Schiffchen (small ship) or folding cap, which required less space in a locker. When wearing this clothing it was possible to identify warrant officers by their more elaborate shoulder straps, which might not be visible in this book reproduction. There are two men at the bottom left: the 3rd and 7th have these shoulder straps. There was no hard and fast rule about commanders wearing white caps, but the fad became firmly established shortly after the beginning of the war. Petty officers can be identified by the obvious corner pieces on their lapels, instead of the gold braid of their jackets.

appear not to have been used. Transferring oil and fuel was obviously done via pipes, while two boats moved at the same speed and in the same direction, something which many inexperienced helmsmen could not do. The flow was turned off the moment a pipe was seen to snap, and the broken pieces were glued together again, but shortages did occur and there were incidents when refuelling had to be abandoned because the receiving helmsman could not maintain speed and course. Waiting for better conditions far out in the Atlantic was not ideal. It is surprising how many managed this complicated task without having been trained to do it.

Loading a U-boat was an art where teamwork was exalted. Sealed tins could go into the wet bilges, but paper-wrapped parcels had to be placed somewhere dry.

Werner von Schmidt in U116 wrote an interesting comment in his log, saying all goods needed to be packed in waterproof containers to prevent the sea from getting at them. One wonders whether he also had the 'pleasure' of being supplied with dry tinned food, such as bread. This was kept in some of the last tins to be opened after fresh food had been consumed, tins which were often stored deep down in bilges where a lot of dirty water collected before it was pumped out again. Instead of soldering these dry food tins, the lids were merely crimped over or just pressed together without soldering and when the men opened them, they invariably discovered the water had got in to spoil the contents – not an ideal revelation when you are some distance from the nearest shop. There are also enough accounts of packages that were ideal for handling on dry land becoming rather cumbersome at sea when water softened the wrapping, but this hurdle was also partly cured with appropriate sailors' language.

Finding exact refuelling positions at sea was not easy and the supply boat would send out radio direction signals for customers to home in on. The opposition overcame this hurdle by providing hunters with special aids for finding U-boats at sea. This was done by printing the German naval grid on transparent paper sheets to fit exactly on top of British and American charts. Thus, it was possible to get instant information for any ambushes. It would seem highly likely a good number of the tricks for this type of secret work were still being used during the Cold War period and we will probably never find out exactly what methods were used to gain the upper hand. Information came into London's Secret Submarine Tracking Room in drips, none of which provided much information on their own until one had a teacup full. Whilst the name of this room sounded grand and the jobs inside it looked interesting, the work there was often most tedious. Yet the effort did make it possible to get well ahead of the opposition. For many of the essential workers, there was certainly no glamour for any of this code-breaking activity. Radio operators intercepted meaningless messages of jumbled letters and everybody from then on worked with this nonsensical order of letters, making the process long and boring and, at the same time, requiring an incredibly high level of concentration all the time. Pencils had to be rationed to stop these people from venting their frustrations by breaking them.

Germany did not know how the opposition was hitting these refuelling sites, but the technique was quickly changed from the earlier practice of only one U-boat being refuelled at a time to having several converging on the same spot at the same time. One boat would then be replenished while the others sat at the extremity of visual signalling distance as additional lookouts. This did not help a great deal since supply U-boats and their customers could not dive quickly. Like many other things at around this time, it seems as if nothing was seriously thought out to any significant depth, and the list of hiccups was almost endless (and well worth a separate book, now so much more material has been released).

There is another, somewhat hidden, point here which made a considerable contribution to the Atlantic war. This came about when American forces drove U-boats away from their coastal waters, leaving them only the Air Gap of the mid-Atlantic as an operations area. This gap had so far been free of land-based aircraft but the U-boats' move into those areas came at roughly the same time as the Allies procured sufficient machines for patrolling this last 'aircraft-free zone'. The other point with this mid-Atlantic Air Gap was that at first the Germans were looking out for huge, very-long-range aircraft and were horribly surprised to see small single-engined fighters. Some of these resembled the cloth-covered types from the First World War and were flown off improvised aircraft carriers made from converted merchant ships with their superstructure removed and a flat wooden deck added.

LANGUAGE AND THE FIRST LETTER HOME

During the years 1941 and 1942 the German language made a major contribution to the codebreakers in England. Men from south Germany spoke a different language from those in the north, and often one could not understand the other. In any case, until after the war, people in the north German seaports spoke Low German or Plattdeutsch rather than High German or Hochdeutsch. This only faded out when many refugees from far-off regions came to work in the ports. These language differences were a considerable problem when the navy was first formed as late as 1871 and remained as a noteworthy hurdle during the First World War. Men joining the army usually ended up with a local regiment, but the navy was far away for many who had to learn what might be a foreign language for them. As a result, all new recruits had to learn naval German and those giving orders had to do so in exactly the same way, using the same words. This made life considerably easier for codebreakers in England when the list of daily Enigma settings, captured from U110 and other ships, had been exhausted. From then onwards codebreakers needed to find their own way of working out the daily crypts for setting the starting positions for their copied Enigma machines. This was done by building several mechanical computers to filter through messages until settings were found which matched the words in intercepted

This page from the 5th U-boat Flotilla's guest book shows how men from U1006 (Oblt.z.S Horst Voigt) saw the loading process in October 1944. If the writing does not reproduce too well, the ship in the background is *St Louis* and the commander is shouting through his megaphone 'Termin ist Termin'. The words 'Gewalt Ausrüstung = 12 std' means 'forced fitting out = 12 hours'.

The great joke came when light transport carriages arrived on the pier at the same time as the air raid warning sounded. Everything which could be moved was then taken back to the safety of concrete bunkers.

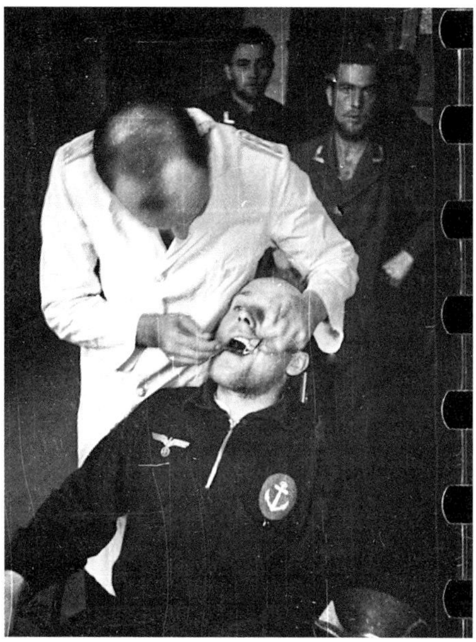

The twenty-five departments of the 5th U-boat Flotilla included dentists, who worked well but were not supplied with a great deal of anaesthetics and visiting them was not always pleasant.

messages. This was done by inducing the Germans to send messages where Britain could make a good guess about what was being said. For example, it was easy for one low-flying plane to put an essential lighthouse out of action. Then, when the harbour master came on air, it was possible to make a fairly accurate guess about what he was broadcasting.

This invisible background Intelligence was given a considerable boost from prisoners who only gave their name and service number when rescued but later talked among themselves and with new 'friends' they made as prisoners of war. Bear in mind, many of these men were hardly trained to serve in submarines, and not all had the experience to resist casual and friendly conversations while chatting about topics they did not consider to be of any great military value.

* * *

The following was provided by Ernst Pfefferle, who published the long and brilliant private series 'Kammeraden auf See'. The original has been slightly modified with information from Franz Selinger and an addition from Wilhelm Winhoff. The author of this first letter home, known only as Ernst, was a south German farmer from Bavaria, where people had considerable problems understanding the north German spoken by Prussians. This difference was not just a case of accent: the two regions spoke totally different dialects,

Almost all the U-boats loading at the 5th U-boat Flotilla base had never taken on board so much as was delivered for their first operational cruise, and many of the boxes would never have fitted through the hatches. So, everything was unpacked on the pier and the Obersteuermann (Navigator) was often responsible for keeping a detailed list of where all the tins ended up, so that the cook could locate them quickly once at sea. The tins did not have paper labels; instead, a code-number, indicating their contents, was embossed on each tin.

Lookout wearing a sou'wester and U-boat leathers.

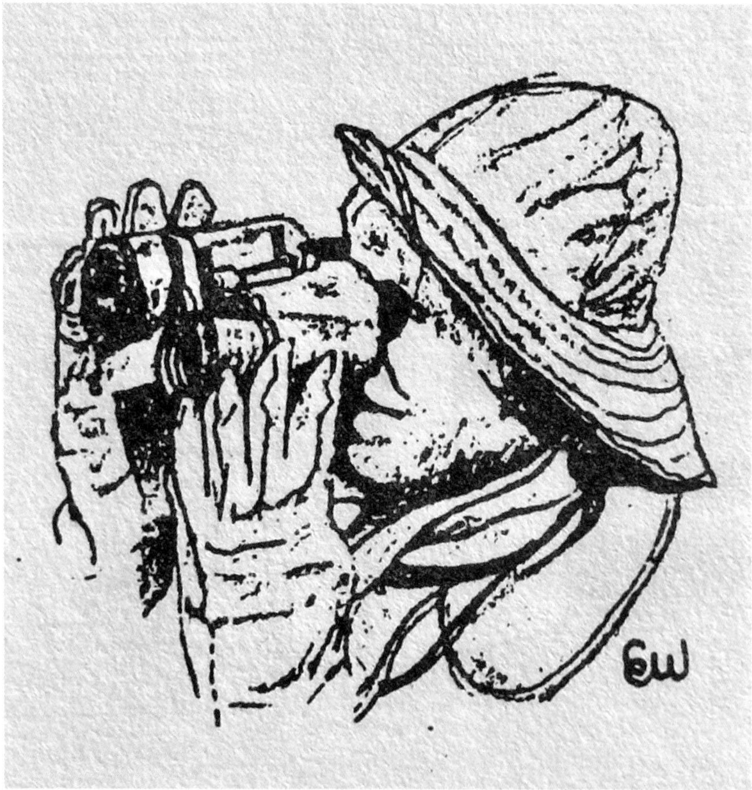

U-boat lookout. *(Drawing: Elaine Womack of Ohio, USA)*

The Ober~steuer~mann. Note the most elaborate shoulder strap on the leather jacket indicating he is a warrant officer with swordknot.

Hans-Diedrich Freiherr von Tiesenhausen (*centre*) aboard U331 around the time he torpedoed the British battleship HMS *Barham* in the Mediterranean. He was first watch officer in U93 under Claus Korth, who is mentioned in chapters at the beginning of this book. Freiherr translates as baron.

often using different words and expressions. Walter Schellenberg, an SS officer and Head of Hitler's Foreign Intelligence in Berlin, used two Bavarians, one on each end of a telephone line, to pass sensitive messages from one office to another because he was sure anyone overhearing them was unlikely to understand what they were saying.

Dear Mother and all loved ones,
It is time I write you a few words. Living with the Prussians is totally crazy. I would much rather be out with the oxen spreading muck than putting up with these bits of fun. I have arrived without a hitch. Have even been a little early but trying to understand anyone is difficult. While lining up on the parade ground some chap from Obereichstätt [A small town in Bavaria, obviously close to where the writer lived] was standing behind me and he was just as confused as me – and he came as a volunteer without having been conscripted. There was another Bavarian as well, who cried when he was being shouted at by petty officers. These barracks are huge and behind us you can see the water, where flying boats are constantly landing and taking off, all making a hell of a noise, enough to drive one mad.

When we arrived, we all had to line up to be divided into groups of ten. Then there appeared a petty officer who looked at us like a shark while asking how old we were. After this he looked at me and said, 'You, you peculiar bird, you will be the room eldest.' [Colloquially, a person with a Vogel is mad.]

I had no idea what he was talking about and asked, 'What's that?'

Then he had a serious go at me.

I had imagined my arrival in the navy would be different. I wanted to join up to learn something, to improve myself. This bloke did not seem to be capable of doing anything other than shout, which the chap from Obereichstätt did not like at all. The petty officer asked every man, including myself, in which ship he would like to serve and what qualities each man is bringing to the navy. When I told him that I came from Bavaria and had not seen any ships, he looked stupidly at me. They don't seem to know any cultural proceedings at all and the one who made me the room eldest was only happy when he could insult others. Life here is not fair and remains as a dreadful memory. People in Bavaria can be pretty rough at times, but one can be pretty frightened when these Prussians open their mouths. My first job now is to learn this new foreign language.

There are ten men in our room, which can be awful. One snores a lot, another drinks beer and one has a definite stammer, so it is necessary not to face him when he is speaking. I did manage to get my own back when our petty officer told me and the Obereichstättner, 'Now at running pace. Quick march.' We ran off and he had problems keeping up with us. Eventually, when he did catch up, he was sweating heavily and after this he made us sweat even more.

The food is good, but I did not eat my lunch yesterday. It was pea soup that looked identical to the food we feed to pigs, except that there was a lot of meat in it. The other men liked it. I have no idea why.

I am going to have to close here. There will soon be a whistle for lights out.

We are wearing grey soldiers' clothing, but I think we will receive navy blue uniforms in eight weeks' time and then we are supposed to move to a school.

With fondest wishes

Your Ernst

THE SECRET SUBMARINE TRACKING ROOM IN LONDON

By 1942 Britain had established a highly secret and very successful Submarine Tracking Room in the Admiralty (London). There was also a better-known Operational Headquarters for the Western Approaches in Liverpool. This London-based and highly successful information source on U-boats came about because of one man, a civilian barrister who had been rejected by the navy because he did not meet the medical requirements. Rodger Winn had contracted polio as a child and his body was slightly deformed. It was not easily visible but when giving presentations he would often stand up leaning against a chair. The polio did not affect his brain, allowing him to study for a law degree at both Oxford in England and at Harvard University in the United States. This legal background as a barrister made him think he might be of use to the navy for interviewing prisoners of war. He had still not settled into a permanent civilian position to do this when he claimed he might be able to forecast what the U-boats were going to do while they were still enroute.

Sceptics were soon overwhelmed by his successes and the ingenuity with which he tackled this complicated task can perhaps be illustrated by an incident with Admiral Max Horton, after he had become Commander-in-Chief of the Western Approaches in

The bunker where the Royal Navy's secret submarine tracking room under Rodger Winn was located is situated close to Admiralty Arch by Trafalgar Square in London and is now overgrown with an incredible vine to make the bland concrete more unobtrusive.

Britain's secret submarine tracking room was housed inside this huge bunker, seen here after the war looking from Admiralty Arch towards Buckingham Palace.

November 1942. Talking to Winn at a conference in London, Horton told him his tracking forecasts were not always accurate. Winn then took him into the secret Submarine Tracking Room to show him how information was collected from a dozen or so sources. Then he asked Horton what forecasts he would make from the material. Horton was speechless, overwhelmed, unable to make sense of the masses of papers, but he agreed with Winn's comment that: 'It was better to get this forecasting right for part of the time than leaving it to always hunt in the dark.' What was more, by the time of this meeting, it was already the end of 1942 and, as Winn said, 'things can only improve'.

Admiral Max Horton, a submariner during the First World War, has been made out by some post-war authors to have led the Western Approaches Command as a magnificent saviour by making enormous changes for the better. He was, undoubtedly, a very interesting man but it is necessary to bear in mind his predecessor, Admiral Sir Percy Noble, was at the helm throughout 1942, when there was a total code-reading blackout and therefore he received very little help from the codebreakers at Bletchley Park. At the same time, the number of U-boats at sea had been the highest of the war. There were between forty and sixty-five during the early part of the year and in September the number reached one hundred, remaining at that high rate until the first months of 1943. Yet during all of this long time the Western Approaches Command managed to keep the U-boats' successes down to less than two merchant ships sunk per month per U-boat at sea. The first clash of titans, when a large wolfpack sprang onto Convoys SC122 and HX229 in the biggest convoy battle of the war, did not take place until March 1943. There were no other huge convoy attacks until this month. So how did Britain and America do it?

Winn's contribution to the war can perhaps be best judged by the fact that as a civilian without any naval training, he was one of the few, if not the only person to hold the rank of Royal Navy Commander and later Captain. The main defensive feature of the convoy war in 1942 centred around Germany being unable to find convoys and for much of the time this was due to careful planning in steering them away from known U-boat positions. The major crunch in this cat and mouse game came early in 1943 when U124 (Kptlt. Jochen Mohr) detected a destroyer escorting two oil tankers; a few days later U514 (Kptlt. Hans-Jürgen Auffermann) spotted the entire convoy TM1 with nine tankers heading from Trinidad off South America towards Gibraltar. Even accounts by respected historians differ about the details, and a good number do not match the original logbooks, which is not terribly important here. The significant point is that the secret Submarine Tracking Room in London did not receive the last-mentioned radio report, yet a multitude of other reports came flooding in at a time when Rodger Winn was hospitalized and absent on sick leave for four weeks. His deputy could not interpret all the essential data, leaving a huge vacuum. As a result, a U-boat wolfpack of ten boats converged on TM1 and sank seven of the nine tankers. Only two reached Gibraltar, making this one of the most outstanding U-boat successes of the whole war. Had Winn been on duty, it seems likely that he might well have spotted the tell-tale signs earlier, when the disaster could perhaps have been averted.

Single and double 20mm anti-aircraft guns were fired in a similar way to a large rifle with two butts, but the quadruple and the larger 37mm versions needed a team of men. The coordination required was incredibly difficult at the best of times and terribly awkward when the submarine was tossed about by waves. What is more, many crews never had the time or the opportunity to practise this satisfactorily.

Chapter 7

The Cruel Atlantic with Spiteful Weather

THE BRITISH ROYAL NAVY PROTECTING CONVOYS

What follows is based on an anonymous wartime account supplied by Commander Richard Compton-Hall (Director of the Royal Navy's Submarine Museum in Gosport). From the named ships, it is possible to identify the convoy as HX231. The author was almost certainly Sir Peter Gretton, who later wrote several books, including *Crisis Convoy*. It is incredible how little high technology was used in April 1943, when the escorts relied mainly on H/F D/F and radar but were helped considerably by aircraft. Only a few years earlier the German U-boat Chief had said, 'Aircraft cannot hurt U-boats as crows cannot hurt moles.'

The following account closely resembles the original, but naval jargon has been removed and additional explanations added.

* * *

Conditions were not pleasant at our western base in Newfoundland, with temperatures well below freezing; they only rose as high as zero very occasionally. Heavy gales with snowstorms added to the discomfort and ice in the harbour made life rather difficult, meaning maintenance became hard work. During the night before sailing, it became necessary for special sentries to move the guns every five minutes to prevent the moving parts from freezing solid. Later, when we sailed the superstructure was constantly washed in spray, which quickly set solid to prevent both guns and depth charges from working. This layer of ice became thick enough to be worrying and the rolling of the ship was too much for sending men out to chip it off again. It was a case of men standing up on an open bridge, holding on to whatever they could and hoping this incredible covering would not make the ship top heavy. Many men were accommodated in the front section of the ship, which was constantly awash with icy water and most unpleasant. [Those men standing on the open bridge were often wearing duffle coats, like the clothing worn by office staff working in cities, and one wonders what incredible conditions they had to endure. Life on those ships was unpleasant, harsh, cold and wet and yet the men survived to do their duty. On the other side, German seamen were issued with superior leather clothing, considerably more suitable in these horrid conditions.]

Luckily warmer weather melted the ice but also gave us a sharp lesson in how not to meet a convoy. The wind blowing spray over the top of us made it almost impossible

The 'CA' class destroyer HMS *Cavalier*, now on display at the Naval Dockyard Museum in Chatham (England). Wartime escorts had an open bridge, without the sun and rain screen which protects visitors these days. Generally, men from the duty watch were not allowed to leave the bridge without permission and the captain's chair was screwed to the deck to prevent angry seas from claiming it. A spell of duty usually lasted for four hours, which might not sound terribly long when active and doing something interesting, but it felt long out on the hostile Atlantic. It was not uncommon for men to return to their post for the second and third time to find the commander had not gone below for a break and was still lurking in the shelter of the glass shuttering. Several veterans remarked they even found the commander was still cracking jokes after such a long hammering of incredible discomfort. The crew did feed him, but there was little they could do to keep him warm or dry.

for lookouts to see anything. When we did eventually meet the merchant ships, we estimated our position was more than 80 miles out from what we had calculated, and we made use of H/F D/F for finding the merchant ships. This incredible error occurred because the weather had not allowed anyone to shoot the sun or stars for days on end. Yet with all the help available it still took two days to make contact. The escort group, which had brought the ships along the first stage of their passage, returned to base, while we set about the cumbersome task of escorting the convoy across the Atlantic.

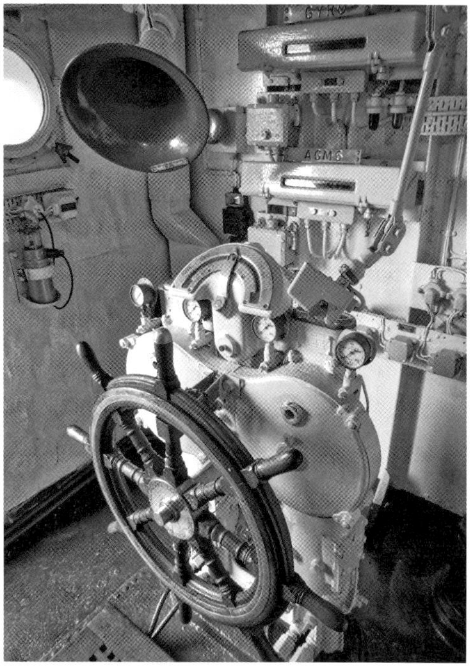

The helmsman by the ship's wheel was down below in a well-protected position. Other than leaving the door open, there was only a small bull's eye to let in a little light but without any opportunities for looking out. The ship was steered entirely on orders from the bridge, which came down through a voice pipe.

The convoy's commodore, a distinguished Admiral, was just as concerned as we were at the sight of this incredible collection of ships. Everything appeared to be in shocking confusion and the first thing was for the escorts to tidy up the merchant ships, to nudge them into formation and then the destroyer *Vidette* was sent out to count them. Visibility was so poor that this had to be done by sailing past each one. There was no way anyone could see the whole formation from one vantage point. This running about used up considerable quantities of fuel and, despite the heavy seas, escorts had to go alongside the oiler to top up. Once under way and making progress, Admiralty informed us of a U-boat signal, suggesting we had probably been sighted. This U-boat was clever enough to run away into that mysterious 'Skip distance' before sending its report back to base. This put it out of our reach until the complete wolfpack had assembled for attacking. To make matters worse, we were now out of aircraft range, meaning there was going to be no further support until we came into range of aircraft based in Iceland. HMS *Tay* was the only ship with a H/F D/F set, so there was little the merchant ships could do to help with making progress and it was 4 o'clock in the afternoon when the direction finder detected significant activity, indicating several U-boats were reporting back to base that they were near us. Although it was impossible to work out how many there were, and we had to make do with an estimate of about eight. To make matters more anxious, shortly before dusk the crow's nest lookout caught sight of a U-boat. It was a waste of time to chase after this intruder because that could be just what he was hoping for, for us to leave a vast gap in the convoy's defences for others to slip through for an attack. In any case, the chance of catching the boat was pretty slim.

Many of the crew were accommodated in a huge room in the bows, where the ship was often battered by the extreme force of the weather. Living space there was cramped and could get extremely unpleasant, especially when the ocean came in to share some of the limited warmth in these tight quarters. Many of these small ships were also without an inside corridor from the galley (kitchen) to the messes, which meant it was not always possible to get a really piping hot meal.

So, all we could do was to wait for what was going to be a busy night. The shortage of ships in those black days crippled all offensive action. U-boats were almost impossible to see at night and our only aid for finding them was 271 surface radar. To make matters worse, U-boats were faster than our corvettes and only one knot slower than a frigate, so catching them in a plain chase was next to impossible. Once we were in position, all we could do was to settle down and wait for the attack. Luckily, the Group's radar and Asdics had all been reported to be in good order. This was indeed a rare situation after the weather which we had been through. The winds and the ice we experienced were powerful enough to pull down ships' aerials. There were too few escorts to form a complete ring around the sixty-five merchant ships, but since we knew a little about U-boat tactics, we left the less likely approach area more open. The H/F D/F direction finder, of course, gave us a good indication of roughly the direction where the majority of U-boats were. On this occasion they were forward on both sides, not an ideal defensive position.

Not long after it was dark there was a flash from the starboard side of the convoy. Nothing further was seen or heard on the Asdic and my first thought was that a

This photo was taken from the US Coast Guard cutter *John C. Spencer* while shooting a bout of Hedgehog or Mousetrap mortars aimed at U175 under Kptlt. Heinrich Bruns, who was killed during the pursuing gunfire.

funnel was on fire. Five minutes later, though, HMS *Alisma* reported 'ship torpedoed'. After some hesitation, I ordered a snowflake illumination, but it was too late to be effective. This display turned out to be most ineffective and resulted in considerable discussion the following day, when it was light, and U-boats were unlikely to attack. The torpedoed ship was Number 22. Carrying a cargo of iron ore. She sank within one minute. While searching astern, HMS *Tay* passed through the survivors swimming in the cold water. There had obviously been no time to launch lifeboats. It is my most painful recollection of the war that we had to shout encouragement to these men over a loud hailer, knowing well that they would probably never be seen again. We could not afford to leave our place in the search scheme otherwise other ships could have suffered the same fate. The search for the U-boat was not successful for two reasons. First was the delay in ordering the illumination to start and the second was that three ships on the convoy's starboard wing decided to break away. One was lucky enough to rejoin the following day. The wolfpack picked off the others.

Then there came a problem from HMS *Vidette*, who reported a contact astern of the convoy, which turned out not to be a U-boat but a tanker with engine trouble. No one could be spared to stay with her and *Vidette* had to resume station. It was now time for a pre-arranged alteration of course which had been planned with the idea of putting the attackers out of position with a drastic change in direction. Since it was difficult for all the ships in a convoy to see each other, there was always the possibility for U-boats far enough away to charge-in to a wrong location. Yet despite this effort, the general situation looked bad. Several ships had been hit, there was one lone straggler and three had broken away. With six hours of darkness still left for U-boats to attack, it seemed likely all the ships would go down before the end of the night. Yet to everybody's surprise, radar and Asdic helped in driving off the next four attacks, and no more ships were hit. Just before dawn it was possible to send back HMS *Pink* to search for survivors of Number 22, but the water was icy cold and without boats they could not have survived for long. At dawn HMS *Tay* closed in on *Waroonga*, which had been torpedoed but was still making headway, to find her crew cheerful and determined. The master wanted to move all men not essential for steaming to an escort, but the weather was too poor for such a transfer. She had a hole in her side large enough for a car to be driven through. The master agreed to keep in position and hoped the engine room bulkhead would hold. [This happened in April 1943 and suggests the U-boats were still using contact detonators

Large sea areas have their own weather patterns and warm air flowing over cold water or cold air blowing over warm water produce some wonderful sights, although these are perhaps not fully appreciated when you are hunting someone who is likely to kill you. This shows how irritating even small amounts of mist can be for lookouts. (*Photo: Jo Field*)

on their torpedoes rather than the more effective magnetic settings, as explained at the beginning of this book.]

The weather now started to improve rapidly and by noon, when we came to a pre-arranged turning point, we altered course to head east. The visibility was maximum, and the sea was calm with a long swell. I had a corvette out on the horizon in the hope that she would put down the shadower , so that this change might not be noticed by the wolfpack.

We were also homing in the first of two aircraft from Iceland, but it could apparently not receive our bearing and it was maddening to watch the bearing missing astern by some distance. The second aircraft was first noticed by plumes of depth charges on our port side horizon. These were followed by the R/T (radio telegraphy) report 'Am over a U-boat', and letting enthusiasm outweigh wisdom HMS *Tay*, the only ship present, was ordered to move out to help. This was a sharp lesson in convoy tactics. Five minutes after we had left position, the escort oiler, Number 62, was hit, with the explosion sending up an enormous column of water. The Commodore reported a torpedo had missed his bows by a few feet. Retaliatory action was started at once. The track had shown where the torpedo had come from on the port side, but despite this clear indication, we failed to pick up the U-boat. It probably dived deep at once. Other aircraft had arrived by now and two of them found many targets.

The situation at dusk was not pleasant. Aircraft reports and H/F D/F bearings showed there were several U-boats on both sides towards the front and the Support Group had signalled they could not join until next day, owing to bad weather ahead of the convoy. We could not possibly avoid the U-boats, with such strength on both sides, and we felt we might even interrupt the Huns' supper. At least, a bad-tempered German would probably make a bad shot.

There was not much time to wait for the first attack of fourteen from the starboard side. Luckily the U-boats usually gave warning of their approach by a tuning signal on W/T and they also failed to synchronize their attacks. They did not all come at the same time. The escorts *Alisma, Pink* and *Tay* were kept hard at it. There was never time to do more than illuminate, which always forced the U-boats down. Then we attacked with depth charges and after the first pattern another was dropped on the same spot on the way back again to resume station. With help of H/F D/F we were able to meet each attack and dawn arrived without a ship having been hit. There were some incidents of note. *Alisma* was narrowly missed by one torpedo; *Tay* and another U-boat were equally surprised by one encounter when the submarine slid out of the darkness across our bows. She was so close that she was inside *Tay*'s turning circle, but the bridge Oerlikon filled her conning tower with lead and the following attack on the U-boat was a good one. [U-boats usually sent a radio message when they started their run-in to attack a convoy, to prevent two from colliding during the same approach. It would seem from this paragraph that this helped the escorts enormously.]

The night rounded off with a tragedy. *Waroonga* reported that her bulkheads had given way and the crew was abandoning ship. She was capsizing and there followed a serious loss of lives. HMS *Loosestrife* was sent to help her and picked up all but one of the ship's crew. It was sad that their brave efforts to get her in had been so ill rewarded. At dawn *Tay* had taken station ahead of the Commodore and was busy counting the ships when the Asdic operator reported an echo right ahead. We were rather sniffy about this, but he stuck to his guns and the order 'stand by' had just been given when the U-boat had the cheek to stick its stern out of the water. It was inside our turning circle and the charge from the port thrower landed just astern of it. This shaking must have been severe enough to prevent it from firing any torpedoes. We got a good view of her stern but in a difficult position and we managed to drop only one more pattern before contact was lost.

An alarming scene then ensued. The convoy started shooting madly at our calcium flare which they imagined to be the U-boat. This had been dropped into the water to mark the position of the U-boat and resulted in six-inch, four inch and smaller shells hurtling in every direction from everybody who had a gun. The streams of tracer from the smaller stuff could be seen clearly. Why no ship was hit remains a deep mystery. In the middle of this scene a Liberator from Iceland arrived, followed shortly by the Support Group, and we passed a very busy half hour. The Support Group had been badly battered by the gales. Some ships were obviously suffering from storm damage, and we learned none of them were fitted with surface radar and only one ship had H/F D/F, but they were invaluable. The tide was turning in our favour. The aircraft made some excellent attacks, swooping down on their victims from the low cloud; although the wolfpack maintained touch, no U-boat got near the convoy again. The next day aircraft came out in strength and again H/F D/F was able to give them many attacks. It was a grand feeling to watch the long line of ships steaming through the North Channel between Ireland and Scotland. The final result had been three ships lost in convoy and three others as stragglers. Two attacks were 'probables' and many others had been delivered. Finally, as the master of the *Waroonga* went ashore, he said, 'Now I must start thinking about another ship.'

ROYAL NAVY ESCORTS

Ships which hunted U-boats

This first one didn't attack U-boats. It is the German torpedo boat *Iltis*, demonstrating the comforts of bridge-duty in damp weather when it is not raining. A considerable proportion of the lower ranks had their quarters in a large bow compartment, where life was most unpleasant under such conditions. The escorts for Convoy HX231 were slightly larger but they also endured considerably worse sea conditions. There was no escape from waves and weather for the men protecting convoys. U-boats, on the other hand, had the advantage of being able to take a little time off for peaceful meals in the depths, where life was motionless and silent, without being constantly reminded how nature was far more powerful than warships.

HMS *Pevensey Castle*, launched on 11 January 1944, is a good example of the type of ship used to hunt U-boats. (*Photo: Jo Fields*)

Destroyers, corvettes and frigates were small warships used for protecting convoys. They may have been successful, but life in them was not terribly comfortable. This is the Flower class corvette HMCS *Owen Sound*, which rescued twenty-three men from U845 (Korvkpt. Werner Weber) after having helped to sink it.

HMS *Versatile*, a 'V' class destroyer, was launched towards the end of 1917 and saw action during the First World War. In 1922 the British submarine H42 surfaced so close in front of her that it was cut it in half with a powerful but accidental ram, killing all the submariners. In 1939 HMS *Versatile* was recommissioned for the Second World War. Note the complicated H/F D/F aerial on top of the stern mast.

The 'F' class destroyer HMS *Forester*, which served throughout the war on anti-U-boat activities and had brushes with several during this time.

The Castle class corvette HMCS *St Thomas*, which saved fifty-five men from U877 (Kptlt. Eberhard Findeisen) after having sunk the U-boat with the new ahead-throwing mortar of Type Squid.

A post-war high frequency radio direction finder high up on a warship.

THE BAROGRAPH RECORDING WEATHER

A barograph was a mechanical barometer for recording natural air pressure on graph paper, usually over a period of one week. An ink pen on the tip of a needle left a trace on a sheet of special paper indicating the number of millibars. The vertical lines of this graph were slightly curved to allow for the hinged pointer rising and falling. A clockwork mechanism was wound up once a week when a clean sheet of paper was also inserted, and the ink topped up.

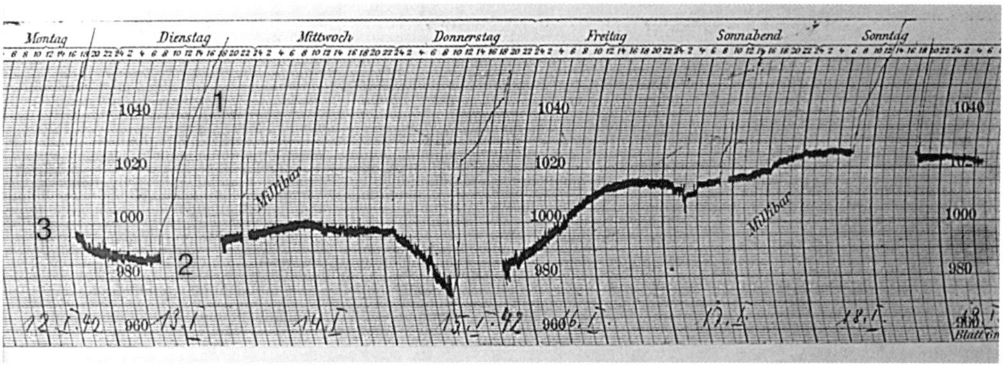

The barograph from U504.

A barograph with its glass case removed.

Korvkpt. Fritz Poske took one of these devices to sea when U504 left Kiel on 6 January 1942. The plan was to sail around the north of Scotland to Lorient in France, where the large ocean-going Type IXC was to be topped up with fuel and provisions to join the third wave of the famous Operation Paukenschlag (a code name for the first thrust against the United States). After a week at sea, while west of Ireland, the boat headed into a ferocious hurricane of wind strength twelve. Germany used the same Beaufort Wind Scale as Britain, with a scale from zero to a maximum of twelve.

A single wave of up to 12 metres in height covered a length of well over 300 metres and while struggling against this incredible force, U504 hardly made any progress over the ground. It was only just possible to maintain its position during the ferocious punishment. Astonishingly enough, the powerful sea hardly affected the men inside the boat. Waves so much bigger than the tiny U-boat made it possible to ride over them like a car driving over an undulating road, but it was too rough for the men to be out enjoying the views and it was not until their arrival in France that they discovered a multitude of damage on the outside. The waves had bent some quite substantial steel, meaning it became a major repair job rather than merely tidying up after the storm. During this dreadful weather U504 met an armed British trawler, but in such rough conditions there was no point of even thinking about using weapons and they passed in peace.

Many years after the war, when Poske stumbled upon this barograph sheet again, he made several copies to hand out at a boat reunion; one of these now hangs in the German U-boat Museum. Normally a barograph would record just one thin line and the thick zigzag impression (3) on the graph paper was not caused by the storm but by the vibrations from the diesel engines. The gaps (2) in the thick trace show when the boat had dived, and one can see the thin line (1) heading off to the top of the page because air pressure increased in the boat the moment the hatches were sealed. Had the barograph not been shaken by the engines, it would have produced a thin line as shown near (1).

THE FEROCIOUS ATLANTIC

Wolfgang Hirschfeld's logbook (*Feindfahrten – Logbuch eines U-bootfunkers* (Paul Neff Verlag, Vienna, 1982)) describes how U109 under Kptlt. Ajax Bleichrodt negotiated a slightly lesser storm while heading west towards Canada, and the following account has been supplemented with information from conversations with both men.

* * *

> While proceeding on the surface during night and day without interference from the British air force, U109 negotiated some lively waves. The Biscay area to the north-west of France did not have the greatest number of light houses along its coasts for nothing and the uncanny turbulence beyond north-west France was not unpleasant for those with good sea legs. Those men accustomed to only German coasts and those from inland locations where they had never seen the sea, also got used to it but failed

Wolfgang Lüth, one of the most decorated men from the U-boat Arm, as commander of U181 on his way from France to the Indian Ocean. He is holding on for dear life to the torpedo-aiming device while the boat's batteries are being charged during a storm. Readers might remember Lüth as the commander who was shot accidentally by his own guard a few days after the end of the war. (*Photo: Walter Schöppe*)

to appreciate the speed with which the Atlantic could change bearable conditions into annoying turmoil. It was around the end of the second watch (8 o'clock in the evening) of 7 October 1941, only two months before the United States joined in the war, when Bleichrodt ordered the first test dive for what was the boat's third war voyage. U109 had hardly levelled out deep down in the cellar when the men were brought to their senses by several exploding depth charges. Seeing some worried faces, Bleichrodt said, 'They are too far away to have been aimed at us. Some others have trodden in the shit.' He was cautious enough not to prompt providence and remained out of the way for a couple of hours, allowing aircraft enough time to go home rather than turn their attention on U109.

Two hours later the boat had still not surfaced completely when the experienced men knew there had been a drastic change in the weather up top. Down in the cellar there was no wave motion and no noise. Men rested or even fell asleep. Those who remained awake talked in whispered tones. It was peaceful and silent; only the air got stuffier but U109 had not been down long enough for breathing to become a problem. Then, before rising to periscope depth, everybody noticed there had been some changes in the weather with considerably rougher waves. Dawn the following morning indicated it was going to be dull and grey, and the lookouts had already donned heavy raingear with safety harnesses. They also kept the hatch shut and when they returned, the inside of the boat was converted into a steaming laundry with clothing hanging to dry in more places than just the engine and electro compartment. Men had come down soaking wet and extremely cold. Had they not been chained in position they would all have been washed off the conning tower. The water often came up as high as their necks and the sheer force of the waves was making even simple breathing difficult. It was not unusual for everybody up top to have to hold their breath and then gasp for air. The Bay of Biscay was living up to its reputation. The men inside did not fare much better. Water no longer dripped but cascaded down through the hatch

Unpleasant weather at sea offered many opportunities for seasickness, even for experienced sailors.

and everything not nailed down joined the Luftwaffe [air force] to fly through the air. Smashed crockery was moving around faster than men hunting the fragments. The broken pieces even found their own way into high up bunks. Breadcrumbs in bed are one thing, crockery chips are even worse, but the men did not change into pyjamas at 'night' and their work clothing protected them from cuts.

Hirschfeld, the leading radio operator, was not much perturbed by the weather or the goings-on in the boat. He had the advantage of being shut off in his quiet little corner, where the news coming through his radio was most disturbing. To be precise, it was not the inflowing news that worried him, but the absence of it. Only a few days ago the crew had watched friends leave and now these men were no longer sending any indication they were still alive. No position reports, no weather reports, even when the radio asked for the information. This bleak silence indicated things were not terribly harmonious ahead. Apart from a short sunny spell when Bleichrodt sent every available man up top to shoot the sun, it remained dull and grey with all the navigation being done by dead reckoning rather than by more accurate positions from shooting sun or stars. Yet the heaving, rolling and pitching did not generate a great deal of concern. It was unlikely the boat would meet anything hard to bump into, but sleeping was becoming a major problem for tired men. The boat's ferocious movement would have thrown them out of their bunks had they not tied themselves down.

Bleichrodt was the type who could find solutions for difficult problems, and he decided the daily test dive was going to coincide with lunch, allowing everybody to enjoy their meal in comfort. Astonishingly enough, the weather did not put many off their food, making the cook's efforts under such extreme circumstances worthwhile. He always had grateful recipients for his cooking. Later, when the barometer suggested the storm was subsiding, the elements quickly changed their minds and instead of improving it was necessary for the men to go through another swearing routine as it got worse.

'Sod this' was Bleichrodt's reaction. He shouted at the LI [engineer officer]. With the engines running and the howling of the sea, normal speech would not have been heard. 'To hell with this wolfpack and our orders. We are going to practise a bit of underwater cruising at the most economical speed.'

Later, when the hatch was opened again and the ventilator started blowing fresh air into the interior, everyone was instantly hit by an unexpected painful chill, cold enough to rattle the bones. 'You have got to get used to this' was all Bleichrodt said. 'We are approaching Greenland and there is a cold wind blowing over from the land.'

When Kptlt. Karl Thurmann (U553) reported the position of the convoy he was shadowing, Bleichrodt cursed again. This gem of a target turned out to be behind rather than in front of U109. The merchant ships must have sailed past the wolfpack while the surface traffic was hidden by the appalling weather. This time the lookouts had good excuses. In addition to painful waves crashing against them, visibility was exceedingly poor with hardly any long-range visibility. The intensity of the storm would not have drowned the noise of so many ships, but sound detectors worked only when the U-boat was submerged and the noisy diesel engines were turned off. The merchant ships could not have passed while the boat was down below. After testing everything, Hirschfeld assured Bleichrodt the sound receivers were in perfect working order and the hypothesis of the convoy having passed while U109 was on the surface had to be correct.

So far, the men had coped with the cold by adding more layers of clothing, but the dampness from drying wet clothing and ejecting water pouring in through the hatch created a vile combination of unpleasant damp condensation. The men had got used to this, but unfortunately the food, especially the bread stored in hammocks, did not develop this indifference, and retaliated by producing an unsightly mould. At first the men polished the bread. Despite their efforts, not all the loaves cooperated. Some had to be thrown out. Much of this bread was finest German black bread, which remained in jolly good condition for two to three months when stored in a domestic breadbin, but did not seem to cope with the Atlantic dampness. Bleichrodt tried to ease the situation by ordering the engineer officer to switch on the heaters, taking the view it would be necessary to return home empty handed if they ran out of food, so they might as well use up some of their fuel for preserving it. The storm did not only physically upset operations, it also played havoc with the radio, and it was not long before Hirschfeld discovered he was not picking up a considerable number of messages. On top of that, no one at headquarters on land was acknowledging those he had transmitted earlier. U109 was cut off from the world.

This stormy torture lasted for more than a week before the inside of U109 returned to some form of normality.

'It is only wind force six today,' Hirschfeld wrote in his log.

If this related to a cross-Channel ferry running from Dover to Calais, then it would be newsworthy. Such conditions would make things difficult for ships passing through the narrow harbour entrances in Dover but the old Hook of Holland to Harwich ferry did not have to worry about narrow passageways and had a reputation for running whatever the weather. Yet a storm force eight would bring the interior of such a ferry to a drastic standstill. Morning tea/coffee would not be served because the crockery had been demolished. The shops would close due to the stock being everywhere except on the shelves, and furniture not screwed to the deck would find its own way into untidy heaps – all in conditions which Hirschfeld described as 'only force six'.

The calmness of force six did not last. Two days later Hirschfeld was woken from deep sleep by loud crashing noises against the conning tower; further investigation indicated the lookouts were, once again, up to their necks in water. This time it was not only the sea, but also a good rendering of snow, hail, ice and thick fog adding to the discomfort. It was obvious the lookouts would not have the slightest chance of drying their clothing during the eight hours before they would be called again to endure more of the torture on the top of the conning tower. Yet it was important to fill the batteries and U109 plodded along on the surface.

Eventually, when it got lighter, it was not only the men who were frozen stiff, but everything else on the outside had turned into one huge block of ice. The guns looked like weird configurations from an alien planet, and one did not need the ingenuity of a U-boat commander to realize the whole contraption was going to get top heavy and turn over. This situation had not occurred gradually. One minute everything was clear, then the lookouts were hit by tons of water pouring over them and the next they knew, the boat had been transformed into a huge lump of ice. Every U-boat had experts in their own fields, who were also knowledgeable in everybody else's business as well, and this occasion was no exception. Wise conversations about how to remove the ice started instantly and it was Bleichrodt who told the men there was no way anyone would be allowed up top to hack it off again.

'Hacking it off will also break away the metal parts of the boat,' he told the men. 'And it will be rather slippery out there. What are we going to do when someone falls overboard? There is no way we will ever get him back in this weather. No. No snowmen.'

At the same time, the old U-boat school trick of diving into the slightly warmer water was also difficult because the vents could not be shut. So, it was a case of going down far enough to clear the vents by pumping out the water that came through on its own until the entire system could be shut down for safe diving. Everybody on board was astonished by this turn of events and even the experienced men realized there was more to being a seaman than the limited knowledge they already had. There was always something new, something one had to learn and to worry about. The eventual dive did clear the ice but once back on the surface it did not take long before the whole process started all over again, all due to a cold wind from the Arctic blowing over the sea. Men were walking like zombies, wearing every bit of clothing they had; despite this, they were still shivering with cold when they joined the Mordbrenner Patrol Line. To add insult to injury, the sacrifice did not help them in finding any targets. U109 returned to France almost empty handed, although it did help to escort a prize merchant ship, the Norwegian *Silvaplana*, to Bordeaux. It had been captured earlier by the ghost cruiser *Atlantis* (Kpt.z.S. Bernhard Rogge) in the south Atlantic.

SOME GERMAN EXPECTATIONS

How some men in the German Navy saw the Atlantic – before they experienced it for themselves. The 5th U-boat Flotilla in Kiel under Karl-Heinz Moehle, a Knight of the Iron Cross, supplied U-boats with everything they needed before they set out for their first operational tour. Someone there had the incredible sense to keep a guest book for visiting U-boat crews and these pages show there were also some highly gifted artists in U-boats. The pages reproduced here provide interesting insights into the minds of the people who were setting out 'to see the world'.

U862 (Kptlt. Heinrich Timm) saw the Naval Memorial in Laboe near Kiel in rain while the Atlantic looked considerably better. This would have been drawn during the autumn of 1943, when U-boats at sea were being hammered to an early death. U862, also a very-long-range boat of Type IXD2, reached the Far East where it survived the war. The boat departed from its last European port, Narvik in Norway, on3 June 1944 and arrived in Penang on 9 September. Now, work out for how long the men were inside their small windowless cruise ship without a great deal of entertainment and a lot of boredom and discomfort.

The men of U859 under Kptlt. Johann Jebsen (from the North Friesian Island of Pellworm in the cold North Sea) appear to have had a wonderful impression of what they hoped to meet on the South Sea islands near the Equator. U859 left Kiel on 4 April 1944, the day when the author was born, and was sunk in September while entering harbour in Penang at the end of its first operational war cruise. Jebsen and forty-six men lost their lives. This was one of the special very-long-range U-boats of Type IXD2.

U843 (Kptlt. Oskar Herwartz) has a naked Aphrodite, the goddess of sexual love and fertility, sitting on the stern of the conning tower and there is a wren on the jumping wire in front of her. The torpedo (code-named Zaun~könig or Wren), is looking out of the water by the stork, calling out the name for the new German acoustic torpedo, which was introduced around the time U843 was getting ready in Kiel. Aphrodite was the name of the new radar foxer, and Wanze or bug (*top right*) was a newly introduced radar detector being sprayed with insecticide. The U-boat has the latest conning tower modification with strengthened anti-aircraft guns. (There was also a Wolfgang Herwartz who died in the British St George's Channel as commander of U1302 on 7 March 1945.)

U265 (Oblt.z.S. Leonhard Aufhammer) has a lady sitting on the conning tower. Neptune at the bottom is saying, 'It will not be long before there are no more merchant ships.' Early in January 1943, the mermaid answers, 'Thank God the war is almost over.' The entire crew died when U265 was sunk less than two weeks later, on 2 February, during an attack by Flying Fortress 'N' from 220 Squadron RAF, piloted by P. Ramsden.

This was part of an illustration about some notes regarding U765 (Oblt.z.S. Werner Wendt). The boat left Kiel on 18 March 1944 and spent a few days in Bergen, before venturing out to the west of Britain where it was sunk a few weeks later, on 6 May. The commander and seven men who were on the bridge at the time were the only ones to survive. This scene was probably drawn a few days before U765 left port.

Chapter 8

The Mid-war Crises – 1943

THE BRITISH SUBMARINE *TUNA* SINKS U644

The key words 'inexperience' and 'schedule is schedule' were now having a significant impact on U-boat operations. The following report of how the British submarine *Tuna* (Lieutenant D.S.R. Martin) torpedoed U644 (Oblt.z.S. Kurt Jensen) on 7 April 1943 is significant because it raises the question of whether this sinking was due to seasickness and inexperience rather than anything else.

In April 1943 there was a U-boat patrol line of considerable size near the island of Jan Mayen, with boats spreading out northwards as far as the ice allowed. When the British submarine *Tuna* was sent into those cold waters to investigate, it spotted U644. Strangely enough, German lookouts appear not to have seen the attacker, despite British submarines having more cluttered conning towers. German lookouts were positioned at the pinnacle of the tower, while *Tuna* had an arrangement of supports above the highest lookout. Closing in to attacking range, *Tuna* fired a salvo of five torpedoes, of which two hit, sinking U644 on the fifth day of its first and only war voyage. The boat had come from Germany, stopped off in Bergen and then continued north. There were no survivors, despite the British submarine closing in to search for people in the water. A solitary man

A famous Catalina flying boat parked at the Imperial War Museum on Duxford Airfield near Cambridge. The wheels could be retracted and the wing tips folded down to serve as floats, allowing the boat to put down on water.

The American escort carrier USS *Card*, seen here with its aircraft parked on deck, was launched in 1942. Several of these escort carriers were hastily converted from merchant ships by removing the superstructure and adding a flight deck. The early types did not have elevators, meaning mechanics serviced the aircraft on the open deck, which must have made for a most precarious existence. Yet despite the crudeness, these carriers were highly successful.

seen struggling in a huge patch of brown oil disappeared before he could be reached. Kurt Jensen, the commander, had served as First Watch Officer in U376 under Kptlt. Friedrich-Karl Marks for less than a year before taking on U644 in the middle of October 1942. Leaving Kiel on 13 March 1943, the boat spent two days in Bergen before leaving again on the 18th; everybody on board was dead by the end of 7 April 1943. It is likely this crew was made up in a similar fashion to that of U570, mentioned earlier.

A few days later, U302 (Kptlt. Herbert Sickel) survived a similar attack from HMS *Tuna* and reported what had happened; it makes one wonder whether the sheer inexperience of the men in U644 was responsible for their loss. There were several U-boats milling around, waiting for the next convoy sailing between the Russian Arctic ports and Iceland, America or the United Kingdom. It would appear exchanges between them, if there were any communications at all, were carried out either by signal lamp, semaphore or getting close enough for captains to shout at each other through megaphones. The U-boats had not compromised their positions by transmitting radio signals. This would suggest the patrol line had been detected by breaking into the naval Enigma code, and probably no one in *Tuna*'s base in Lerwick (Shetland Islands) had any knowledge of the code-breaking breakthrough. All they would have been told is there might be a German patrol line at sea. It is unlikely the British submarine knew the positions of the U-boats when it set out and the U-boats were found by searching for them. Hunting U-boats with submarines was not part of usual procedures because it was exceedingly difficult for one low-profile submarine to spot another, especially in the north where fogs often shrouded the horizon.

There were no quiet corners inside U-boats and tables were in the main corridor, meaning they had to be put away when people moved around. Finding somewhere for the all-important paperwork was not always easy.

Being shut inside tight quarters for much of the time, men were more than happy to have a picnic on the deck when conditions permitted. This man has an injured left arm and is wearing his submarine escape apparatus, which could also serve as a lifejacket.

The next time you see those pristine soldiers on parade with a caption saying they were killer Nazis out for a brutal attack, then also look at this picture to realize life in U-boats was neither posh nor conducive to good etiquette. The men only ate out on the open deck in 'very' safe areas, if and when such places could be found.

Engineer Officer Schmitt of U355. The thick 'book' he is supporting on his lap is a large piece of cheese, and the 'truncheon' in his hand is a salami sausage. Hard cheeses were used for eating and a pile of them sometimes served as temporary seat.

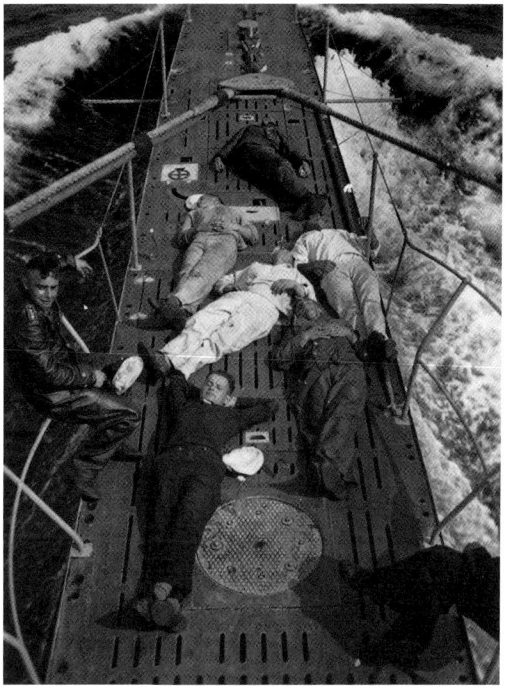

Above and below: The military drives its men to the limit of their endurance and then, after that, still expects them to carry out their normal duties. 'Professor' Gus Briton said that way you learn to sleep anywhere, at any time and under any conditions. Seen here are two crews taking it easy in safe conditions where someone else is doing the hard work.

The weather and the sea were reasonably calm on the day of U644's sinking. It was cloudy, with visibility changing from 8 to 12 nautical miles, and a moderate wind was whipping up the sea to produce large rolling waves up to about a man in height. Similar conditions prevailed early on 14 April 1943 when, at 0738 hours, one of the lookouts on U302 calmly reported a school of whales or porpoises breaking through the waves about 2 kilometres away. These had closed in to about 600 metres when Sickel, the commander, realized he was not looking at local wildlife but at a salvo of torpedoes. Driving the diesels to maximum power, the boat turned sharply onto a parallel course to the approaching destruction, to present the torpedoes with the smallest possible target. Then, still not sure whether this was a torpedo attack or whales, his fears were confirmed by an explosion some distance away, after the eels had passed the U-boat. The confusion in recognizing this dangerous situation came about as a result of the relatively calm sea and the high waves. To hit a submarine, the torpedoes would have been adjusted to their minimum depth, making it possible to see the torpedoes when they came to the crest of each wave. The illusion of them being whales was further strengthened by the wind. There was just enough to blow plumes of water a little higher than a man, resembling the spray blown up by marine mammals. Still recovering from the shock, U302 dived deep while the commander ordered absolute silence, and the U-boat quietly crept away. HMS *Tuna* was probably also submerged. No one on the German side saw the attacking submarine.

Aircraft on an open deck in rather exciting weather – exciting only if you don't have to experience it yourself.

A Swordfish aircraft in difficulties aboard HMS *Chaser*. Although introduced as late as 1936, these aircraft resembled the 'string bags' of the First World War, but they were highly effective naval aircraft. (*Photo: Tim Kirby*)

It is questionable whether anyone in U302 had seen marine life before, but they had been at sea for a whole month on the day of the *Tuna* encounter, so it was likely the men had found their sea legs and were not suffering from sea sickness, which could well have been a decisive factor in the loss of U644. This was also U302's sixth war voyage, making the majority of men seasoned sea dogs, well in tune with natural conditions. The commander, Herbert Sickel, had been 1WO in U73 for almost a year before commissioning U302, so he came with considerable experience. Another significant and often used comment in personal reports is the domineering feeling of tiredness, which occurred even when the men were confined to lying in bunks or hammocks for long periods. Sleeplessness is a wonderful tool for slowing the thinking process and making automatic reactions much more lethargic; add a touch of seasickness and you have a deadly combination.

HM Submarine *Tuna* has another 'hidden' event to her credit. On 24 September 1940 she torpedoed and sank the catapult ship *Ostmark* close to the French coast, prompting Dönitz to change procedures and send a short signal when outgoing U-boats had reached the Atlantic side of the Bay of Biscay. The latitude of these signals could be determined by British radio direction finders and was used by the secret Submarine Tracking Room in London to make an educated guess as to where they were going. Knowing the average cruising speed of U-boats, it was also possible to estimate when each would arrive in its operations area.

BREAKDOWNS AT SEA

Mechanical failures causing breakdowns at sea had been a major issue since before the start of the war and the following account, derived from a logbook, is just one example.

* * *

For the majority of Germans, work and school started at 0800 hours, the same time as U989 (Kptlt. Hardo Rodler von Roithberg) left Kiel for its first operational war cruise on 11 January 1944, some five months before the D-Day Normandy landings. By this time most of the U-boats' teething problems should have been recognized and rectified. It was a bitterly cold day as several boats waited for escort as far as the Skagerrak and the south-western tip of Norway. Once clear of the narrow danger zone, they were free to head west on their own, all in a slightly different direction. The following is a description of what happened once the brand-new U989 was on its own. Although this was the boat's first operational voyage, the commander was by no means a novice. Rodler von Roithberg had joined the navy in 1937 and spent six months aboard the destroyer *Karl Galster* (Z20) as watch officer before starting his U-boat training. Following this, he saw serious action as second watch officer in U96 under the Knight of the Iron Cross, Kptlt. Heinrich Lehmann-Willenbrock, before moving on to command the training boat U24 for a year. He took over command of U71 from Walter Flachsenberg on the last day of June 1942 and stayed with it for almost a year. So, he was no beginner.

Now, out on his first war voyage in U989, there was hardly any contact with the opposition, but plenty of cursing to deal with a chain of mechanical disasters. Only on one occasion were men terrified by an aircraft illuminating them with a Leigh Light, but its pilot was obliging enough to switch it on while still a long way off, giving U989 plenty of time to disappear from the surface before it got close. By the time the U-boat was out of sight of land, having left minesweepers and escorts, the crew had already repaired three major leaks in different parts of the boat. All of these were in places where ducts passed through the pressure hull in accessible spots, making the unwanted intrusions relatively easy to deal with. The fourth leak, a few days later, was more difficult and more puzzling. Water was flowing in through a ventilator. At home workmen from a shipyard were called to deal with such disasters but here there were no workmen and no one else to help. The crew had only themselves and the problem seemed to be on the outside, under the hard iron shell of the superstructure. The most obvious place to look was under the fairing aft of the conning tower, an area which had become a rather cluttered mishmash with several modifications added on top of the original design. The gun platforms had been enlarged and ready-to-use ammunition containers added wherever there was space. Originally, in the olden days, it would have been a simple matter of turning a few nuts and bolts, a sort of large screwdriver job to get into the empty space between the upper (outside) deck and the pressure hull. Now the men needed a cold chisel, hammer and crowbar to lever away some of the obstructing new

Martlet aircraft being launched from a US aircraft carrier.

A Swordfish aircraft with anti-submarine rockets under its fuselage.

A Seafire aircraft crashing on HMS *Chaser*. Sadly, the pilot did not survive. This aircraft type was a specially manufactured naval version of the famous Spitfire with adaptations for landing and taking off from aircraft carriers. (*Photo: Tim Kirby*)

fittings before they could open the hatch into this tiny space. Once inside, they repaired the head valve of the ventilation shaft. This stopped the water coming in, but it would have been much quicker had there been an easy-to-open doorway. One must bear in mind the safest time to carry out this type of work was in the dark when there was likely to be less interference from aircraft. Waves were also uncooperative enough to make the process hard going for the men squeezed into this tight spot. Water was constantly washing in through the huge vents along both sides of the fairing – and remember, it was still January, and U989 was not too far from Norway. It was an exciting time of the year to be close to uncooperative waves.

The men, feeling pleased with themselves for having completed these awkward repairs, then turned their attention to the radar detector's aerial, which had snapped for the second time since leaving Kiel. Reinforcing the stalk with timber was easier than trying to replace several broken ceramic insulators, but the men got the system up and running again. Having recovered from their cold and wet exertions, they dealt with a faulty torpedo and after that discovered two high pressure oil pumps had seized up. Among other things, these powered the mechanism for raising and lowering both periscopes, meaning muscle men were now required to wind them up and down by hand. Those with more skill and less muscle tackled the pumps. All this was going on while men were coping with seasickness and quite extraordinary waves, making sure the newcomers knew the Atlantic was a good deal more restless than the Baltic. Those not employed with the tricky jobs had to deal with some loose twisted grating which had unhelpfully bent one of the gun barrels. No one was terribly worried about losing their large 37mm anti-aircraft gun. During recent regular maintenance checks it had not yet produced a decent rate of continuous fire. Earlier, this semi-automatic gun failed to eject the first cartridge, making it impossible to fire any more until someone had serious words with the jammed instrument – and this happened at a time when the opposition prevented the boat from hanging about on the surface for long enough to take the contraption to pieces.

Things were not harmonious in the engine room either, where men had been standing in water for some time. Not only was it deep enough to be annoying but it was also dirty, with a definite black colour, and traces of oil with lumps of grease floating on top. The ballast pump was making a hell of a lot of noise, reminding the engineer officer he needed to find other ways of getting rid of the wet intrusion. Allowing it to flood into the accommodation area had to be prevented because there it could find its way into the battery compartments to mix with acid, producing the vilest choking gas. If this were not enough to keep the men on their toes, the gyro compass at the back of the central control room protested in sympathy before going on strike as well.

Later, when U989 got close to several convoys and tried to use homing signals from other U-boats to find the merchant ships, the men discovered these radio impulses were

At the beginning of the war, German leaders still held the view aircraft could not hurt submarines because it was possible to dive out of harm's way before anything got close enough to attack. This antiquated view proved to be incorrect after the start of the Second World War when aircraft spotting became a major activity aboard U-boats. On the left is a periscopic radio aerial and on the right, nearest the warrant officer in the middle, is the sky or navigation periscope with the large head lens. Lower right, in front of the commander, is a sighting compass set in gimbals.

identifying themselves by using the names of their commanders instead of their boat numbers and U989 had not been given a list of which commander belonged to which number. The men must have had a frustrating time. To make them even more miserable, when they reached France, they had their leave curtailed to face rather an intensive training programme before setting out for their next war voyage. Men were often most amiable but having your leave curtailed was a heavy punishment, especially when you hardly ever got an opportunity to go home, and everybody was working for more than a normal seven-day week without breaks.

Herbert Sohler, the Chief of the 7th U-boat Flotilla, in St Nazaire (France), talking to Gerhard Bigalk, commander of U751, shortly after he had sunk the escort carrier *Audacity* during a bitter battle on 21 December 1941.

Yet U989 was one of the more successful boats, having sunk one ship and damaged another during seven hair-raising voyages. Incidents like these show German U-boats didn't need Allied opponents to fight the war: they could do all the fighting themselves with their own machinery.

TO SEA FOR THE FIRST AND LAST TIME

U533 (Kptlt. Helmut Henning) was one of the later large, long-range boats of Type IXC-40. The following is based on an account by Gottfried Zestermann (radio operator) and supplied by Ernst Pfefferle. Additional information has come from Arthur Banks, who wrote the book *Wings of the Dawning* (Images Publishing, Malvern, 1996). It seems likely Gottfried Zestermann left the boat during the refit in France and was therefore not aboard when it sank.

* * *

'Our boat is a good, sharp weapon,' said Kptlt. Henning before ordering the flag to be hoisted for the first time on U533. Nobody was terribly keen on long speeches during commissioning ceremonies. It was usually an easy day for the workers in their Sunday best. The crew parading on deck were also wearing their finest uniforms to mark the momentous occasion with a bun fight accompanied by a plentiful supply of beer. The men were proud of their new boat. It looked smart with impressive guns, but most of the crew, still in their late teens, had never been to sea before. These youngsters knew U-boats had been lost at sea, but they did not know how many. Gottfried Zestermann, the radio

By 1941 the best-dressed gunners aboard U-boats had exchanged their soft hats for something a bit harder. Both men are also wearing uninflated lifejackets. Statistically, wearing tin hats considerably increased the number of head injuries. The reason might not be obvious, but a bullet through the head when not wearing a hard hat meant death, while with the helmet many survived.

operator, guessed it to have been around thirty-five to thirty-eight. Not a bad figure after almost forty months of bitter fighting. It was a while before he got to know the real number. On 25 November 1942, U533's commissioning day, the losses were around two hundred. This helps to understand how young men could be enticed to go to war without knowing where they were going or what they were volunteering for. It was the same in all countries. Neither Germany, Britain nor the United States had learned the lessons from the First World War about the misery of human losses; and judging by what is going on in this present time, modern leaders have also not yet learned those lessons either.

The men of U533 learned to master their complicated machinery by sailing around the Baltic and it was April 1943, the month before 'Black May', when they ventured out for their first operational voyage. There was not the slightest indication of anything untoward happening, and even their baptism of fire did little more than wake sleeping men. The little damage inflicted by an air attack was repaired with tools on board and the boat was back in full action by the same time on the following day. The worst incident involved Boots~manns~maat Buttkuss (Boatswain, a petty officer without swordknot). Able to get around the boat like a monkey, he offered a whole crate of beer to anyone who could jump on his head. He might have been faster down the conning tower than the majority,

The result of a dramatic air attack on U505 in 1942 while on its first mission with the new commander, Kptlt. Peter Zschech. A Trinidad-based Hudson scored a hit on the loaded 37mm quick firing deck gun, causing a massive explosion. The aircraft crashed into the sea, killing the crew of four. Several men on the bridge were seriously injured as well and the damage was severe enough to prevent U505 from diving until repairs had been made. Zschech killed himself around the time the Americans boarded his boat on 24 October 1943.

but he failed to take into account the irrational fear injected into men when they sighted aircraft. This had already been a frightening experience long enough for everybody at sea to know aircraft had become 'the' killer for all surfaced U-boats. Just seeing something in the air, even if it was a long way off, was bad enough to send terrifying shivers down men's backs. U533 was somewhere to the south of Iceland when someone succeeded in meeting Buttkuss's challenge, leaving the commander having to use medical clips to stitch up the resulting 6cm-long gash in his head. The men's subsequent indifference with a Sunderland flying boat was even worse. This time Boots~manns~maat Buttkuss was shot through the thigh, Matrosen~gefreiter (Able Seaman) Fekken through the lower leg and Matrosen~gefreiter Ludwig through the lower arm. In addition to these injuries, many men were suffering from seasickness severely enough to have problems doing their jobs. Each compartment had a bucket with a little old engine oil in it. This oil was poured onto anything with a more offensive smell until the effect of depth charges spread the putridity around the surrounding walls.

On two occasions, while heading west towards an expected convoy, the men were driven into the depths without the new radar detector giving the usual warning of any activity around them. The crew assumed there must be something wrong with their receiving equipment. Once nearer the convoy, the boat was again attacked by huge, long-range Sunderland flying boats. These did not get close enough to attack but made life more difficult and frustrated the men in the U-boat trying to drive home their attack. Despite this, Henning, the commander, did eventually manage to get close enough to be attacked by depth charges. In the end, while running out of air and electricity, all U533 could do was to slide away at an incredibly slow speed, at which it was almost impossible to hear the motors. After this, although life was nowhere near easy, the most amazing thing happened: without the U-boat making any effort, a convoy sailed towards U533. Everything was ready for the first attack, but the procedures were complicated and so were the variety of levers, handwheels and taps. Men working the torpedo tubes in the bow compartment did something in the wrong order, causing tons of water to flood in. This turned out to be more than just an exciting interlude. It became life-threatening. The engineer officer kept the boat afloat by driving the engines to a fast speed while setting the forward hydroplanes to 'up' and bringing every possible ballast pump into use. Following this, there were more air attacks, including one with a Leigh Light during a dark night. Having heard about these new searchlights, the U-boat crews nicknamed them 'Leichen~licht' (Corpses' Light). It happened terribly quickly, without warning:

Meeting with supply submarine U116 (Korvkpt. Werner von Schmidt) are U94 (Oblt.z.S. Otto Ites) on the left and U406 (Kptlt. Horst Dietrichs) on the right. U116 was a large minelayer of Type XB; these were used as supply boats before the purpose-built supply boats were ready to go to sea.

In the olden days it was common for people to write messages on the front of postcards, while the address always went on the back. This card has a rather poignant message, saying: 'The last time we were together in Hamburg in June 1943 at the Alotria.' The Allotria (misspelt on the card) was a variety theatre on the Reeperbahn from 1936 until it closed in 1956. Several veterans said it was easy to make good friends in the navy, but it was also damn easy to lose them again without a further word about what happened to them. People just vanished, as if by magic, and often without a funeral.

The lookout is wearing a raincoat, and it appears the weather has improved since he came on duty with other men having been given permission to smoke up top. This was the only way many could sample fresh air and changed the habits of many non-smokers. The two stars on the shoulder strap indicate this man's rank and the two anchors show his trade. He is an Ober~boots~mann, making him the Ober~steuer~mann or navigator, who was also the third watch officer. His hat is the so-called Schiff~chen or small ship, which was favoured because it folded flat to occupy only a little locker space.

Kptlt. Siegfried Freiherr von Forstner immediately after he had been awarded the Knights Cross in February 1943 as commander of U402. He was killed in action when the boat was sunk less than a year later.

There was some natural segregation in bars visited by Germans, with the higher ranking focusing more on select establishments while sailors often chose small bars, where there were fewer opportunities for saluting. Drunkenness was dealt with within some purpose-built military bases by having special sinks for being sick in.

A cold day in February 1942. Kptlt. Herbert Sohler (on the right), Commander of the 7th U-boat Flotilla, welcoming home U751 under Kptlt. Gerhard Bigalk (*left*) and U85 under Oblt.z.S. Eberhard Greger. Both boat commanders died before the end of the summer of 1942. Waiting for incoming U-boats was often a time-consuming, drawn-out process, with dignitaries having to wait because no one could predict the exact arrival time. Officers who did this regularly had some especially warm greatcoats with thick fur lining. These were incredibly heavy and felt like wearing armour.

A makeshift refuelling of U758 (Kptlt. Helmut Manseck) from U221 (Kptlt. Hans Trojer), with seriously damaged bows. U221 had rammed U254 (Kptlt. Odo Loewe) during appalling conditions. The damage was serious enough for the boat to sink while the huge waves made it possible to rescue only four of her crew. An investigation back in port declared this to have been an unavoidable accident. With U221 having to return to base due to the torpedo tubes being bent, it was decided to hand over some of the spare fuel to U758, but the combined pipes from both boats were not long enough and the fuel was passed over in metal containers tied to lifejackets. The containers had to go back and forth several times. Since there was no way of pouring it into the fuel tanks, they were emptied into the bilges under the inside deck and from there pumped into the fuel tanks. All this took place a few days before Christmas 1942, not a good time to be at sea in a storm.

> One moment it was pitch black, then we saw the light, the gun crew had not yet started shooting when we heard metal hitting the U-boat, loud enough to wreck one's nerves. Being in the radio room for much of the time, I did not experience this light display myself, but it certainly rattled those up on the bridge. The glare of the light was intense, making it impossible for the gunners to see the position of the aircraft for accurate aim. In any case, shooting back into that dazzling glare was not easy and we had enough wounded men to know for certain this was not the sort of moment for hanging around on the surface.

In the end it was the Royal Navy, rather than the Royal Air Force, which put paid to U533's further action against North Atlantic convoys. During the night of 5/6 May 1943 the U-boat was rammed by the corvette HMS *Sunflower*, causing serious damage but without sinking it. U533 crawled back to France, arriving in Lorient on the 24th. The boat may not have sunk any ships, but the men were lucky to have brought it back, to earn themselves some home leave and a little prestige.

The men of U533 had negotiated Atlantic gales powerful enough to derail convoys, had come to terms with seasickness and had survived terrifying depth charge attacks. Now they were ready for more action, for more failures and for their final end. Joining the Monsoon Group, U533 sailed towards the Indian Ocean, where rich Europeans now go for their holidays. In 1943 the ticket meant far worse conditions than the tight seating of airlines' tourist accommodation. The journey started on 5 July 1943 and ended in the approaches to the Persian Gulf on 16 October, after a series of disasters. In the end there was only one survivor from an air attack, Seaman Günther Schmidt. He was picked up after having been afloat in the water for more than 24 hours. Some sources say he reached the shore, while others state he was picked up by the Indian auxiliary patrol boat HMIS *Hiravati*, which is more likely. Arthur Banks wrote 'the known presence of the enemy in the form of a real German prisoner resulted in both air and ground crews being spurred into more action, making them realize they were not in a desert backwater but fighting on the front line'.

Writing the story of this mission as a novel would be futile. No one would believe a plot with such a devastating series of failures, all of them far beyond the control of the men in U533, and all these disappointments have now been lost in a sea of statistics. The men of U533 did not sink anything despite having been at sea for a long time, although all but one paid for their ticket with their lives while doing their duty for their country.

A reprovisioning moment in warmer, southern waters showing the use of an inflatable life raft. Paddling it was most cumbersome.

THE LEIGH LIGHT

The Leigh Light became operational during the second half of 1942, and the following explanation comes from Britain's secret Anti-Submarine Report:

> The two types of illuminants proven to be of value for night attack on the U-boat are the Leigh Light and the 4-inch high-intensity flare. It must be remembered attack by night is a very specialized task and must therefore have a much greater amount of training than for the day-attack. This, in turn, demands the allowance of training aircraft for night squadrons be greater than for day squadrons. In the absence of this additional training, only small dividends can be expected from the average air crews.
>
> The Leigh Light in the Wellington has proved itself to be an effective means of delivering night attacks on U-boats. The manoeuvrability of the Wellington, with its good pilot's view, combine to make it very suitable for this type of attack. Nevertheless, good crew drill, with a high state of ASV homing efficiency, are also essential to achieve success. The candle power of the Leigh Light is approximately 22 million. The Leigh Light in a Liberator aircraft is a newer project, which requires a higher state of crew training than with the Wellington. The reason for this is the lack of manoeuvrability inherent in larger aircraft which renders it less simple to make last-minute corrections during an approach; a Liberator pilot is more reluctant to reduce height sufficiently when doing this than the pilot of a Wellington. The pilot's view forward is restricted by the long nose, and if the target is picked up on the starboard (right hand) beam it may be impossible for the pilot to see it.

A Type XB, probably U234 (Kptlt. Hans Fehler), which surrendered at the end of the war while enroute to Japan. The mineshafts were full of cargo and more watertight storage containers had been attached on top. The straps holding these are clearly visible. There is a radar and a radar detector aerial of Type Hohentwiel by the elbow of the man holding on to the periscope support. At the front of the conning tower wall is the hole for the retractable radio direction finder. Also note the top of the schnorkel in the deck and the bracket for holding it, when raised, by the head of the man on the left.

> Night attacks with the 4-inch High Intensity Flare were adopted operationally in late 1943 when two Halifax squadrons became available for night-time anti-U-boat operations. Here, again a high state of training is necessary to achieve success. The flares should be dropped from 750 feet [228m] at approximately 1.25 miles [2km], or slightly less, from the target. The aircraft then decreases height as quickly as possible, consistent with safety; on picking up the target visually for a normal low-level attack.

Each flare lasted only for about three or four seconds, so it was necessary to drop a lot of them during a single attack. What is more, the aircraft could not fly below the U-boat's radar and therefore had to approach within the enemy's radar beam. If the aircraft were below 750 feet, then the flares were likely to fall into the water without illuminating. Using them was a simple matter of dropping the flare through a tube, which ignited with a slight delay to get it clear of the aircraft. Each flare had an intensity of 2 million candle power and was thus nowhere near as intense as the Leigh Light. Aircraft used in the Atlantic were often called flying coffins because many had been modernized to carry more fuel than in their original design and the additional weight of many flares became critical. Leigh Lights, on the other hand were more powerful and could be powered directly from the aircraft's electrical system.

Other weapons, such as the Hedgehog, Mousetrap and MAD (Magnetic Airborne Detector), played an important role, but these were hardly noticed by U-boat crews and are therefore not included in this volume. Ahead-throwing Hedgehog mortars could

Tirpitz Pier in Kiel Harbour with a Type VIIC boat on the left and the largest U-boat, a minelayer of Type XB, on the right. The raised box on the bows is the top of the mineshafts for holding standard moored mines. Just forward from it is the head of the rotatable sound detector and forward of that is the detachable head of the capstan.

be used only on British ships with strong decks, due to the heavy recoil of the launcher. The American version, named Mousetrap, fitted on ships with weaker decks, had the firing charge inside the projectile instead of the launcher. Both had the advantage of only detonating when they hit something solid, thus the explosion did not interfere with Asdic (sonar) activity. Depth charges were launched by dropping them off the stern of a ship or by using special launchers to throw them sideways, and they exploded at a set depth, which could be adjusted shortly before discharging them. Throughout the war there were more than 5,100 depth charge attacks resulting in about eighty-five hits, while the Hedgehog was used in just under 270 attacks, resulting in forty-seven hits. The first U-boat to be sunk by a Hedgehog was U628 (Kptlt. Heinrich Hasenschar) on 3 July 1943, and it is likely all hits on other U-boats resulted in a sinking with no chance of anyone escaping from the submerged target.

ATTACKS FROM THE AIR

The following account is based on the boat's log, with a report written by the commander when he returned to base.

U228 (Oblt.z.S. Erwin Christophersen), a Type VIIC, left St Nazaire on 4 May 1943 and crossed the Bay of Biscay early on the 7th, heading west some distance to the northwest of Spain. The sea was choppy but still smooth enough not to have worried passengers, had there been any on board, and visibility was good except for a number of high clouds in an otherwise blue sky.

> Log entry for 7 May 1943. Second War Voyage.
> 10.15 hours. Aircraft approaching. Both engines to top speed ahead. Action stations with men wearing life jackets. All guns are operational and ready, having been fired for maintenance earlier in the day. At a range of 2 kilometres our guns started shooting, causing the plane to veer off and circle around us at a respectful distance. The aircraft dropped lower while our guns continue to shoot. Our aiming is good. When the guns stopped to change magazines, the aircraft turned to attack again. Coming in from the front, our gunners could not shoot [*because all our guns face backwards*]. Still at top speed we make a hard turn to port (left) while the aircraft shoots and then throws six bombs. Two of them were pretty close, only about twenty to twenty-five metres from the boat, causing a considerable shaking towards the stern. Aircraft flies low over us. Our defensive fire is good with shells hitting the aircraft. Aircraft does not come back for a second attack. Cleared the decks and then dived. It is possible the four-engine aircraft of type Lancaster came down in the sea. If it did, it caused considerable damage to the boat, which we set about to repair the best we could.
>
> Experiences collected during our first war voyage have produced good results for us in all aspects. The crew met all the demands in all situations and was ready to defend the boat. Aircraft attacks were repelled on three occasions. Damage resulting during these attacks was repaired as far as possible. Engine and radio personnel did everything they could to make good any disruption and damage. The

men were depressed because two were injured during the first attack, which limited the operational capacity of the boat significantly, but they all recovered very quickly, and the general humour and good atmosphere returned quickly again. When the boat received orders to operate further south, we entered a zone with completely new conditions for everybody on board. The performance of the men remained the same and their achievements were satisfactory.

The demands put on the lookouts were considerable and in areas where air attacks were likely, we used only our best men. We could have done with more seamen in those areas as well, especially when the anti-aircraft guns had to be made ready. The sun sector lookouts and the radar detection operations were manned by engineers and mechanics rather than seamen. In addition to the normal men on the bridge, we could have done with four more to man the smaller calibre machine guns. Instead of our usual four-hour long watches, the men were kept on duty for only two hours, which produced successful results. Health issues were satisfactory for all except one man, who seems to have caught a sexually transmitted disease shortly before leaving port. He was treated the best we could and isolated from the rest but still presented a significant burden for the others. The two men wounded during the first attack recovered quickly again. One of them was handed over to the supply U-boat [*U488 under Oblt.z.S. Erwin Bartke*]. Both food and water provisions were sufficient although it was necessary to ration things.

The constant knowledge of being surprised from the air demanded an exceptionally high level of concentration and devotion to duty and the three air attacks created a definite nervousness among the men. The men remained in high spirits, despite periods of depression caused by us not having had any success in attacking the expected convoys. [*U228 left France on 4 May and did not return until 19 July 1943, a period of seventy-six days or more than two months.*]

Signed
Erwin Christophersen, Oblt.z.S.
On board U228, 19 July 1943.

ESCAPING THE FIRST ALLIED ACOUSTIC TORPEDOES

The following is based on mid-1980s research by Hanns Parsch, second watch officer of U760, who was helped by the commander, Otto-Ulrich Blum. One wonders how the two men reacted when they discovered their boat should have been sunk by an aircraft dropping a mine. This was most unusual. Mines were dropped for ships to run into; they were not aimed at specific targets. Later, the two discovered the mine in question was not a mine at all, but an American sound-detecting torpedo with a misleading cover name. This was something totally new. Neither the men of U760 nor the U-boat Command had ever heard of such weapons being used. The German sound-detecting torpedo, the Zaun~könig (Wren) or T5, did not come into service until a few weeks after U760 left port, so it is quite likely no one who took part in this drama knew anything about such

In the foreground is a sea-going Type VII with a small coastal boat of Type II as size comparison.

futuristic weapons. The newly appointed consultant for the T5, Kptlt. Otto Köhler, with his torpedo mechanic from U377, Heinrich Böhm, were appointed in Germany around the same time as U760 left France.

The stories about this incident are very variable, with every source containing different information, and it is difficult to work out from published sources exactly what did happen. Therefore, the following is based exclusively on the long and detailed research by Hanns Parsch and Otto-Ulrich Blum, which was carried out shortly after the decoding secret of Bletchley Park had been published.

* * *

Two VIIC boats, U760 (Kptlt. Otto-Ulrich Blum) and U262 (Kptlt. Heinz Franke), left La Pallice in France on 24 July 1943 to cross the Bay of Biscay together, hoping their combined anti-aircraft fire could fend off any interference from above. Progress was good and no one appeared to trouble them; both boats were almost 300 kilometres from the coast before they had their first encounter. During his research, Hanns Parsch discovered this was a Catalina flying boat with a Magnetic Airborne Detector (MAD). This weapon, a type of flying indicator loop, was fitted to aircraft for locating submerged submarines down to a depth of almost 80 metres and it was used for the first time some four months before U760 set out. It produced reasonable results in deep Atlantic waters where it was unlikely to pick up wrecks on the seabed. It was especially good at locating submerged U-boats immediately after they had left the surface.

Neither boat was hindered for long by the Catalina, and they continued their journey to the American side of the Atlantic. While still a long way from land, U760 was refuelled from U664 (Kptlt. Adolf Graef) and two days later was lucky to avoid a fatal attack by carrier-borne aircraft, which put an abrupt end to the supply U-boat. Britain's secret Submarine Tracking Room, in a bunker by the side of Admiralty Arch in London, used decoded intercepts from Bletchley Park and about ten other sources for Rodger Winn to work out the approximate position of U760. Thus, when a very-long-range Liberator was sent out for 'free submarine hunting', it could be directed to the most lucrative area. U-boats themselves contributed one further piece of useful data for the secret Submarine Tracking Room in London by sending a short radio signal to confirm they had successfully crossed the dangerous Bay of Biscay. The latitude of this could be determined by British radio direction finders. Knowing where the boat had come from made it possible to make a reasonably accurate guess about its possible destination.

U219 (Kptlt. Walter Burghagen) in Kiel, probably during the commissioning ceremony.

The Liberator that U760 encountered during the mid-afternoon of 12 August 1943 had a crew of nine under the leadership of the first pilot, Lieutenant T.S. Thueson, and carried three depth charges, adjusted for attacking surfaced submarines, plus two Mk 24 mines, code-named 'Fido', for continuing the onslaught after the target had dived. (The weight of armaments had been reduced in favour of carrying more fuel.) This new acoustic torpedo could detect and chase a submerged submarine running at fast speed but could not find it on the surface or when it was running on near-silent drive. Although the aircraft's radar was switched on, it was the second pilot, R.W. Lane, who first spotted U760 at a range of 8 miles, having noticed the boat's wash rather than its dark shape. The aircraft sent a sighting report back to base in Argentia (Newfoundland) while starting its attack before all the men could get to their action stations. The quickest way down meant hitting the U-boat from the rear and it was not long before the airmen saw heavy anti-aircraft fire coming up to greet them. Not only was this visually impressive, with every third shell being an illuminated tracer, but it was accurate enough to produce an irritating noise as the shells deflected off the aircraft's armour along the bottom of the hull. This armour was most effective but would have been too heavy to cover the whole aircraft; thus, it provided only limited protection for the essentials. On this occasion the pilot decided it would be better to abandon the approach in favour of going in from the front. It was well known U-boats' anti-aircraft guns could only fire backwards. This whole procedure was most disturbing for the airmen, who were used to monotonous flying at a few thousand feet, rather than going in so close to a retaliating target. Their training was based on U-boats diving in less than 30 seconds once they had sighted the aircraft, but this obstinate one did not do that. It remained on the surface. With the new improved anti-aircraft guns manned, it was going to take much longer than the usual 30 seconds to dive. This incident also took place just a few weeks after the fateful month of Black May, when it was thought better for U-boats to remain on the surface for a shoot-out rather than being caught during the diving process.

Life in these aircraft must have been horrific, or they would not have been referred to as flying coffins. Everybody on board the Liberator had more than one job, the men were jammed into an even smaller space than submariners had, and for most of the time they were fighting with accurate navigation, boredom or the weather. There was no other in-flight entertainment after their repertoire of jokes had run out. The second attack, five minutes after starting the first, was more effective because all the airmen were now at their action stations, ready to shoot with every available gun. Coming in from the front this time, three depth charges were dropped from a height of only 100 feet (30 metres). The airmen hardly noticed what was happening. They must have been as terrified as the men on the conning tower, possibly never having been so close to a target before. All the while thinking they were going to hit the water, they expected the U-boat to dive, making it possible for the aircraft to launch the two acoustic torpedoes. The aircraft was without sonar-buoys, meaning it was important to keep the target in sight until a third attack could be launched.

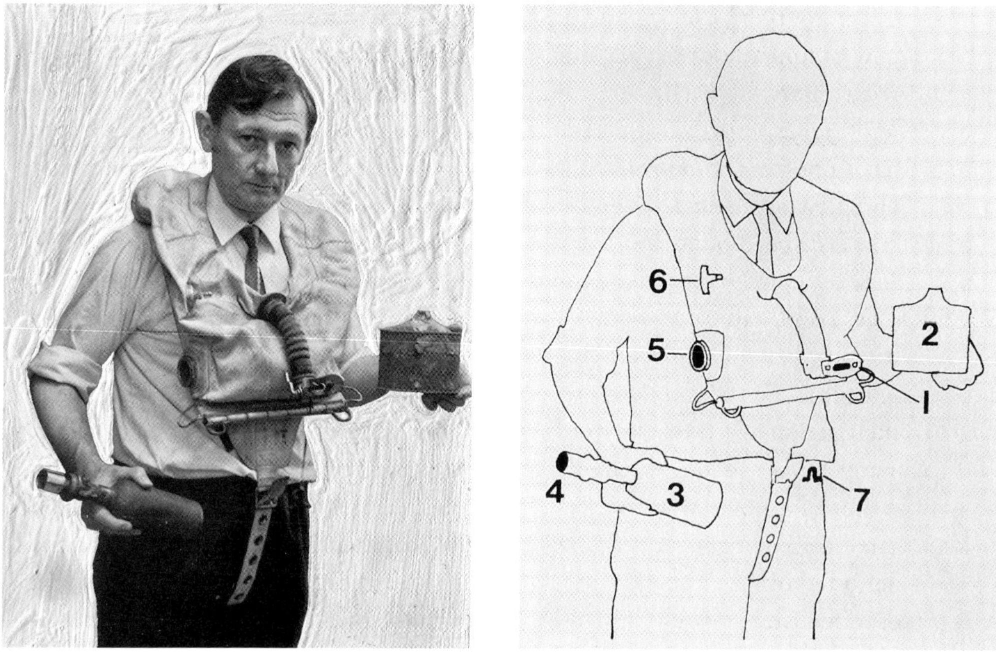

Ray Freeman of the Imperial War Museum in London demonstrating the Dräger Tauchretter (U-boat Escape Apparatus). The mouthpiece (1) should be in his mouth but on this occasion, as the equipment was not exactly in prime condition, Mr Freeman was reluctant to give a full demonstration. The goggles are missing, and the nose clip (7) is hardly visible. (2) is a tin containing a chemical for absorbing carbon dioxide from exhaled air. This would normally fit inside the bag at the bottom of the breathing pipe. (3) is an oxygen cylinder, which also fits inside the bag and could be used to inflate the device when it was needed as a lifejacket. (4) is the tap for the oxygen cylinder. This normally stuck out through the hole (5). (6) is an outlet valve for deflating the air bag.

(Sonar buoys transmitted noises made by submerged submarines to the aircraft flying overhead.)

The weather had been getting worse for some time, the aircraft's radar had stopped working, fuel was getting low and communications with base varied from difficult to impossible. It was obviously time to head for home. Hanns Parsch described this weather as having been deep black with an incredible thunderstorm, which raged while they were looking for Able Seaman Günter Werner, who had been washed overboard during the attack.

Once back at base, the pilot was praised for his efforts. Seeing photographs of the attack convinced the Intelligence officers this was indeed a terrific performance against a retaliating U-boat. The lack of photos showing the results of the main weapons suggested the U-boat had been damaged but not necessarily sunk. U760 was indeed exceedingly lucky in not having dived and later, when it did leave the surface, it had to move slowly with the engines making hardly any noise. As a result, the acoustic torpedoes were lost in the vastness of the Atlantic and would have gone on all day long without finding the target had they not run out of power. Of course, the sensitive sound detectors could have been damaged if the aircraft had dropped them from too great a height.

Most of the men in U760 had hardly any knowledge of what was happening on the outside during such an attack. All they knew was their mundane life had suddenly become rather unpleasant. Hanns Parsch got over this vacuum in information by passing his initial research on to the commander, Otto-Ulrich Blum, who saw most of this action from beginning to end, and added the following details:

The American researcher Geoff Birst in the U-boat Museum in Cuxhaven-Altenbruch holding a partly inflated Tauchretter or submarine escape apparatus, which was known as the Dräger Lung, after the firm which made it. It could be used for about twenty minutes for breathing under water or in poisonous fumes. Once on the surface, it could be fully inflated to act as a flotation aid. U-boats also carried a variety of ordinary lifejackets for men working on the outside in difficult conditions.

> The concluding analysis by the American Intelligence officers is grossly undervalued. The damage to our boat from the depth charge, and we counted only one, was considerable. [This suggests two depth charges detonated at the same time, otherwise it would be difficult to explain damage to both ends of the boat.] In addition to a fault with the diving valve, which prevented us from leaving the surface, we had a severe steering failure, all four bow torpedo tubes were damaged, the engines were put out of action, the navigation or sky periscope was damaged and the main radio aerials were no longer functioning. The inside looked like a ruin with glass and crockery smashed. Later, when an emergency aerial had been set up to report the damage, we received the instruction to return home but to hand over some of our fuel and provisions to U84 (Kptlt. Horst Uphoff) which was on the way back from the Caribbean.

Once again, Bletchley Park decoded the details, Rodger Winn added his magic and U84 was sunk with all hands less than two weeks later, before it got back to base.

Standing on the top of the conning tower, Blum was still wondering what to do next. He did not know whether the Liberator had more bombs. Then the radio room reported more radar impulses from another aircraft, which made up his mind for him:

> I did not want to be caught out by another attacker at a time when our guns were unmanned while diving or surfacing, so I decided on the safe option of going deep. At

this stage the attacker reported seeing the boat trying three times to leave the surface but somehow it did not manage to get below the waves, which was correct. One valve after another could not be closed properly, meaning it was necessary to remain on the surface while we adjusted them with crowbars. Once down at a safe depth, I was dithering about my order to dive and wondered whether it might be better to meet the newcomer with all guns manned. Again, my mind was made up for me. A roll call revealed our Günter Werner must have been washed overboard when the depth charge exploded. It was common knowledge that several boats appear to have been lost as a result of having taken too long to dive and U-boat Command had instructed us, quite correctly, to remain on the surface during any doubtful situations. We did go back to look for Werner, but he was not found.

During one of the longest voyages of the war, a man from U181 is using a Dräger Lung as a diving device to examine the bottom of the hull. The bag is almost deflated, and he is probably wearing a weighted belt as well. U181 set out from Bordeaux on 23 March 1943 and returned on 14 October to the same port, having been in the Indian Ocean. The following year this very-long-range boat undertook another voyage under a new commander, Kpt.z.S. Kurt Freiwald, leaving La Pallice in France on 16 March 1944 and arriving in Penang on 8 August, without having put into any other port on the way.

There was more action with surface ships but U760 managed to travel almost all the way back. One diesel and then the other needed to be stopped for repairs until both refused to go any further while still some distance off Cape Finisterre. Having previously maintained radio silence, Blum now had no choice other than to use the emergency aerial for contacting U-boat Command. The answer came back: 'Try to reach Vigo in Spain for repairs. Do not destroy secret materials.' U760 did eventually reach its destination in a neutral country where both boat and crew were interned for the duration of the war.

ONE OF THE FIRST U-BOATS SUNK WITH ROCKETS

U752 (Kptlt. Karl-Ernst Schroeter), a Type VIIC with an experienced commander, had just made contact with Convoy HX239 when it surfaced around 21 May 1943 to transmit a sighting report. What happened next depends a little on which account one reads, but every source seems to agree that U752 did not sink any ships but instead became the first U-boat to be sunk with rockets.

The newly introduced rockets had a terrific advantage. They could be shot ahead of the aircraft, and, unlike some other weapons, it did not matter whether the target was on the surface or submerged. It seems likely the boat was first spotted by a Swordfish aircraft from HMS *Archer*, which got close enough to drop depth charges while the boat was diving. Then, knowing there was a U-boat in the vicinity and being able to roughly calculate when it was likely to resurface, another Swordfish, piloted by Sub-lieutenant H. Horrocks, took off with the rockets. What a sight this must have been! A string bag of an aircraft, looking almost as if it had been left over from the First World War, carrying the latest technology for blasting submarines into the depths. U752 had only just returned to the surface, with the lookouts still settling into position, when this combination of antiquity and high-tech pounced, shooting one rocket after another. The fourth was seen to hit and must have surprised the pilot as much as the Germans:

> It was shortly after midday when bombs hit us badly enough to cause water to leak into the officers' quarters, making the boat incapable of remaining submerged. Once

A photo taken by the Hamburg Fire Brigade showing the firestorm during the summer of 1943. In the middle, below the clouds, one can make out a block of flats with four or five floors. (*Photo: Hans Brunswig*)

> back on the surface the gunners kept three more carrier-borne aircraft at bay while the boat gave the impression of behaving normally. The hole must have been nearer the top rather than the bottom of the hull. Yet with two destroyers having been sighted, and with such an abundance of aircraft, there was little point in continuing the fight, especially as ammunition was running low. Our return fire was intense enough for all of it to be used up, thus making the guns rather useless. The commander ordered the boat to be made ready for scuttling and for the crew to get ready to abandon ship. Following this, the commander and officer cadet Scharmer were both killed by gunfire from an approaching aircraft. Realizing what had happened, the first watch officer ordered the engines to stop and for everybody to abandon ship.

Whether it was planned or not will probably never be known, but the opposition now made every effort to help the men from the U-boat by dropping a large life raft and several small one-man floats. It is possible the Royal Navy was hoping to arrive in time to get a boarding party on board, but if that were the case, they were out of luck. The rocket had already done its job. U752 was sinking fast. From what happened next, one can assume the Royal Navy was not certain whether the U-boat had sunk or dived, and they must have known there were other U-boats nearby. Whatever, none of the ships remained around to be torpedoed by other U-boats. After picking up a crowd of a dozen or so men, they made off. It was less than four hours later when U91 (Kptlt. Heinz Hungerhausen) arrived to pick up the last survivors. One wonders what must have gone through the minds of the men who saw their comrades being picked up and then their only apparent hope for survival making off at high speed. The final toll was: 13 men became prisoners of war, 4 were saved by U91 and 30 died. Strangely enough, U-boat Command classed U752 as missing rather than sunk, although they knew from survivors what had happened. It was more than six months later before the boat was listed as sunk. Were they deliberately cooking the books?

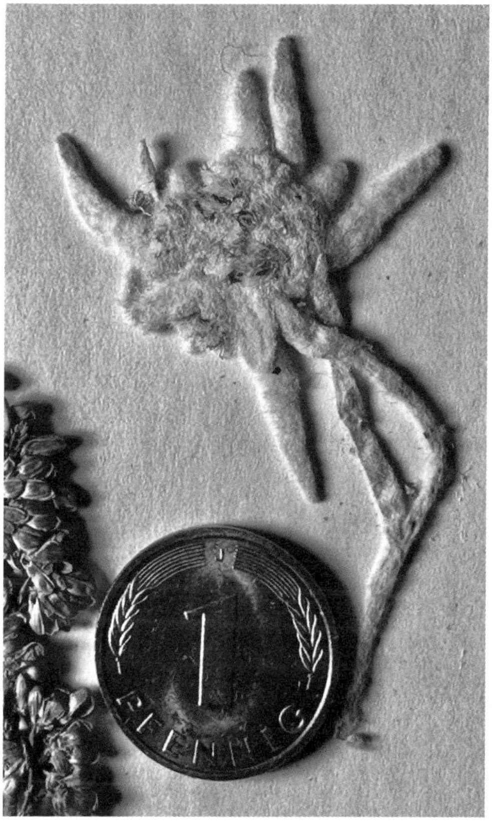

During the great firestorm of July 1943 my mother cycled several miles each time to take drinking water to survivors. She also brought some food to a man who did not know the area and was somewhat lost amidst the thousands of corpses in the streets. He thanked her by giving her this pressed Edelweiss, which he kept in his wallet as reminder of his home. I still have it as one of the most valuable items from this gruesome time when the Allied air forces concentrated on killing and torturing to death civilians – women, old people and children.

U91, a Type VIIC under Kptlt. Heinz Hungerhausen, was having its own problems with aircraft. At 0900 hours that morning, 23 May, it was faced with a battle against a four-engined Liberator. When this aircraft approached for the first time there was no gunfire, no bombs nor any depth charges. Perhaps it was mystified by the U-boat's reaction. Turning away at fast speed, the boat's rudder jammed hard to port, making it difficult to do anything else other than run in a circle. A second attack was fended off with the anti-aircraft guns. Again, not much happened, probably because the aircraft knew the Royal Navy was approaching at high speed; on the U-boat, lookouts spotted mast tips of vessels still beyond the horizon, which triggered an emergency dive. The sound gear quickly confirmed there were two fast small warships approaching; both had probably been called in by the aircraft, but again nothing happened, and the warships did not come close enough to annoy the submerged U-boat. It was not until later in the day, at 14.45 hours, when lookouts spotted men swimming in the water. There were several of them, some distance apart, and not easy to make out among the choppy waves. Lookouts on the U-boat had spotted the life rafts dropped from the British aircraft, and a rescue went ahead quickly, with the boat collecting all those who were not floating head down in the water. This rescue was still going on when another Liberator made two attacks, probably unaware the boat was picking up survivors. The men from U752 were only just brought on board U91 when more ships were sighted, making it necessary to dive deep again. The men from U91 brought some of the almost dead bodies on board to try to resuscitate them, but this failed. After four hours it was certain that some of the rescued men could not be revived, and they were given a quick sea burial. There was not enough time for any prolonged ceremony. It was more a case of disposing of six dead bodies. U91 returned to Brest with four men from U752 on 7 June 1943.

Archives are full of survivor stories from both the good and the bad sides of the humanity spectrum. Some shipwrecked U-boat men were treated with the best of respect and reverence, while others were shot in the water or cut to pieces by the propellers of 'rescue' ship reversing into them. The photos here show the humane end of the spectrum. Scrambling nets, as seen here, were a vital part of the equipment carried by many ships, but many men lacked the energy to climb up them and ships could not delay for fear of being attacked. Life was cheap and dying not pleasant. I have not yet seen a memorial to those who stopped to save the lives of many.

SINKING THE SUPPLY TANKER

The supply U-boat U487 (Oblt.z.S. Helmut Metz) was sunk on 13 July 1943. This account is based on a report by Funk~maat Bernhard Pötter.

* * *

It was one of those days where a deeply relaxed atmosphere dominated the proceedings. Being so warm, we were dressed in only light gym shorts while everything in the radio room had been shut down. Quite a few of us would have been happy to go about naked, had naval regulations not prohibited complete nudity. We were only allowed to strip off completely when washing. Visibility was brilliant, making it possible for an aircraft to see as far as its radar, and it was therefore unlikely to be using it. Our radar receiver on board was switched off and the lookouts were warned to keep a special eye open for anything in the air. Being some 600 nautical miles south-west of the Azores, in an area unfrequented by the usual nautical traffic, we were drifting along, waiting for our next customer who needed supplies. This idyllic peace was disturbed by a large wooden crate. A huge cube, each side about two metres long, and a long way off. The commander eyed it up carefully and then called the engineer officer, suggesting he help to get this object on board. 'There might be something interesting inside,' he said. Tinned fruit was highest on our wish list, although a crate full of such tins would probably not float. The obvious comment by several was, 'there's got to be something light inside'. It turned out to be compressed cotton wool, wrapped up well to cope with the Atlantic weather, and it was perfectly dry. The commander ordered every available sack to be brought up for filling with what had become a rare commodity in Germany. Cotton wool would be welcomed by many back home. The whole process of heaving the box on board and repacking the contents to fit through our hatches made a welcome change to the usual dreary routine and sacks full to the brim were wedged on the deck and on the top of the conning tower, waiting to be stowed away.

It was soft, good for sitting on, until some rotter came along to spoil the party, and this intrusion arrived with little warning. The lookouts were expecting large, long-range aircraft to appear this far out in the Atlantic, but during the early afternoon we were surprised by some small, fast-flying American fighters, coming at us with the bright sun behind their tails. Gunfire from the aircraft caused the stacked sacks to burst into flames, making us realize we were dealing not with pure cotton wool but with highly flammable and explosive gun cotton. (This low-grade explosive was used commercially for the manufacture of several everyday items, including billiard balls.)

In addition to shooting, the aircraft also dropped bombs, one of which detonated a short distance behind the boat, putting the entire steering system out of order. Jammed at a slight angle, all the boat could do was run a huge circle with a diameter of about a kilometre. This made things rather critical, and the commander was still

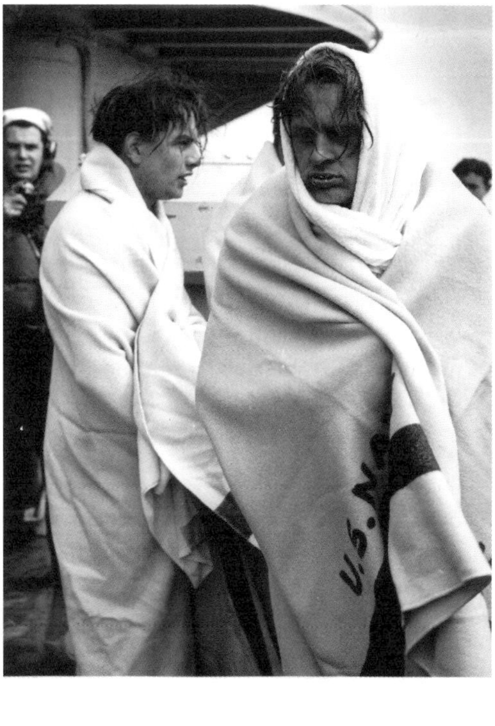

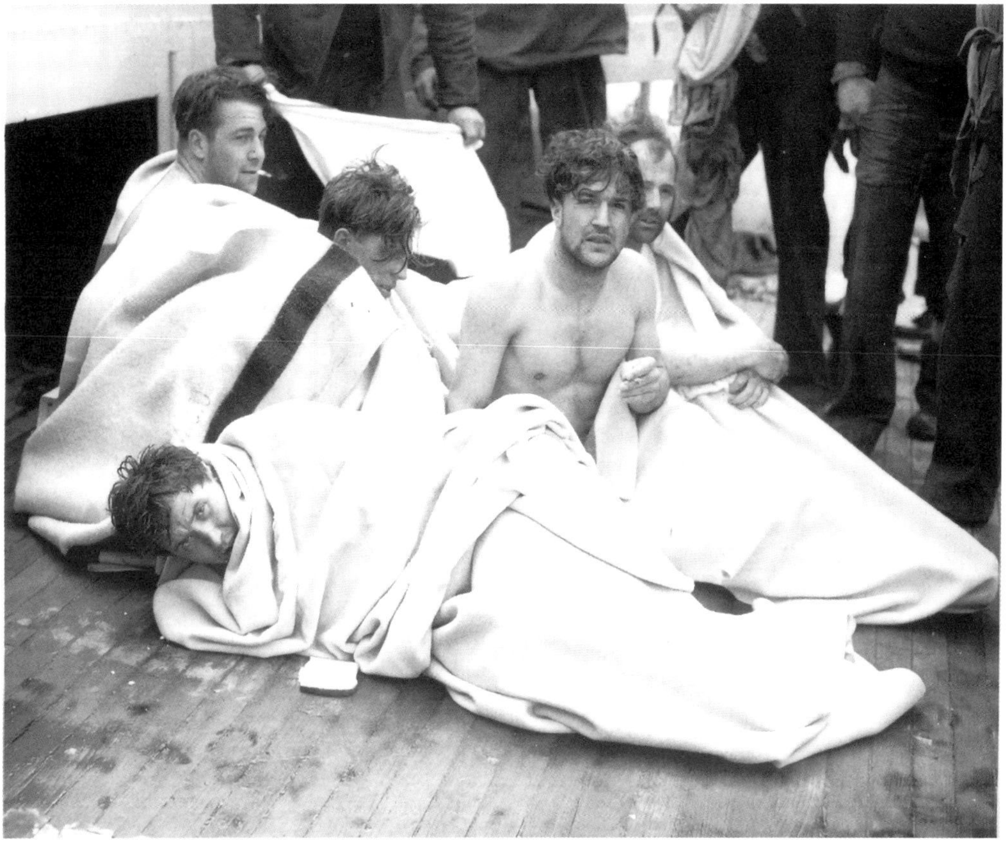

Above and opposite: It seems likely these photos show survivors from U175 (Kptlt. Heinrich Bruns). The American crewmen are wearing lifejackets, while the U-boat survivors came on board with their submarine escape apparatus. The U-boat crew had scuttled their own boat due to damage from an attack by USCG cutters *Duane* and *Spencer*. A group of men from *Spencer* climbed on board the U-boat before it sank but they arrived too late to salvage anything.

wondering what to do when his mind was made up for him. Leaks were reported in the pressure hull where water was seeping in. His first reaction was to order the men to shoot back with the 20mm quadruple gun aft of the conning tower. The trouble was this instrument had only two barrels. It was a 20mm twin with two wooden poles to make it look more impressive for any passing attacker coming close to case up the joint. These twins were easy to operate. They were fired in a similar fashion to a rifle with the main weight being taken by the pole that attached the gun to the deck. It balanced perfectly. The gunner should certainly have gained his marksman's lanyard by shooting down the next attacking aircraft, which was another fighter, obviously flown off an aircraft carrier. The puny little gun kept aircraft at bay for well over an hour until the leaks in the pressure hull had allowed in enough water to flood the magazine under the radio room. Twenty minutes later the commander had no alternative other than to order everybody out of the boat.

I (Funk~maat Pötter) tried to send a distress signal but the hatch in the watertight bulkhead between the radio room and the central room could no longer be opened. The explosions must somehow have jammed it. When the boat came up to the surface again, we found only the commander on the bridge with another aircraft approaching. Taking refuge behind the conning tower, I saw the old man sag together, as he was hit by heavy gunfire. The men who had jumped overboard remained in the water for several hours, to be picked up later by USS *Barker*. The Americans took pity on us dressed only in gym shorts; we were given clean clothing as well as a welcome set of toiletries such as soap, shaving gear, toothbrush and toothpaste. The Americans also made a concerted effort to deal with several wounded, including Funk~maat Fischer, who had been shot through the chest. We were even more surprised later when the Americans sent several of our wounded to special trauma clinics to deal with some of the more unusual injuries. They were very good to us.

JUMPING INTO FEAR – THE END OF U458 (Kptlt. Kurt Diggins)

What follows is based on an account by Georg Brandhuber and conversations with Kurt Diggins, and with help from Paul Tenholt.

* * *

We were standing in cold, knee-deep water, coughing, hardly able to get any air when the loudspeaker suddenly sprang into life. It was still running on emergency power.

'Abandon ship and save yourself,' came as an order from the commander, to produce a feeling that cannot be described in words. This weird sensation crept up through the body, making me feel hot, but it did nothing to help in making an escape. The boat, which had been our home for more than a year and taken us on eight voyages, had now become our prison. The submarine was filled with the latest technology, with cables, dials, switches, levers, handwheels, buttons and indicator lights. A lay person who saw this would be amazed. It is incredibly complicated, yet the crew worked all of this in the same way as other people put on their socks in the dark. The crew's reactions and actions were always quick and automatic. Like robots. No one had to think about what they were doing. They merely obeyed orders, doing only what they had been taught and now, suddenly, every man had to think. Think for himself about what to do next. Well, how do you get out of a stinking sinking submarine? We had never done that before. We had practised everything and gone through many motions, but we had never seriously thought about how to get out of this dark coffin during an emergency.

None of us were happy or comfortable at the time of the short announcement, despite it having made us think hard enough to wake those who were already almost dead. We had endured two hours' worth of depth-charging. Machinery had been

It is highly likely this shows Lockheed Ventura B-6 of US Squadron VB-125 in Newfoundland, after it had sunk U174 (Oblt.z.S. Wolfgang Grandefeld), while piloted by Lieutenant Thomas Kinaszczuk. One wonders what went through the minds of the four crewmen as they flew over miles of featureless water with only two engines and no possibilities for making an emergency landing.

smashed, but flexible bodies remained intact. Strangely, it was not our bodies but our minds which were now beginning to give way. You cannot describe a depth charge attack. The noise is horrendous, much worse than any thunderstorm and there is no vocabulary to explain this. For two hours we were thrown around in this incredible din and in darkness where anyone shouting at you could not have been heard. It turned people into rigid ghosts. Some were thrown against hard protrusions to receive painful injuries. People were screaming, bleeding and there was no one to help. It was pitch black in many places and at times the dim essential emergency lights went out as well. In such situations it is a case of every man for himself. And two hours of such torture is an eternity. Water spraying into the interior immediately turned into mist, making people look like fading doomed faces in a horror movie. There was no clarity. Only God knows how the Old Man remained standing at his post. He didn't flinch. He still gave calm orders while the boat was thrown exceedingly violently at times. Then, at the end of this ordeal, we felt the boat was swaying on waves, to give us an indication we were now on the surface, but without any idea of what was going on up there.

The inside of Catalina P-I under Lieutenant E. Dryden of US Navy Squadron VP-53 which had sunk U156 under Korvkpt. Werner Hartenstein. There were no survivors. The insides of all U-boat-hunting aircraft were cramped, uncomfortable and often lacking in basic comforts or in-flight entertainment once the repertoire of jokes had run dry. There have been cases where the wives of men who served in these aircraft refused to go inside museum exhibits because the interior was too cramped, and one lady was in tears when she saw the conditions in which her husband had worked and lived as a young man.

I ended up in the galley, where there was a hatch to the outside. This was used as the front door in port but was now securely locked shut with three additional safety catches, in case some idiot accidentally tried to open it at the wrong time, or a depth charge got too close to do the same job. Depth charges were worse than the idiots and, in any case, we did not have many on board. The cook working in this tiny kitchen had plenty of headroom, after all, he was always making loads of steam, and the wheel for opening the hatch was high above his head, too far to reach. [*The ladder used in ports was removed once the boat put to sea.*] Several men had to come forward for me to stand on their shoulders to twist it open. The fog inside the boat was now getting considerably thinner, making it possible to see complete faces near me but this did not help in pushing the hatch. Even climbing up higher and pressing with my back against it, did not seem to make it budge. The men behind me were getting anxious, creating a dreaded crush where it became difficult to think or to move the locking mechanism. Stupid really. All I had to do was to release the safety catches and then twist the wheel, but such an easy, everyday operation was now trying to kill us.

Then, suddenly, without realizing it at first, I found myself in the open. It was as dark as the inside of the boat, only searchlights indicated there must be others about. It is a strange situation to be surrounded by a ring of English warships with their guns pointing at you. It was too dark to see them, but you could hear them loud and clear, hammering away at us. While sitting on the deck I heard bullets banging

Depth charge damage on U534, which is now on display at the ferry pier in Birkenhead, near Liverpool. The rectangular window in the side contained a small ejection device for an Asdic foxer. This created a mass of bubbles in the water to make it difficult for any pursuer to focus on the submarine.

against our hull, which was too strong for the small calibre being shot. The worst happening was from one of the larger shells breaking a thick steel cable, which ran from the top of the conning tower to the deck, the so-called net deflector. This also served as radio aerial and as a secure fastening for safety harnesses. Being under considerable tension, it whipped back, hurling a man into the water. After a while, still not knowing what was going on, I became aware there were no more men coming up through the hatch and water on the outside was slowly rising up towards me. Usually, I would have known right away what was happening, but on this occasion, it all seemed to be rather mysterious, like a bad dream. It took a while to realize the water was not rising but our boat was sinking.

So, what next? Sitting on deck, recovering from the earlier exertions was not going to see me through. I had to do something and there was no one giving any orders. No one telling you what to do is something incredibly damning for men who are used to reacting only to orders. Ever since joining the navy, private decisions had been driven out of us and now I had to decide what to do for myself. Well, what can you do? Assessing the general situation, I realized I was not sitting on a stationary deck. The electric motors were running. We were still making headway. Then a thought came to me: our sinking boat would be capable of dragging me down with it into the depths. I had to get off, but as weird as it seemed I hesitated to jump into the water. I was already soaking wet but somehow felt apprehensive about abandoning the ship. Somehow my mind was searching for something solid to step onto. Stupid really. I also became aware I was wearing my submarine escape apparatus. Only God knows how I got into that silly situation; I was also wearing a life jacket. Why wear both? The escape lung also served as life jacket. No one ever wore both at the same

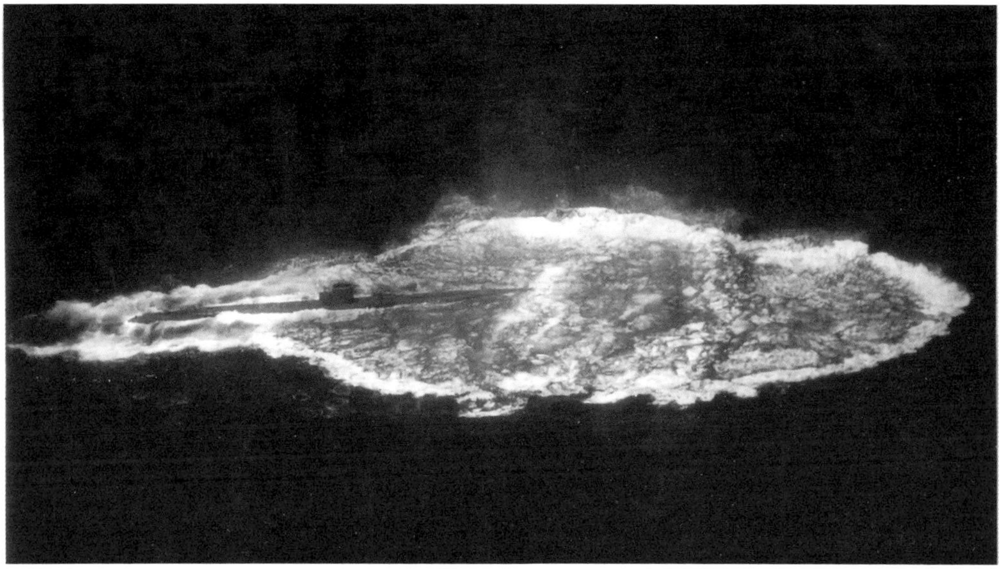

The U-boat is travelling from left to right, meaning it missed the full blast of the explosion, which was close enough to have inflicted serious damage.

If the caption on the back of this photo is correct, then this shows the end of U159 (Oblt.z.S. Hermann Beckmann) and was taken a short distance south of Haiti by a Mariner aircraft, VP32, piloted by Lieutenant R.C. Mayo of the United States Navy. The attack was a textbook example of how it should be done and there were no survivors.

time. When I did jump, I noticed the confounded din had gone quiet. The shooting had stopped, and I could hear cries for help. At the same time, I became aware of a burning sensation on my back. While swimming this developed into a piercing pain. Not knowing what to do, I decided to move in the direction of the cries for help and eventually managed to push a few worse-off mates into a rubber boat. This made it obvious there were men with even more injuries than the mere pain on my back.

I can't remember what else happened. The water felt warm when I jumped in but now, after having been wet for some time, I felt horribly cold and the fear of dying started to grab me again. There was nothing to do. It was dark. No solid land. My teeth were chattering. I then felt in my pocket to find a small torch. It wasn't of much use, but it gave me a little confidence that somehow, we might survive in this black darkness. These thoughts were somehow interrupted by a siren, giving me a dreadful start as a ship appeared by our side. This has got to be the imagination going haywire or was I already dead and my brain was still pumping away, sending me stupid ideas? I had never been dead before, so there was no way of assessing the general situation.

Even approaching this monster ship was not easy. My first thoughts suggested I might be killed by being squashed against the hull. Eventually I ended up on the

The end of U405 (Korvkpt. Rudolf Hopman) on 1 November 1940.

deck. Two men pulled me up. My clothing was still wet, making me wonder why it was not dry. Taking off my trousers, an easy task in normal times, was difficult. There was no energy for doing anything. Somehow and I don't know why but I felt a raging fury against these men who had saved me. I ended up lying on deck next to motionless men. Wondering whether they were dead or alive I touched the one next to me, who did not move but felt warm, so he had to be alive. We were totally naked now, probably part of their survival training to prevent us from being cooled further by our wet clothing. When we were handed blankets, I felt that earlier burning sensation again. Pulling on the blanket, I noticed it had stuck to my back. I must be bleeding. There was something not quite right. Assembling on deck, we stood close to someone lying in such a weird way that he had to be dead. When going inside, several of us were hit by a strong feeling of thirst. I asked a sailor for some water, but he ignored me, he did not speak and walked away. Almost immediately another man appeared with water, and he also gave us some cigarettes. We were aboard the Greek auxiliary cruiser *Pimtos*, sailing under the British flag. Eight men died during this escape from U458, but thirty-nine of us, including the commander, became prisoners of war. It felt bloody good at the time.

Here, its increased anti-aircraft armament almost hidden by the impressive spray, is U1065 (Oblt.z.S. Hans Panitz), photographed less than a month before the Instrument of Surrender was signed at Field Marshal Montgomery's headquarters to the south of Hamburg on 4 May 1945. There were no survivors.

Men from U805 (Korvkpt. Richard Bernardelli) after their arrival in Portsmouth, USA. Although this photo was taken after German's capitulation, the Americans were still frightened enough of the U-boat men to point guns at them.

AIR RAIDS

This section is based partly on a brief account by the boat's WO, Friedrich Hartel, the boat's log, and conversations with Wilhelm Schlegel (of the Hamburg Water Police), who was stationed close to Blohm und Voss. Further information has come from conversations with Hans Brunswig, who wrote the book *Feuersturm über Hamburg* (Motorbuch Verlag, Stuttgart, n.d.) after the war.

* * *

Ruins look almost the same wherever they are. The bombing information collected by the Hamburg Fire Brigade was confiscated by British troops after the war and almost certainly destroyed. The Museum of Hamburg History was not allowed to collect or display exhibits of the bombing. Much of this horror has now vanished in time with a concerted effort still being made to conceal the destruction, atrocities and deprivation created by the Allied air forces. Both American and British authors have stated this destruction did not affect the U-boat war in any way but many Germans who experienced it have said the opposite, saying it made them more determined to continue fighting. (*Photos: Hans Brunswig*)

Unexpected cold weather reminders from what had been a harsh winter were still displacing the warmth of spring when the crew for U989 assembled at the Blohm und Voss Shipyard in Hamburg early in 1943 for their so-called 'Building Instruction'. The shipyard is still located close to the southern end of the old tunnel under the ½km-wide Elbe River. This made it possible for men to be accommodated in the city on the other side, to walk to work rather than endure the squashed and unheated workers' ferries. Due to air raids having become a frequent feature of daily life, the men had strict instructions to seek out shelters when the warnings sounded. So far, the maximum number of people killed by a single raid had been just over a hundred, but well over a thousand families had been made homeless. U989 was still lying by the shipyard, waiting to be commissioned, towards the end of July 1943, when the British and American air forces launched incredible terror attacks against civilian housing areas. In two days they tortured to death almost as many civilians as were killed in the United Kingdom during the whole war. There were more than 125,000 injuries, while the fire brigade counted 5,900 serious fires, many of them in blocks of flats some five storeys high. The bombers were not interested in putting heavy industries on the southern bank out of action, but concentrated on highly populated areas, bombing, burning and painfully punishing the civilian-dominated population. One of Hamburg's fire chiefs, Hans Brunswig, apologized after the war because his figures of 42,000 dead included only the corpses which had been picked up for burial. He said, 'I should have included those who walked away with serious injuries and survived long enough to die elsewhere.' His post-war estimated total came to almost 60,000. Brunswig also explained how large areas were cordoned off by piling walls of bricks across roads, leaving the corpses there for rats and flies. There was not enough manpower to deal with the vast devastation. Anyone seen in the cordoned-off area was shot on sight for pilfering. It was a huge area, as big as a small town. Now all dead except for flies and rats who thrived on the corpses. A real no-go area and you could smell it as well.

After the war, the Knight of the Iron Cross, Kpt.z.S. Hellmuth von Ruckteschell and others were sentenced by war crimes tribunals to ten years in jail for having attacked too aggressively. Von Ruckteschell was told he should have stopped his wartime shooting much earlier than he did. His sentence was later reduced to seven years, although he died in June 1948, some three years after the end of the war. Yet this devastation of German cities, with immense suffering by civilians consisting predominantly of children and old people, was 'legal', according to the new post-war military army of occupation.

Some men from U989, accommodated on the edge of this intense firestorm, came out of air raid shelters to find their lodgings gone. These men may have lost their few belongings, but they had the advantage of finding a bed inside their submarine. Many of the civilian survivors had been bombed out, leaving them only with what they were carrying, and thousands of people ended up in open parks where they slept under the open sky and sheltered in the shade from trees during the sunny days. For many Germans, this deprivation created an incredible resolve to go out and do your duty.

Winston Churchill is often quoted as having said: 'The weapon that worried me the most were the U-boats.' Yet the Allied air forces never made any serious attempt to put the construction yards out of action. Throughout the whole war not a single U-boat was ever seriously damaged until the very end, when they were no longer a threat. What is more, this destruction continued long after the war, when many of the boats on the building slips were demolished by land-based soldiers. Harbour installations such as cranes, railway lines, high-water flood defences and hundreds of factories were destroyed after the war as well, when people still died in significant numbers. After the war, bombed-out people living in disused air raid shelters were punished further by being turned out to live without roofs over their heads while the victors of the war demolished stairs and entrances in some of the larger air raid bunkers to prevent them being occupied.

With everything in the city in utter chaos, all U989 could do was to leave, but even a simple voyage along the Elbe to Brunsbüttel, at the southern end of the Kiel Canal, required serious organization, with minesweepers sailing ahead of valuable shipping. Leaving Hamburg against this huge burning backdrop, the watch officer Friedrich Hartel recorded: 'All we could see were thick black clouds of putrid smoke with an incredibly unpleasant smell as we sailed away from the disaster zone. We never lost sight of that dreadful cloud. We could still see it from the entrance of the Kiel Canal and having arrived in Kiel we found the black cloud was thick enough to darken the midday sun, despite us being a hundred kilometres to the north of Hamburg.' The men of U989 had experienced the worst baptism of fire the world had ever seen, making them extra determined to become fully qualified as a front boat as quickly as possible.

One wonders how much the men knew about what was going on at sea. It is quite likely they were not told about the serious losses nor of the terrible suffering men at sea had to endure. There is a description of a short verbal exchange between Hans-Georg Fischer, commanding officer of U109, and his radio operator, Wolfgang Hirschfeld, who had just come back from visiting an old friend in the radio room at headquarters. Hirschfeld asked whether they had passed their training or whether they were being sent back for more exercises. (This conversation took place during the early summer of 1941, not during the black days of 1943.)

'I suppose you would like some more training?' asked the commander.

'Well, yes, why not? It seems to be rather hellish out there in the Atlantic now.'

Fischer jumped up and exploded. 'You radio operators are all the same. You know exactly what is going on everywhere, but you must keep your mouth shut and not talk about this. Is that understood?'

'Klar, Herr Kaleu.' ('Of course, sir.')

It is also interesting to look at events later in the war, when long-distance boats were starting to operate in the Indian Ocean, where there was a strong likelihood of meeting Japanese submarines making their way to German bases in France. The entire crew was instructed not to mention any problems the U-boats were facing in the Bay of Biscay, and no one was to talk about this being an especially dangerous area.

Chapter 9

The Failure of the Costly U-boat Comeback, Autumn 1943

The wolfpack battles named Leuthen (now Lutynia in Poland) and Rossbach (Bavaria) were ingrained in Prussian history as dramatically as Trafalgar and Waterloo still dominate Britain's past. In 1757 small Prussian armies won decisive victories over much larger and more powerful Austrian armies in those locations.

THE VIEW FROM THE WAVES

On average about twelve U-boats were lost each month from November 1942 to April 1943, when losses suddenly shot up to a total of forty-four in what became known as Black May. Twelve may not sound many, but a dozen U-boats adds up to well over 500 men, and each boat was pretty expensive in terms of construction man-hours and the war materials it consumed. Three of the forty-four boats lost in May were damaged during air raids on ports, the rest just vanished in the vastness of the seas. The horrified U-boat Chief, Karl Dönitz, by now an Admiral and Commander-in-Chief of the whole German Navy, responded with the unorthodox step of asking commanders of front-line boats to hold a secret ballot. Every member of the crew was to vote anonymously on whether they wanted to continue going to war or whether they should remain in port for the time being, to wait for the new boats already under construction. The result was overwhelming support for not giving up, whence Grand Admiral Karl Dönitz chose the dramatic names Leuthen and Rossbach for the U-boats' comeback offensive in the autumn of 1943. (I have not seen any written records of this vote, but the information was carefully weeded out of veterans WITHOUT asking them directly nor suggesting such an event had taken place. Several men visiting the U-boat Museum in Cuxhaven-Altenbruch then mentioned a confidential vote in their boat, which they were told not to mention to anyone.)

To spur on his troops, Dönitz told U-boat crews:

> Following our heavy losses in May, we are constantly considering whether we should give up our struggle at sea and wait until the new boats, already under construction, will be fully operational. I am aware of the heavy burden you are carrying but you are saving considerably worse punishment for your families at home. You are keeping thousands of fighter aircraft and more than two thousand four-engined bombers away from Germany. If you were not at sea, these aircraft would fly daily bombing raids over our cities.

The museum boat U995 by the Naval Memorial in Laboe near Kiel. Note the enlarged anti-aircraft armament and the later, but still ineffective, wind and spray deflectors. There were two double 20mm guns on the upper platform and the 37mm towards the left was often replaced by a semi-automatic quadruple 20mm weapon.

This decision, whether to give up or continue with the sea war, remained Karl Dönitz's biggest worry until the end of his life. Long after the war, after having been released from Spandau Prison and when meeting with old wartime colleagues, he often asked whether his decisions had been correct. Those who knew him well reminded him that nobody in the German Navy went to war with the slightest hope of ever winning. Everybody knew, right from the first day, there was no way Germany could win a war against Britain and there would be no hope at all once the United States and Russia joined in against Germany.

Now, back to the late summer of 1943. The Leuthen wolfpack comeback battle started in what had been the mid-Atlantic air gap around 13 September 1943 with twenty-one boats, while the second wave, named Rossbach, was formed on 26 September with twenty-five boats. The initial assembly point was roughly halfway between Spain and Newfoundland, and from there the boats moved northwards to intercept Convoys ON202 and ONS18. Before this, throughout the first five months of that year, there had been almost sixty named wolfpacks, so attacking with a group of U-boats aimed at the same convoy was nothing new to anyone, least of all not to the opposition.

The hastiness of how this all started can perhaps be seen by looking at U448 (Oblt.z.S. Helmut Dauter), which had left St Nazaire on the first day of August. A day or so later it was recalled to join one of these two groups. The significant reason for waiting until

September was due to the unexpected news of an early delivery of the first new acoustic torpedoes called 'Zaun~könig' (Wren) and known as T5.

In addition to this new wonder weapon, all the boats were modified with additional anti-aircraft guns. The basic configuration had an enlarged upper gun platform with room for two twin 20mms and there was an additional platform aft of this, a little lower down. Type VII boats were given a quadruple 20mm on this lower platform, while Type IXs were usually fitted with a single semi-automatic 37mm. However, shortages and distribution hold-ups meant some VIIs had a 37mm instead of the quadruple and there are photos showing Type IXs with the quadruple gun. These conning towers also had additional armour to protect the crew. None of this armour turned out to be terribly successful but various designs were fitted in time for the comeback action. Fixed holders for accommodating smaller, usually 9mm, machine guns were also fitted. These guns were not designed for anti-aircraft use, and they were not watertight, so they had to be taken below when the boats dived.

The other new defences for these boats included radar sets as well as radar detectors. The radar detectors for identifying enemy activity were now of two types. One of them told the crew when there was someone near them using radar, while the other, less sensitive, receiver indicated when the opposition was close enough for an attack to begin. Ideally, the boat should have dived to safety when this second set activated. Later radar equipment did away with the double receivers and had only one, capable of searching several channels at the same time. During the summer of 1943, for the first time, the deeply ingrained operational procedures of fast diving to safety were changed for the Leuthen boats. Instead of diving when the radar got 'hot', commanders were told to remain on the surface and take on approaching aircraft in a shoot-out. This initially rattled the airmen, who were ready to perhaps hit a diving boat before it vanished from view. Now, suddenly, they were greeted with rather a lot of impressive firepower, meaning a change in response was necessary, but first they had to get over the shock of the new tactics.

The German crews at sea did not think a great deal of this new method. It created a noteworthy increase in injured men and not all the guns could work all the time, meaning there were times when only one or two gunners were coping with major attacks. The main cause for complaint seems to have been the 37mm. It was liable to jam, and its firepower was insufficient for huge land-based long-distance aircraft. A twin version of this single barrel gun did come into service before the end of the war, but it was not fitted to many boats. Winding the wheels to move the quadruple gun was not easy and required more training than there had been time for. Seeing comrades being brought down with bleeding wounds, even when these were only minor injuries, was most depressing for the rest of crew, who obviously could only hear what was going on outside. Many of the old lags were by now priding themselves on the speed at which they could dive, and those critical seconds were made drastically longer due to there being many men up top. The crew did not like it and seeing the blood made life considerably worse.

Having torpedoes for homing in on sounds meant they could be used against small warships coming towards the U-boat head-on at fast speeds – something that had been impossible before. Acoustic torpedoes would, of course, go after anything noisy, such as a merchant ship and even the U-boat which had just fired it. It wasn't fussy. Therefore, it was necessary for the U-boat to dive in silent drive until the torpedo was far enough away. It had also been foreseen that this system could easily be fooled by a target towing a noisy decoy or 'foxer' at the end of a long rope. The T5 was especially designed to cope with such deception. Once it got close enough to the sound, the torpedo would turn into a tight circle and go around the sound source. Having turned into this tight circle, the sound detector, at the end of a funnel-like tube on the front of the torpedo, could no longer 'hear' the foxer, but soon this sensor would point towards the towing ship's propeller and engines and then head off towards this new sound source. Once again, the torpedo would turn into a circle, but ships were bigger than the radius of the circle, to result in a pronounced bang. Collisions with the target were rare because the torpedo was deep enough to go under the ship where a magnetic detonator fired the explosives.

A size and hitting power comparison: the ammunition used by the 37mm anti-aircraft gun on the left and 20mm on the right.

In theory, these new weapons were going to make it possible for U-boats to beat the opposition on all counts. But there was a built-in snag, which the Germans took some time to discover. The magnetic detonators did not work very well and only about one in ten or twelve sank their target. Of course, the U-boat had dived, so all the crew heard was the explosion, and by the time it resurfaced the scenario would have changed sufficiently for the U-boat men not to notice their target had not sunk. Both British and American sailors were rather annoyed at this new device because some explosions were close enough to give the men on board a serious shock. Sometimes they also found their ship was dead in the water due to their propellers having been blown off or bent by the blast, but not too many torpedoes got that close.

* * *

U-boat life during 1943 was harsh. One of the few boats to have made it this far was U448 under Oblt.z.S. Helmut Dauter, who also became one of those rare survivors of Black May. Five months earlier, it had stopped off in Bergen (Norway) after leaving Kiel for its first operational tour on 30 January 1943. The stopover was necessary to make repairs to prevent the periscope well from filling with water when diving deep. Several aircraft attacked while U448 was near Bergen and the men on the top of the conning tower watched in amazement as one of the escorting patrol boats shot one down. U448 did eventually reach its operations area in the Atlantic. The weather there was deplorable, and nothing had been sunk by the time a shortage of fuel dictated a return. Making for St Nazaire in France, U448 ran into the incredible Bay of Biscay opposition. Alarm dives to get away from aircraft became too frequent to keep count of them and in any case the men were far more worried about the lack of electricity in the boat. The batteries seemed to be constantly empty, making it essential to remain on the surface long enough to fill them again. Yet every time they tried this, aircraft forced them down again, preventing the batteries from being anywhere near satisfactorily full. Although U448 saw plenty of action, albeit without sinking anything, in the fifty-four days since leaving Kiel, the men learned a lot.

Oblt.z.S. Gerhard Kluth, the last commander of U377, wearing his coat like a cloak during the Leuthen battle in September–October 1943. As a result of his injuries, with both arms bandaged and in slings, he handed command over to his first watch officer, Ernst August Gerke. Once in safer waters where quick diving was unlikely, he came up to the bridge. Gerke stood in for two other commanders in U382 and U650 before having his own command in U678 and later in a new electro-boat of Type XXI. He was lucky to have survived the war.

Putting out for the next voyage was as difficult as the run into port. Once assembled in the patrol line far out in the Atlantic, U448 was attacked by escorts as well as aircraft, but managed to avoid the full force of several nearby depth charges. The second night of the attack was worse. This time, several other boats from the same wolfpack reported they could no longer dive, due to being constantly pushed away by both escorts and aircraft. U448 continued the hunt and did not leave the convoy until it was too close to land. Very little shipping had been sunk and to make matters worse, a quick count showed the monthly figures for sunk U-boats had risen dramatically. The men in U448 would not have known the exact figures, although hearsay from the radio operators did get around when they heard many boats not answering calls asking them to send in weather or position reports.

The next voyage, starting on 17 April 1943, took U448 far enough west to need a supply ship. This turned out to be U459, one of the purpose-built supply submarines under the command of a dashing character known as 'Wild Moritz', from his name Georg von Wilamowitz-Moellendorf. Born in 1893, he was one of the oldest U-boat commanders of the Second World War and he had been a watch officer in four U-boats of the Imperial Navy. The radio equipment in U448 kept giving up the ghost at crucial moments and the engineer officer, Oblt.z.S.(Ing.) Norbert Ehinger, lost a small finger in the refuelling process, otherwise all went well without serious interruption. The real problems did not start again until they had to cross the by now infamous Black Pit of Biscay. Once again,

U377 coming into Brest on 10 October 1943 after a small aircraft had crashed on the boat. This incident has hardly been clarified and caused considerable argument at the debriefing for 'Jumbo' Gerke.

attacking aircraft became a major problem, making it obvious U-boats were hanging on by a thread rather than sinking anything.

Shortly after leaving St Nazaire for its next war cruise on 1 August 1943, U448 was faced with something most unusual. Instead of the battering from aircraft, the radio room received orders for the commander to return to port. The Atlantic Comeback had started to boil. For U448, this happened on 6 September 1943. U448 survived the Rossbach drama and was not sunk until April of the following year. The commander and most of the crew were rescued following an intense depth charge and 'Hedgehog' hunt. Nine men were killed by gunfire as they abandoned their sinking wreck.

While assembling out in the Atlantic to become the Leuthen and Rossbach Groups, those boats already at sea had other pressing problems. At first, they did not meet any aircraft due to the sea being covered with thick fog, and this was followed by a storm severe enough to tear some anti-aircraft guns from their mountings. When the men, wearing heavy safety harnesses, eventually managed to stand on deck without support, it became a case of cutting away parts of the damaged gun mountings before welding the guns temporarily back into some sort of working condition. Once back in action, U448 was attacked four times by a Sunderland with depth charges; it seems the aircraft eventually crashed near or in the convoy, probably hoping someone would notice its demise to alert a rescue ship.

Later, when U448 surfaced accidentally amidst a hunter killer group, there was a direct acoustic torpedo confrontation. The men in the U-boat reported hitting two of the escorts, while the third kept a good distance to rescue men from the other two. One of the T5 torpedoes detonated more than ten minutes after discharge, by which time the men in U488 could no longer see the escort. Comparing records after the war, it would seem nothing was sunk all day, and only the corvette HMS *Rhododendron* observed a passing torpedo, but without any reports of any hits. At least the Germans came home jubilant, after their imagined successes.

Other boats were not so lucky. Some just vanished without trace. Take U338, for example. Its last hours at sea were recorded by U-boat Command in the radio logbook, which reads as follows: 'U338 (Kptlt. Manfred Kinzel) left St Nazaire in France for its third operational voyage on 25 August 1943.' There was no more news after this, and it must be assumed the boat was lost with all hands. At the time of writing this book, there is still no known cause for U338's sinking. British records suggest the boat was probably seriously damaged by Liberator F of 120 Squadron RAF, but it could also have been helped into the depths by the Canadian corvette HMCS *Drumheller*. What happened appears to be rather unclear, and it is possible an acoustic torpedo from U338 exploded close to the corvette. There is room for further study.

The Australian Wes Loney sitting in the pilot's seat of a Liberator in the Cosford Aircraft Museum reflecting on the time when this was his 'office' for many hours each day.

The last radio signals from U338 on 20 September 1943 read as follows:

09.21 hours	Have a convoy in sight.
16.10 hours	Enemy aircraft is shadowing us.
17.07 hours	We are under attack by an aircraft.
17.13 hours	Remaining on the surface to fend off aircraft with anti-aircraft guns.

The commander, Manfred Kinzel, had served as naval officer with the Luftwaffe from October 1937 until August 1941 and started his U-boat training the following month. Before taking command of U338 he had served as second watch officer in U404 for not more than four months, while Kptlt. Otto von Bülow was in command. He had been to sea for only fifty-nine days by the time he became commander of U338.

The British Admiralty summed up the events of Leuthen and Rossbach by saying: 'The renewal of the U-boat offensive in the North Atlantic, which started in September, has proved to be a costly failure for the enemy.' Many of the Germans who took part would agree.

THE VIEW FROM THE AIR

The following is based on an account by Australian Wes Loney, with additional material from John Dixon, the surviving men of U377 (who were not aboard for the final voyage) and notes from C.R. Vincent in Canada.

* * *

In 1943 I found myself captain of a Liberator crew of 59 Squadron, RAF Coastal Command, based at Ballykelly in Northern Ireland. On 16–17 October a convoy battle took place in the middle of the North Atlantic, because five or six U-boats were sunk and two others damaged for the loss of one merchant ship and two aircraft. On the first day, I was involved with two other Liberators of 120 Squadron from Iceland in a half-hour long battle some 40 miles ahead of the convoy, which resulted in the destruction of a Type VIIC U-boat. After our final attack the U-boat disintegrated and shortly afterwards, we counted about fifteen men in the water. After dropping a marker buoy and reporting their position to the Senior Naval Officer of the Escort Group (Commander Peter Gretton in the destroyer *Duncan*), I set a course for base.

A few weeks later my navigator, co-pilot and I were summoned to Coastal Command HQ at Northwood in London for further interrogation about the attack. Photographs we had taken showed a much heavier armament on the U-boat to what had hitherto been experienced. Apparently, the boat in question had been identified by two survivors picked up by HMS *Duncan* as U470 under Oblt.z.S. Günther-Paul Grave. Unfortunately, the men we had seen in the water had drifted far apart by the time rescuers reached the spot, and the Royal Navy managed to pick up only

Gerhard Tacken and Heinz Knappe. Knowing there were U-boats in the area, it was unwise for escorts to search for other possible survivors. Although called Flak Boats at the time, U470 was not an aircraft trap as such with the additional heavy armaments forward of the conning tower. These had incredibly high casualty rates in the Bay of Biscay. U470 was one of those boats converted to what became known as Leuthen and Rossbach Packs. There was an additional point of interest here for the Intelligence staff. Although we did not experience this ourselves, several other aircraft reported U-boats were using their anti-aircraft weapons effectively while submerged. This sounded a bit farfetched; the Intelligence people were set on delving deeper into these reports and finally concluded the reports originated when a surfaced U-boat moving at fast speed through slightly turbulent seas had its upper (outside) deck awash with waves gushing over it while the anti-aircraft guns at the top of the conning tower were blazing away.

It may be of interest to add U470 was the first boat to have been sunk by using the new sonar buoys for radioing engine noises to the aircraft above them and it was also one of the few boats with the rubber Alberich matting, which made it difficult for sonar operators to get a decent bearing when it was submerged. The sinking of U470 took place during the middle of October 1943 and our next serious engagement with a U-boat did not occur until January 1944. This boat, with strengthened anti-aircraft guns, gave a good account of itself, but eventually we managed to bag it. There was not much to see other than it dived suddenly at a steep angle with the stern lifting clear of the water for us to see the propellers and the red paint of its lower hull. Our gunfire must also have hit several of the men on the top of the conning tower because there were several motionless bodies floating in the water, but we did not see any evidence of having sunk the boat. The assessment, once we got back to base, was a 'probable' sinking.

Nothing further transpired for forty-three years until 1987 when I read the book *U-boats under the Swastika* by Jak P. Mallmann Showell. Mallmann's father, also Jak, had been lost without trace in January 1944, and from its last known position and the date it last sent a signal back to base, it seemed likely this was the boat we attacked on 13 January. So I wrote to Jak Mallmann, who was then living in Shropshire. He replied immediately, assuring me we were not responsible for his father's death, but we had, in fact, attacked U621 (Oblt.z.S. Max Kruschka), which had sustained serious damage but managed to return to Brest for repairs. Some of the crew had been injured, while those who died were stitched into hammocks with weights to be given a sea funeral. U621 was finally sunk in August 1944, but Jak was able to put me in touch with the medical officer, who was not on board for the last voyage. Jak also put me in touch with the German U-boat Museum and after a little persistent research I managed to get in touch with some of the survivors and, even more exciting, I managed to fly to Europe to meet these men, all of which was one of the most rewarding events of my life. I also managed to help Gerhard Tacken from U470 by putting him in touch with Admiral Sir Peter Gretton, whom he remembered as a fine officer and gentleman.

Things got even more exciting when Gerhard took me to the Moehne Dam, which had been broken by the famous Dam Busters and where an old school friend of mine, Les Knight, was awarded the Distinguished Flying Cross from the Royal Air Force. The other most momentous occasion was when Jak took us to the Aircraft Museum at RAF Cosford, where I was allowed to sit in the pilot seat of a wartime Liberator. My mind drifted back to those dreadful days of long ago. The man from the museum who opened the aircraft for us said this sort of memory flashback was not uncommon and he told me about wartime pilots spending several hours just sitting in their old positions while their wives wondered how men fitted into such tiny and highly confined spaces for such long flights. Jak told me afterwards I sat there for a long time, totally motionless, but with my eyes open the whole time. I can't remember any of that. For me I just saw images from the war that I had not even thought about for a long time. It was a weird experience.

My wife and myself had come to Europe with a friend, John Dixon and his wife, for a retirement holiday but now found ourselves in a fantastic journey of marvellous discovery. We later met Dr Klaus Steen in Hamburg before going on to Kiel to meet half a dozen survivors from U621. This was indeed an especially momentous occasion because I wanted to pay tribute to the crew and especially their commander, Oblt.z.S. Max Kruschka, for his masterly handling of his boat. His evasive action upset my tracking on two occasions and probably also saved his boat from total destruction. Kruschka survived the war but sadly lost his life in a fishing accident in 1948.

* * *

Attacking U-boats with Liberators was not easy due to the pilot's view being obscured by the huge aircraft nose in front of him. If his target was towards the right-hand side, he could not see it at all. Attacks with large aircraft required especially well-trained crews.

The two ladies were visibly shocked when they saw the interior of the aircraft. They were standing on the ground looking in through the bomb bay and refused to go any further, saying the whole space was exceedingly cramped. They questioned the men about the tightness of the space wondering how a whole crew could have fitted into it. A similar experience occurred sometime later when Elsa Patzke, the widow of U377's Petty Officer for the Central Control Room, watched men from the Kiel Machine Museum start their U-boat diesel engine. This was in a huge hall-like place with an incredible noise where Elsa burst into tears saying she had no idea of the noise her husband had to endure in the U-boat. Neither airmen nor U-boat men were given much space nor much comfort.

Wes also wrote:

> Not all my friends in Australia approved of this fantastic experience in England and in Germany, but I felt the burying of the hatchet was long overdue and we in Coastal Command had the highest regard for the courage and seamanship of the U-boat crews. They must have had the very worst job of the war, and this visit convinced me they were only young men, like ourselves, simply doing their job the best they could. Our attacks on U-boats were made at very low levels, so low that a good number of aircraft did not climb back into the sky again. We could clearly see the faces of our adversaries. I still retain a vivid image in my mind of a wounded gunner desperately clawing his way back to his gun seconds before being blasted into eternity. At that moment, I mentally awarded him an Iron Cross, whoever he was.

SONO OR SONAR BUOYS

The following was first printed in 1944 in the Royal Navy's Anti-Submarine Reports. This was printed at a time when supplies of Sonobuoys were still limited but it was hoped production could soon be stepped up.

* * *

> The ERSB (Expendable Radio Sono Buoy) is a method of providing aircraft with a means of listening to underwater sounds. It weighs 14 pounds and is about 45 inches long and 6 inches in diameter. It consists of a hydrophone (underwater microphone) which is released from the base of the buoy when this strikes the water and is then suspended some 24 feet below the surface. There is also a transmitting set and a short antenna, which transmit sounds by radio to the listening aircraft. The buoy has a life of 4 to 8 hours, after which it will sink. Those currently in use have non-directional hydrophones but a directional model is being developed. In order that the aircraft may know which buoy is transmitting sounds they are made in six frequencies, each buoy being painted a distinctive colour corresponding to its frequency. A circling aircraft should, therefore, get an easy and immediate indication of where the sound source is located.

> The range of detection of a submerged U-boat's sounds depends on the speed of the boat and upon the surface sea conditions and are approximately as follows:
>
> U-boat speed 2 knots = Range of detection 300 – 1,000 yards
> U-boat speed 4 knots = Range of detection 1,000 – 6,500 yards
> U-boat speed 6 knots = Range of detection 3,000 – 10,000 yards
>
> The range of the transmitter is 35 miles when flying at 5,000 feet altitude and 30 miles at 3,000 feet.

The idea was for an aircraft to drop a visual marker, such as a smoke buoy, at the point where the U-boat dived and then to fly in any direction, but at best along the course of the U-boat for about 2 miles and then fly in a square of about 4 miles, dropping a sonobuoy in each corner. The radio operator can then switch from one frequency to another by following the right colour sequence to give some idea of the U-boat's location. In addition to the obvious uses, the device could also be used for investigating oil slicks and signals from Magnetic Airborne Detectors.

Men from U108 wearing woollen hats. These were standard naval issue rather than having been knitted by granny back home.

Chapter 10

Alberich,* Anti-submarine Mines, Defying Orders and Alleged Suicide Orders

The U-boat Arm had a good number of remarkable storytellers. Admiral Karl Dönitz (U-boat Chief) would have been delighted, had he known they continued with their wild stories after becoming prisoners of war. Interrogation reports circulating within the British Admiralty about the new Alberich skin being applied to U-boats suggested this rubber coat was being added to make bombs bounce off, and as a side-effect it also made boats more streamlined. Such documents can't be genuine, yet they don't look like fakes, either. Fakes or not, the U-boat skin was real, it did exist and U480, launched on 14 August 1943, was one of the first boats to have had such a covering added during the construction stage, when a breathing pipe was built-in at the same time. The German word 'Schnorchel' was apparently coined by Dönitz and quickly modified by the Royal Navy as 'schnorkel', a term continuously used in Britain throughout the war. The Americans called it 'snort' or 'snorkel' instead.

The Alberich skin was a rubber sheet, smooth on the outside and with another section containing masses of small bubbles nearer the inside for absorbing sound (Asdic) impulses. The problem was no one had yet invented a suitable glue for attaching it to steel. Carpenters of those days brewed up a powerful mixture of cow horns and hooves in a small pot which was kept constantly hot by being immersed in simmering water. There wasn't much else as strong as this glue for smooth metal. (Although the famous German glue 'Uhu' had been invented shortly before Hitler came to power, the formula and method of application were still in their infancy. The high quality, modern 'super' glues had not yet been invented.) The concoction of glue had to be applied to a scrupulously clean surface away from rain and dust. Even then, it did not last terribly long, so metal fasteners were attached as well. Despite these difficulties, this invention seems to have worked, if it lasted. Parts often detached themselves and flapped like a group of seals performing an especially loud clapping act with their flippers.

One of the most interesting Alberich stories emerged not during the war but in 1998, when a team of divers under the leadership of Innes McCartney explored a VIIC U-boat wreck with such a covering near the Isle of Wight, on England's south coast. When this news first broke, people said he could not have found an Alberich boat because they were exceedingly rare and none of them ever got into the English Channel. People pointed to official documents telling us how Operation Cork, the blocking-off of the English

*. Alberich was a dwarf from Nordic legends. Despite having the strength of more than ten men, he was overpowered by the hero, Siegfried, wearing his cloak of invisibility.

Channel and especially the D-Day invasion beaches, was exceptionally successful, with many U-boats having been sunk on the Atlantic side of this barrier. Hardly anything got through into those precarious Channel waters. Yet McCartney could identify his U-boat types. He had probably dived on more than anyone else and this was definitely a Type VIIC with a rubber skin, despite this layer having been missed by many previous divers. Since he could not solve the riddle from existing papers, he approached the Naval Historical Branch at the Ministry of Defence, where Bob Coppock provided the necessary information. This was not easy, but the chap was a professional who could not be beaten by what others had written before him. Finally, he concluded this could only be U480 (Oblt.z.S. Hans-Joachim Förster), although that boat had been sunk on 24 February 1945 off Cornwall, some 200 miles further west, in the Operation Cork zone.

A diver like McCartney, breathing bottled air and with his head in the water, can be excused for messing up the history books by finding one U-boat wreck where it shouldn't be. After all, this sinking happened towards the end of the war, when activity in English waters increased to a point of being so exceedingly hectic that nobody could see the overall picture of what was going on. U-boats could no longer surface or use their radios and commanders were given more latitude for making their own on-the-spot decisions. The trouble was, Innes McCartney was starting to make habit of finding U-boats where they shouldn't be, and it was not long before he had a respectable list, and the Naval Historical Branch was obliged to rewrite the details of several wartime sinkings.

As it turned out, McCartney's discoveries also uncovered some previously unknown and highly intelligent British skulduggery. Knowing the German Navy was reading the British Merchant Navy's radio code, the Admiralty sent instructions to its ships at sea with details of safe routes through dangerous minefields and told the ships how to get into harbours without bumping into their own explosives. Hoping the Germans would decode this information and perhaps make use of it, some of these routes were laced with special deep anti-submarine mines. A merchant ship could pass harmlessly over the top, but they would catch submerged submarines trying to use the same route and Innes McCartney found several 'unknown' wrecks in those trap areas.

As a result, in addition to U480 (Oblt.z.S. Hans-Joachim Förster), U325 (Oblt.z.S. Erwin Dohrn), U400 (Kptlt. Horst Creutz) and U1021 (Oblt.z.S. Wilhelm Holpert) fell foul of these anti-submarine mines. The details are included in the latest edition of Axel Niestle's *German U-boat Losses during World War II* (Frontline Books, London, 2014). Each of these boats was recorded as having been depth charged to the west of Land's End in Cornwall, but they were later found to be lying in British coastal waters.

Alberich protection has had an indifferent to negative press, which seems to be a little misleading because those who used it were enthusiastic about the protection it provided. It may not have absorbed all the Asdic impulses, but it certainly helped to confuse operators, making it difficult for them to get an accurate fix on the submarine. Although only a little is known about U480's last cruise, we do know this was not its first excursion into the English Channel. The boat was taking part in Alberich trials off Norway when the D-Day invasion burst upon the Normandy beaches on 6 June 1944 and the following day it was dispatched to make for the English Channel. With the German High Command not sure about how things were developing, U-boats at sea were told to make for the huge bunker in Brest, to await further instructions until the situation could be assessed. A purposeful engagement was thought to be better than just mingling with the crowds. In any case, progress from Norway to France was exceedingly slow. Schnorkeling speed had to be less than 5 knots, and the normal electric submerged speed of a U-boat was also less than 4 knots. So U480 was a little late in arriving and it was 3 August 1944 when it left Brest to operate between the Isle of Wight and Cherbourg in France. The constantly submerged submarine did not need any special listening gear to establish a lot was going on in those waters. The noise everybody could hear inside the boat did not sound terribly relaxing. Far-off exploding depth charges and propeller noises were present as constant background noise and Asdic pings from submarine hunters also appeared at regular intervals. It was all rather unsettling.

Having reached the operations area, the men in U480 were none the wiser and not sure exactly where the centre of action was located. Since they did not get any direct instructions from headquarters, it was decided to explore the Isle of Wight on the English side rather than go sightseeing along the French coast. From a fighting point of view, this was the right decision. U480 ran into the most horrific action, with several ships dashing about directly overhead for more than six hours at a time. The men were confident the Alberich covering was mainly responsible for their miraculous escapes. The hunters on the surface were coming close but did not seem to be able to get a decent fix on the submerged submarine, although U480's sound detectors picked up the opposition most clearly. The boat had remained submerged since its first dive into deep water off Brest, sticking up the schnorkel only for brief periods to recharge the batteries. Since the men could not open the hatch, there were no opportunities for getting rid of rubbish and by the time these intense hunts were under way, the inside of the boat resembled a fully laden garbage truck. The smell of rotting food was everywhere, and nothing could be done to get rid of the intensely putrid smell. It must have been excruciating. Even ventilating the boat through the raised schnorkel did not bring a great deal of relief as the stench was more powerful than the fresh air streaming in. To make this situation even worse, the men had stacked up with fresh food in Brest, leaving them with considerably more waste than when using tinned provisions. The inside of the boat must have been sheer hell, yet the men did get back to the huge bunker to hand in the logbook and to get thoroughly drunk on local hospitality.

The general situation in the town was also horrific, with the Allied air forces having bombed it often enough to demolish much of it, leaving a significant number of orphans who were being fed by the German Navy. So, although critical and most precarious, with many secret documents being thrown onto bonfires in anticipation of an evacuation, life on land under the open sky was considerably better than being shut up inside a small steel coffin.

Early in 1943 the U-boat Chief, Admiral Karl Dönitz, was promoted to become Supreme Commander-in-Chief of the Navy and therefore moved his headquarters to Berlin, to be near the Military High Command, from where he could attend high level meetings with Hitler. Several highly experienced U-boat commanders were given more authority to deal with the goings-on in their immediate coastal waters. On hearing the news of the Normandy invasion, Dönitz took the same view as Field Marshal Erwin Rommel, saying the attackers must be thrown back into the sea at all costs. Yes, the words 'at all costs' were recorded by several German sources. They had been spoken. This made several officers raise their eyebrows at Dönitz's decision, who then made it clear this was a terribly dangerous situation for Germany. All boats, with an emphasis on 'all', had to be made ready for going into the English Channel. At that time, three basic U-boat types were being made ready in Brest, the nearest U-boat base to the invasion area. Some boats, like U480, were built with an Alberich skin and with a schnorkel, while a few more had these aids added at a later stage. There were many more boats with schnorkels but without the matting on the outside, and there were even more old submarines without schnorkels.

Later the same day, when Dönitz was sure this was 'the' Allied invasion, and not merely a grand commando raid, he ordered Konter~admiral Eberhard Godt (Head of the U-boat Operation Department) to send the boats to sea. Godt knew full well this meant 'all' boats, as had been discussed only a few hours earlier. He did exactly as he had been ordered, except that he sent the non-schnorkel boats into the mid-Atlantic where nothing was going on; only those with schnorkels were ordered into the English Channel. This action was a direct refusal to obey his commanding officer and long after the war, in the 1990s, there came an opportunity to confront Godt with this most serious breach of discipline. Photocopies of the orders were placed in front of him. After having studied them in detail, he looked up and said: 'Yes. You are right, but I cannot remember this incident.' The conversation continued until late in the night, with Konter~admiral Godt requesting copies of the necessary papers, but the reason why and how he defied the high command has never been clarified. Whatever, there are many men who owe their lives to this remarkable character, who sent them away from a certain death.

The local commander for the Normandy and Biscay area was Kpt.z.S. Hans Rösing, with the title of Führer der Unter~see~boote West (FdU West = Flag Officer for U-boats, West). On D-Day he was obviously hovering in a black void, not knowing exactly what was happening and what should be done about this massive landing. His headquarters were near the French Biscay coast, so all he could do was wait for clarification. U-boats in port were put on immediate standby, while their commanders were called to an urgent meeting to discuss what could be done. One of these commanders, who settled in the United States after the war and later wrote a best-selling autobiography, revealed how commanders were ordered to sail to the invasion beaches, expend all their torpedoes and then kill themselves by ramming any target, even if it were only as small as a landing craft. Long after the war, when his book was published, it was rather difficult to confront Rösing with this incredible suicide order. This was awful. He had given the order for hundreds of men to kill themselves for little or no gain. The search for further details was made considerably easier when a list of the attending U-boat commanders was found, and one could approach each man to give an account of what had happened at that fateful meeting.

People present agreed such a ridiculous order was never discussed or given, but afterwards, while taking some light refreshments, individuals came up with the wildest schemes for fending off the Allied invasion and it seems likely this is where the story of the suicide order originated. It was never given as an order. This 'alleged order' was of special interest to the author of this book because his father's U-boat disappeared at the beginning of 1944 and could have been given a similar suicide order. (It was not until the end of the twentieth century that Dr Axel Niestlé discovered how U377, then under command of Oblt.z.S. Gerhard Kluth, had been sunk by depth charges from the destroyer HMS *Wanderer* (Lieutenant Commander R.F. Whinney) on 17 January 1944 and those details are in his book *German U-boat Losses During World War Two* (Frontline Books, London, 2014). The book by Captain Reginald Whinney, *The U-boat Peril – An Anti-Submarine Commander's War* (Arrow Books, London, 1986), is also of interest.

The torpedo aimer with binoculars clipped in position. These binoculars were similar to those used by the men, giving a plain picture without a grid, which is incorrectly shown in many films. These glasses were water and pressure resistant, meaning the boat could dive with the binoculars in position without damaging the optics. In this photo there are two plain metal tubes screwed to the front to prevent rain and spray from clouding the front lenses. The men are wearing normal raingear with sou'westers. Boats also carried sets for heavy rain, like modern dry suits.

Chapter 11

Schnorkels and East Prussian Evacuations: The Collapse of the Ostmark

THE FIRST GERMAN OPERATIONAL SCHNORKEL, THE AGRU-FRONT AND EAST PRUSSIA

U235, commissioned on 19 December 1942, and U236, commissioned on 9 January 1943, were both sunk four months later during an air raid on Kiel. They were raised to be made ready for a second time and during this repair work they became the first operational boats to have schnorkels installed. Thus, on 29 September 1943, U236 under Oblt.z.S. Curt Hartmann became the first operational boat with a schnorkel, and U235 was the second when it was returned to service on the same day one month later under the command of Oblt.z.S. Hans-Erich Kummetz (not to be confused with Admiral Oskar Kummetz.)

The following report about U235 is based on papers Horst Bredow asked me to photocopy during an exceptionally busy day with many visitors. Unfortunately, I did not make a note of the author's name, but Horst confirmed he was a reliable source. Months later, when I looked in the Archive again, there was no longer any trace of the original. It had probably been filed in the wrong location.

* * *

Since U235 had been training successfully in the Baltic, the men expected to be sent into the Atlantic as soon as they had completed their final shakedown cruise, and they were already joking about how this would improve the dwindling successes out there. This urge to go to war was instantly frustrated when Admiral Hans-Georg von Friedeburg (Head of the U-boat Arm's Organization Department) handed the commander his operational orders. The first objective was to stay in the Baltic to test the new schnorkel or breathing pipe for running diesel engines without surfacing. At the same time, the men were to suggest modifications before the device went into mass production. Another order then dashed all earlier expectations about running into the Atlantic. After these tests, U235 was to remain in the Baltic to teach other crews how to use the new invention. The urgent process of installing schnorkels and teaching crews how to use them was on a considerable scale, meaning lessons with visiting personnel lasted for only a few trips in U235, to learn the basic essentials. The rest had to be self-taught in their own boats.

Mark in this case means border area or Marches.

The schnorkel for existing U-boat types consisted of a rigid pipe, hinged at the base of the conning tower. When not in use, it was stowed in the space between the pressure hull and the upper (outside) deck. The original design to raise the device as high as an extended periscope by using an electric motor pulling on a cable did not work and was quickly replaced by a more efficient hydraulic system. Once raised, the pipe locked into a bracket at the top of the conning tower. The head valve, which closed automatically when it dropped below the surface of the water, was often covered in radar-absorbing rubber and had a radar-detecting aerial on the top. German experts were under the impression this rubber would probably be superfluous to requirements because the head valve was too small to be detected by radar. Unfortunately for Germany, they were wrong and only discovered this error elsewhere around the time of the first schnorkel trials.

An illustration from an official naval booklet instructing people about the intricacies of the 'Kali~patrone' with a Dräger emergency breathing tube. Sleeping with one or even sitting with it was cumbersome, and when having to work while wearing one, the interior of the submarine would have been on the dimmest illumination as well. Hardly ideal conditions at the best of times.

German experts thought radar could work only with long radio wavelengths until a new and much more sensitive short-wave British radar set was recovered from a crashed bomber near Rotterdam in Holland early in 1943. It took several months to reconstruct it, meaning it was around the time of Black May and the famous Leuthen comeback, during the autumn of that year, when they knew for certain this new 'short wave' gear was much superior to anything there had been before. British veterans meeting at the Arctic Convoys Museum by Loch Ewe in 2013 confirmed this new short-wave or Centimetric radar could detect *and alert* an operator when just a small periscope head was visible above the surface of the water at a range of up to 2,000 yards or 1,800 metres, and thus the new radar had no great problems when searching for a larger schnorkel head.

Water accidentally flooding down the schnorkel pipe ended up in a sump from where it was pumped out again, while the huge existing duct took the incoming air to the engine room. The diesels then sucked their air out of that compartment without there being a direct air supply for the engines. When the head valve was closed by waves, the diesel engines continued running until they were turned off manually. There was no warning system to tell the men the head valve had closed, and they only noticed this by the air pressure difference. This meant there was always a time lapse when diesels sucked air out of the boat, making it most uncomfortable for the crew.

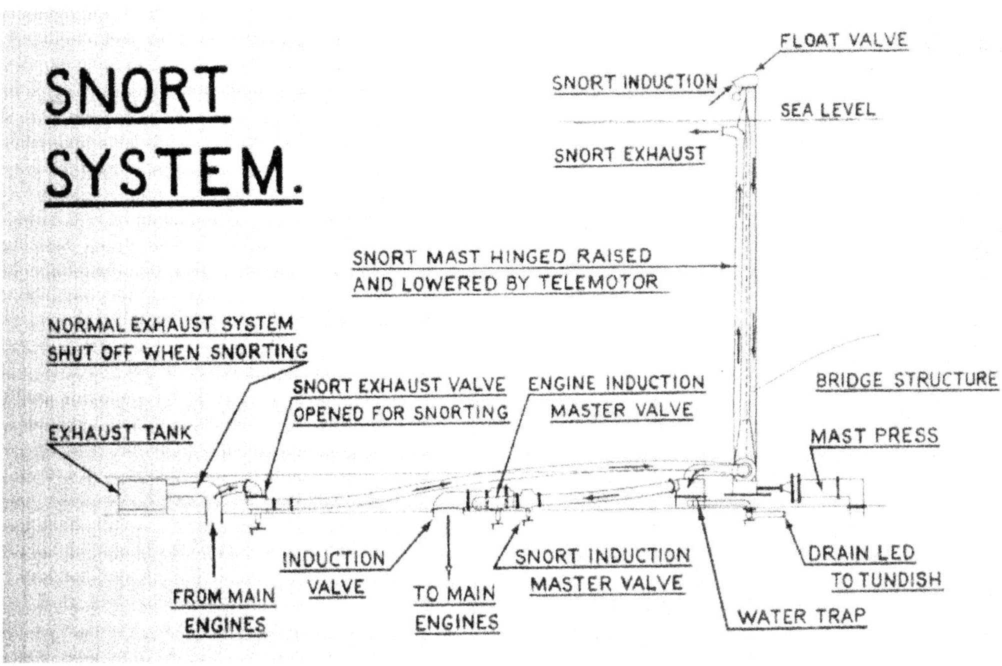

The American instructions for the German U-boat schnorkel. Throughout the war the Royal Navy used the anglicized name schnorkel while the Americans called it snort or snorkel.

Making this pressure difference considerably worse, each diesel exhaust system was fitted with a valve by the outlet to prevent water flooding backwards into the engine through the exhaust pipe. This was an additional safety feature in case the outside water pressure was greater than the exhaust pressure. If such a rare accident should occur, then the valve would open to vent the choking and poisonous exhaust gases into the interior of the boat. Obviously, this could only happen when the boat was on the surface, at a time when the hatch was open or could be opened very quickly. Each man also had his own personal breathing equipment for the rare occasions when things went wrong. The schnorkel now added a terrific disadvantage because the diesels would be running at a time when the hatch could not be opened, thus there now was the possibility of filling the boat with choking smoke and deadly poisonous carbon monoxide in addition to rapidly increasing obnoxious carbon dioxide.

As far as the first trials were concerned, it was necessary to find a way for men to cope with the constantly varying pressure. The biggest problem was the Eustachian tube between the back of the mouth and the ears, which can be kept comfortably open by swallowing or yawning. Years ago, when aircraft pressurization was not as good as it is today, airlines handed out boiled sweets for passengers to suck to help relieve any slight pressure differences during take-off and landing. The pressure variation inside submarines was far more intense than expected and no one knew how much a person could cope with. But the German Navy had not been idle with its research into human problems, and it was easy to arrange for specialists from the Naval Medical Research Institute to come along for a few trial runs.

As daft as it might sound, cows' milk was used for neutralizing exhaust gas poisoning until something more powerful could be found. Submarines had for many years carried testing kits for determining carbon dioxide levels and they had means of absorbing this gas from the air, but not for the high levels which occurred when using the schnorkel and, even worse, when the emergency exhaust valve ventilated poisonous gases directly into the boat. Without going into the details, one can quickly see this new introduction was like a huge mud bath with no one capable of seeing through it. Yet despite the difficulties and discomforts, the top leaders did not pass the buck and even Grand Admiral Dönitz came to U235 to experience these problems for himself.

A schnorkel head inlet valve with ball float to shut the air duct when the intake dropped below the surface of the water. Many were covered in rubber to absorb radar impulses and usually there was a radar detection aerial on the top.

On 8 March 1944, U235 was moved away from the air-raid danger area of Kiel to Hela (Hel, now in Poland) to join the Agru-Front. This technical branch, its name derived from 'Aus~bildungs~gruppe – Front', was the last stage in the instruction process between training and going to war. Experienced specialists went aboard each boat to provide a punishing schedule where instructors determined machinery failures and other accidents the men might have to face in future. Somehow, there was a definite problem with this stage. Many of the men were keen to get to the front and looked upon this additional process as unnecessary bureaucracy. Claus Korth, who served with the Agru-Front for a while, told me how some crews were openly hostile to instructors and would not even provide them with a space to sleep, despite being at sea for several days on end. Korth also explained how the Agru-Front was under pressure to pass boats on as quickly as possible: 'We rewarded the best boats by failing them,' he said. 'The general training was nowhere near good enough to face the rigours of the Atlantic and by failing the good crews for more training meant they had better chances to survive at sea.'

Hela (Hel) was nothing more than a delightful, overgrown village or tiny town at the bulbous end of a 34km-long peninsula or barrier beach. This was some distance off the mainland and in places not much wider than the road and railway running along it. In those days it was possible to travel from Gotenhafen (Gdynia) to Hela by ferry or by train, with both journeys taking about ninety minutes. The faster train obviously had a considerably longer journey and it stopped in several places on the way. The small harbour with its tiny U-boat base, situated some 3 or 4km west of the town, was simply cordoned off with barbed wire and the distance from the main gate to the harbour was another 1½km. It was an idyllic open space, far away from the normal rigidity of life. All the buildings there faced away from the open Baltic to protect them from the weather. Shipping coming past would have seen only the magnificent lighthouse above the trees. The commanding officer of the naval installation allowed his married staff to bring their wives, a most positive plus point. Hela was very much an idyllic backwater, quiet and naturally interesting, and the families took full advantage of being there to get away from the intense bombing in the west. From June 1944 onwards four married members of U235's crew lived there as tenants of local house owners. This was an official arrangement and being registered with the police meant they had their own ration cards without the navy having to fiddle the accounts.

Men in training came to Hela to try out the new schnorkel system and, of course, all of them experienced several incidents where the head valve was deliberately shut to produce the incredible unpleasantness. Hans-Erich Kummetz, the commander of U235, became most concerned when several of his men started suffering from what he thought was a gradual poisoning, and he asked for the entire crew to be examined by the flotilla's senior medical officer. The result was astonishing. Three-quarters of the men were no longer suitable for U-boat service. Kummetz wrote an official report, but never received a reply, which made him so concerned that he refused to put to sea on more than one occasion. As a result, he got a sharp reprimand from a land-based commander, who told him officers who refused to obey orders would be court-martialled. Not wanting to be a push-over, nor responsible for poisoning his men, Kummetz communicated his fears to higher officers of the U-boat Arm rather than to desk-bound retirees from surface ships. In doing this, it became apparent Hans-Georg von Friedeburg, the Admiral of the Organization Department, never received the poisoning information; he reacted immediately by creating two crews for the boat. The idea was for one crew to be resting in fresh air while the other was in the U-boat. He granted the affected men a six-week long holiday in a naval convalescent home where they were allowed to take their wives. U235's alternative crew was under Oblt.z.S. Rudolf Kleinschmidt. The U-boat Arm was quite liberal. After the war, several lower-ranking sailors confirmed that when they complained to flotilla commanders or higher U-boat authorities, action to help them was usually instantaneous, without recriminations or messing about.

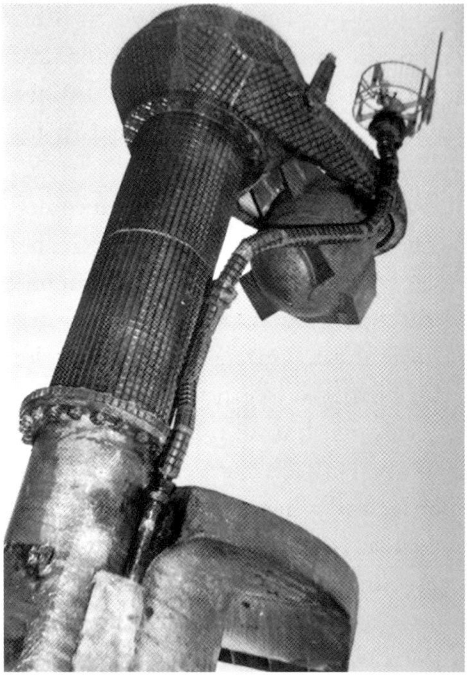

The schnorkel head valve with radar detecting aerial and lower down a diesel exhaust.

LAND DEFENCES AND EVACUATION OF THE OSTMARK (the old eastern border areas)

Hela, both the tiny settlement and the peninsula, remained as an oasis of peace until the autumn of 1944. Of course, the Schnorkel School was not the only small teaching unit in Germany's far eastern Baltic. There was also an Acoustic Torpedo School and several more in other small, out-of-the-way locations. All they needed was a U-boat pier with special fenders to prevent the huge depth rudders or hydroplanes from scraping against anything solid. Other necessities, such as food, water, oil and fuel, were easily provided in any small harbour and only untoward happenings made it necessary to seek out bigger towns for repairs or for specialist help. Supply matters, personnel issues and any additional support were handled by the U-boat flotillas, all of which were administrative rather than operational units. U-boat flotillas hardly ever operated as a unit of several ships going into action together. By 1944 Anglo-American air raids on the west had forced a good number of training facilities to migrate to the far east, where U-boats were out of reach of the massive bomber squadrons, and therefore used several small locations, many of them at some distance from larger conglomerations. There were also a significant number of operational boats in the far east, seeking out small but efficient shipyards for repairs and maintenance.

* * *

The following account, by Werner Ebner of U1192 and Karl Heinz Krause (a man with technical naval range finder qualifications) describes what happened to boats under the jurisdiction of the 22nd U-boat Training Flotilla in Memel (now Klaipeda in Lithuania) on 3 November 1944 when the Russian Army was crossing the border into Germany.

> With many of the senior naval commanders not having any operational control, they could only obey orders from higher authorities and this new emergency of Russians crossing the border came without much warning. The first alarm order was to reduce the submarine crews by about fifty per cent, allowing twenty men from each boat to be drafted into a new force for defences on land. Over the whole area to the east of Danzig [Gdansk] this added up to a total of about 500 to 600 men, making up a mishmash from many naval sources, including surface ships, to supplement army units, with Home Guard (Volks~sturm) and others who happened to be there.
>
> It quickly became obvious the authorities issuing these orders had no idea about what was going on or about the lie of the land. The men from U1192, for example, were kitted out with tools for digging ditches in what turned out to be wet marshy ground saturated with water. They were also given some close combat weapons for putting tanks out of action (Panzer~faust) and guns manufactured during the First World War. Each man could take as much ammunition as he could carry. At the time none of the men knew these bullets, of an unusual calibre, were no longer manufactured and there were no further supplies. This bedraggled and helpless collection was pitted against much superior firepower from heavy artillery, which they could not even see. As a result, the German casualties were enormous and, at times, deeply soul destroying. A good number from U1192, sent out further east as a reconnaissance unit, got snarled up in hidden barbed wire entanglements where they were horrifically injured within sight of both their German comrades and advancing Russian snipers. Their screams and cries for help lasted until late in the night when death relieved them of their agony. No one from the German side could get out of the water-filled trenches to help without having his head blown off. The advancing army

U516 after the end of the war, showing periscopes and schnorkel. On the left is the sky or navigation periscope with the large head lens. In Type VIIC boats this could be viewed only from the central control room and could therefore not be raised as high as the attack periscope with the smaller head lens. The schnorkel's air intake at the top has a circular radar detector aerial attached to it and the engine exhaust pipe is visible at the bottom.

> was much more efficient than the meagre defences, yet this standoff lasted for almost two weeks before the pressure from the east became too great and the few German survivors were forced to evacuate back to Memel, which was by that time also within reach of the Russian artillery. The casualties on the German side were incredibly high.
>
> Once back in the town, the local naval commander realized the men from U1192 were specialists, who were in great demand further west, and therefore he ordered their immediate evacuation to a still considerable U-boat force located around the naval base in Gotenhafen [Gdynia]. Getting there by sea was considerably easier than going overland but arriving was unpleasant and depressing. Despite the horrific savagery of the past few weeks, the men from U1192 were still taken aback by the misery of the long refugee columns they saw on roads and among the surrounding countryside. Thousands of wretched people, without food, warmth or shelter, stretched into what looked like never-ending columns plodding on foot with heavy loads from small towns and villages towards what they thought would be organized evacuation points. Once the U-boat men who had been sent back arrived in the naval base, the senior U-boat commander there was most critical of their intentions and sent them back to Memel, where they had come from. They were needed to help with the land defences. The lucky survivors were those who were injured and taken to western hospitals. The majority died somewhere, but no one knows where or how. They just vanished into the morass of expendable humanity. Frozen stiff, some of the corpses were used for surfacing still muddy sections in roads or for filling holes torn by bombs. War is always cruel, and some wars are more cruel than others.
>
> When U235 was ordered west, there were still four wives living in the Hela base, who were not allowed to be evacuated with their husbands and therefore had to be deserted, to be left alone to whatever fate they would face and without much support, food, clothing or shelter on their lonely, long trek to a safer location. The boat's commander, Hans-Erich Kummetz, may have been a little harsh at times, but there was no way he was going to desert the wives. They were given naval uniforms and told to hide their long hair under sou'westers. Having trained so many newcomers onboard U235, the crew was used to accommodating additional people and placing the women in the officers' quarters worked quite well, allowing U235 to reach Kiel, where some urgent remedial work lasted until the last day of March 1945. When the air raid warning sounded, Kummetz used a bicycle as the fastest means of getting from the naval barracks to the U-boat in the harbour. He did not see any sentries by the gate and hearing the shooting of bigger anti-aircraft guns, he pedalled on, only to be shot and wounded by a guard. Luckily the skill of a naval surgeon meant he made a full recovery.

The Hela Peninsula was of no strategic value to any advancing army and from the end of 1944 onwards it became crowded with refugees. The local authorities there even created a special field post stamp for mail carried west by U-boats. Gosh, one must marvel at the bureaucracy. The conditions under which this was done were horrific and beyond the scope of this book. Unlike the evacuations at Dunkirk, these refugees were mainly civilians, women, children and old people walking and often sleeping out in the open even when the warmest part of the day did not reach much above the magic 'minus fourteen' number. [Magic, perhaps only to schoolchildren, because minus fourteen degrees Celsius is the same as plus fourteen degrees Fahrenheit.] Incredible efforts went into providing transport and although the situation was chaotic, the discipline of many of these pitiful characters remained exceedingly high, despite the intense suffering. There is a story of a retreating army commander coming across refugees and finding no food other than beans and sugar. He ordered his men to bring bathtubs from deserted nearby houses. These were placed over open wood fires to heat the beans, providing the only hot food many had eaten for a long time.

It was around January 1945 when the remains of the 22nd U-boat Training Flotilla, stationed in Gotenhafen near Danzig (Gdansk), was ordered to disband and to distribute its men among the defences on land. The snag was the men did not have the weapons, tools, clothing or physical stamina for such activities. They did not move far in U-boats, where exercising had always been a great problem. None of these boats was in a good state of repair, with a high proportion having been relegated to training duties because the machinery could no longer withstand the rigours of the Atlantic. To make matters

A schnorkel being fitted to an older boat. Bearing in mind this was something totally new, the device came without installation instructions and the whole process was rather complicated.

worse, many of the men had brought their wives and children to live in what had been an area safe from air raids, and now they were ordered to sacrifice everything they had in what many saw as a pointless defensive exercise. There was nothing, no weapons nor any other resources, to stem the rate at which the Russian armies were moving westwards at an incredibly fast and efficient speed.

The flotilla commander, Korvkpt. Heinrich (but better known as Ajax) Bleichrodt, had not only resigned his U-boat command in U109 while at sea, but also announced his intentions over the general airwaves for others to hear. Once he had done so, U-boat Command ordered him to hand over his command to the first watch officer and take a prescribed medicine to subdue his nerves. Bleichrodt may have been at the end of his nerves, but he had enough energy to realize that this officer was in no position to refuse taking command and there was no way Bleichrodt was going to burden the man with such a momentous responsibility. Thus, on 23 January 1943 he returned to Lorient in France as commander of his boat. The average officer would, no doubt, have been shunted into a penal institution or, at best, into some other sideline, but Bleichrodt was a Knight of the Iron Cross with Oakleaves, which meant he won the award twice, and men of his calibre were becoming a rarity. Too many with such awards were either dead or in prisoner-of-war camps. So Bleichrodt was pushed quietly into what became a most unenviable training flotilla in East Prussia, far away from the hubbub of naval life. Talking about this, Bleichrodt explained how as early as 1942 commanders and crews were totally finished and their nerves shredded. 'Just look at the huge number of commanders who were relieved of their positions,' he said. 'Too many dropped out because they were in such a pitiful mental state and there was no safety mechanism which allowed them time off to recover. Instead of granting them some leave, these men were pushed further into the world of insanity.'

Bleichrodt was not the type to obey pointless orders and there was no way he was going to desert his men or their families. In January 1945, only four months before the end of the war, he told his commanders: 'Prepare for an evacuation to the west and sod the orders.' In addition to the U-boats, there was also the depot ship *Weichsel*, whose crew was supplemented with wives, fiancées and children: a total of 357 souls, almost twice as many as normal. The journey was going to be crowded and uncomfortable. People were told to bring clothing, a cooking pot, a kitchen knife (plus a small knife for peeling potatoes) and a few spoons. Many military units kept pigs, to make good use of leftovers from the messes, and Bleichrodt ordered these to be brought down to the harbour as well. Shot on the quay side, the butchered carcasses were laid in the lifeboats. Icy temperatures at around minus 18 degrees Celsius meant they were unlikely to go bad before being eaten. 'Throw the pigs out of the lifeboats when we start sinking,' he told everybody.

If the U-boats were to dive to avoid an attack, then the *Weichsel* would not have had enough firepower to defend itself. Therefore, the plan was to sail west as a closed group. No one was allowed to start shooting until Bleichrodt aboard *Weichsel* gave the order, and then every gun was to open up at the same time. The ammunition was especially doctored in favour of having an unusually high proportion of tracer shells. It worked: the resulting fireworks display was brilliant and none of the attacking aircraft came close enough to molest anyone. Everybody got through, but only just.

Not far away in Gotenhafen was the cruise ship *Wilhelm Gustloff*, taking on board far more people than it had ever carried before. The immediate post-war estimates were that it boarded about 5,000 people, but modern research suggests the figure was over 10,000. One of these was the wife of Oblt.z.S. Ludwig Fabricius, commander of U721. When Bleichrodt learned she was likely to give birth during the voyage, he suggested she should be brought over to *Weichsel* to be looked after by his wife Carla, a doctor and experienced gynaecologist. Mrs Fabricius duly gave birth to a girl, who long after the war won a magazine competition for the most unusual birth. This collection of ships left Gotenhafen on 28 January 1945 to plough through the ice on a westerly course. *Wilhelm Gustloff* was sunk two days later while heading west. Sailing behind it was a smaller ship, also over-full with refugees. The commander, Korvkpt. Otto Köhler, of what had been the Eastern Branch of the Acoustic Torpedo Shooting School, said watching the catastrophe and not being able to stop to pick up any more people was one of the hardest tests he faced during the war.

Kptlt. Heinrich (but better known as Ajax) Bleichrodt commanded U48, U67 and U109, before he resigned at sea during an operational tour and announced this decision over the open radio for all to hear. Following this, he was shunted sideways to become the Chief of the 22nd U-boat Training Flotilla and led the Flotilla's evacuations from East Prussia at the end of the war.

BREATHING PROBLEMS IN A LONG-SERVING U-BOAT WITH AN EXPERIENCED CREW

U218, a Type VIID, was almost identical to the VIIC except for an additional section aft of the conning tower containing five vertical mineshafts, each one holding three shaft mines. These were bigger than torpedo mines, but the crew could not access them once at sea; therefore, last-minute adjustments could not be made before dropping them one at a time. This additional section also contained tanks and fuel bunkers, meaning the Type VIIC's maximum range of 9,500 nautical miles was increased to 13,000 nautical miles.

U218 (under Richard Becker and later under Rupprecht Stock) is an interesting boat. It was commissioned on 21 January 1942, at about the same time as the United States 'officially' joined the war and a time when the tide had turned against U-boats. It sailed on at least a dozen significant voyages, placing it among the top 30 per cent of all U-boats, and one wonders how many new boats suffered similar disasters and failed to make it back to port due to lack of experience (see Table 2).

Much of the following information probably comes from Wilhelm Foehner, who must have devoted a considerable time to establishing the history of his boat.

Voyages undertaken by U218, 1942–1945.

Port	Departure date	Return date	Days at sea	Days in port
Kiel	25. 08. 42	29. 09. 42	34	–
Brest	25. 10. 42	21. 11. 42	26	24
Brest	07. 01. 43	10. 03. 43	33	46
Brest	18. 04. 43	02. 06. 43	44	38
Brest	22. 07. 43	23. 07. 43	0	28
Brest	29. 07. 43	06. 08. 43	14	5
Brest	19. 09. 43	08. 12. 43	48	43
Brest	12. 02. 44	07. 05. 44	84	65
Brest	13. 06. 44	09. 07. 44	25	31
Brest	10. 08. 44	23. 09. 44	43	43
Bergen	06. 10. 44	12. 10. 44	5	12
Flensburg	17. 10. 44	17. 10. 44	0	4
Kiel for major refit	08. 03. 45	16. 03. 45	7	161
Horten	19. 03. 45	20. 03. 45	0	2
Bergen	22. 03. 45	08. 05. 45	46	1
Totals:			409	503

Notes: Departure days and arrival days are not included.
Total number of ships attacked during all voyages: 4
Total number of ships sunk during all voyages: 2

The four commanders on the right are (*from left to right*) Günther Heydemann of U575, Horst Kessler of U704 and later of U985, Otto Tinschert of U267 and Friedrich Mumm of U594. Someone wrote the names on the back of the photo. There was also a Herbert Mumm of U4 and U236, who survived the war, and there was an Ernst Heydemann who went down with U268. On the left is Georg-Wilhelm Schulz, who commanded U64 and U124, and is seen here as Chief of the 6th U-boat Flotilla with the ruins of St Nazaire in the background.

U218 had been in dock in Brest for two months, where repairs were finished off with the installation of a schnorkel. Trials to test the new equipment had to be curtailed because the High Command demanded the boat be sent immediately into the D-Day invasion area and, as everything appeared to be functioning reasonably well, the men set off on 13 June 1944 without running a full set of tests. Leaving under cover of darkness with a small group of U-boats accompanied by three minesweepers, U218 had been at sea for a little more than an hour when the main rudder controls ceased to work, making it necessary to leave the escorts. The boat continued on its own, steered by the emergency manual rudder wheel in the rear torpedo compartment. After this, the electric motors stopped working as well and the following hours of daylight were devoted to saving electricity by lying on the seabed. The boat surfaced in darkness for twenty minutes to empty buckets and to throw garbage overboard. Then, while schnorkeling, U218 was detected by an aircraft and there was a small fire in the engine room, caused by fuel dripping from a joint to ignite when hitting the glowing hot exhaust pipe. The fire was put out with an extinguisher, but the turn of events left the men with an uneasy feeling due to having heard rather a lot of Asdic noises. These were often loud enough to be heard by all, not just by the man listening with the sound detector. The Hamburg-born Kptlt. Richard Becker, who had been in command since the boat's commissioning two years earlier and had led seven operational voyages, took several other breakdowns in his stride, making sure all possible manoeuvres were tried out in a dangerous but open part of the Atlantic before closing in on his objective in the English Channel to the south of Cornwall. Although an idyllic part of the world with pasties, serpentine and wonderful scenery, U218 never had an opportunity to enjoy this magic county from close quarters. The Channel there was thickly laced with prickly hostility.

It is hardly necessary to understand the technicalities of what happened next but the results from the disasters were horrifyingly astonishing and could well have led other boats to their deaths. Without much warning, the emergency valve opened, venting powerful diesel exhausts into the interior without there being an escape to the outside. The boat was submerged at schnorkeling depth. Those who could, immediately grabbed their escape apparatus (with its own air supply) while the boat surfaced for a thorough ventilation. The first time this happened was at around 04.00 hours, shortly before sunrise at that time of the year. The engineers worked feverishly on the problem, and it was shortly after midday when everything was ready for another trial. The decisive factor for surfacing in broad daylight appears to have been an acute shortage of electricity rather than testing the ventilation system. There were no problems with raising the schnorkel, but then the same irritating combination happened for a second time. As a result, the boat was forced to surface into a lively sea of Force 3 with brilliant visibility. Only five minutes were required to clear the air before settling down to schnorkel again. The first incident was probably caused by a valve having been jammed by a nearby depth charge, and the second incident could have been caused by too much water in the ducts, which the low pressure from

U217 of Type VIID with mineshafts aft of the conning tower. Each shaft could hold three ordinary moored mines, which were considerably larger than torpedo mines. They were jettisoned one at a time. This photo was taken during the commissioning ceremony on 31 January 1942 when the national flag was hoisted for the first time. In the foreground is a single 20mm anti-aircraft gun. The water is white because it is covered by ice and snow. The entire crew, under Kptlt. Kurt Reichenbach-Klinke, died near the Azores on 5 June 1943, after having taken part in three operational voyages.

Depth was controlled by these two hydroplane operators, who are holding on to firm handgrips for support in rough conditions. There is a large button under each palm working the electrical controls for going either up or down. If these fail, the men can stand up and manually turn the large wheels, which are connected to the hydroplanes by long shafts with flexible joints. Should both of these controls fail, then there was a third set, with the necessary dials, in a well by the hydroplanes in the bows and stern. The dials above their heads were for the helmsman, who sat facing forwards, at right angles to these two facing the side. The operators are obviously posing for the camera because the engine dial shows 'stop' and the large shallow-water depth gauge indicates the boat is on the surface.

In the German armed forces men were not allowed to collect money for any cause without the permission of a senior officer and games where money could be won were prohibited. This obviously shows a game of chance where toy money was used.

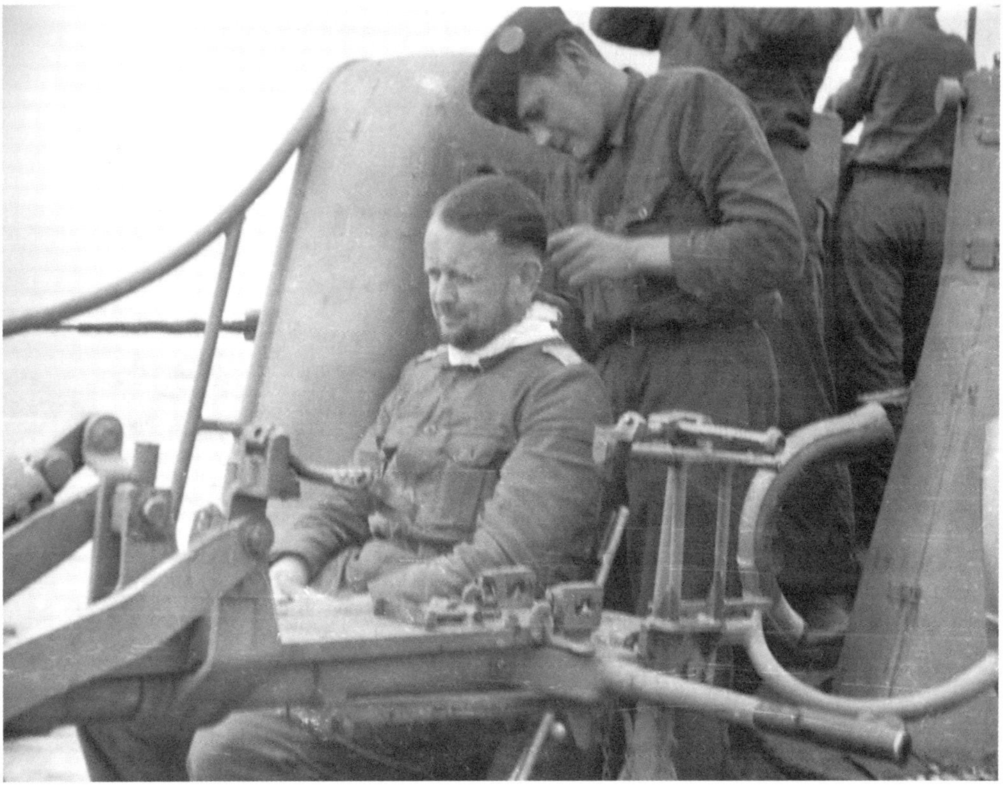

The Munich-born Wolf-Harro Stiebler, who commanded U8, U17, U21, U61 and U461, having his hair cut.

Dr Carla and Kptlt. Heinrich Bleichrodt. He was a Knight of the Iron Cross with Oakleaves, making him a significant celebrity, although here he is wearing only the Knight's Cross without the Oakleaves, thus dating this photo to the early part of the war. The star above the three sleeve rings indicates the seaman's division and the ribbon in the top buttonhole indicates an Iron Cross Second Class. His wife Carla, an accomplished gynaecologist, was on board the overcrowded escort ship *Weichsel* during the evacuation to the west, where she helped another officer's wife to give birth.

earlier engine damage could not blow out. Whatever, the consequences were most dramatic and could well have led to less experienced crews embarking on their final plunge into the depths.

The presence of the concentrated exhaust gases resulted in several men having to be withdrawn from normal duties and by midday two-thirds were out of action, complaining of strong headaches, stomach pains, feeling sick and with the strong urge to vomit. Although the rest were also complaining of strong headaches, they did find enough people to man the essential positions while extra personal breathing devices for absorbing carbon dioxide were distributed. The men had also guessed they were suffering from carbon monoxide poisoning rather than having inhaled too much 'stale' air (carbon dioxide). Attempts to get the men back on their feet took a while. This must be taken literally because several had their balance affected and were seen crawling about on all fours. To make this serious handicap even worse, two days later, at almost the same time of 04.00 hours in the morning, someone up in the air detected the extended schnorkel head to unleash sixty hours' worth of depth charging. At the end of this ordeal the crew considered themselves to be fully operational again, although several men still reported light headaches. It is a wonder they all remained sane and alive.

Chapter 12

Shortly Before the End – Beaten but Not Completely Dead

THE END OF U1023 IN THE ENGLISH CHANNEL

Kptlt. Heinrich Schroeteler, commanding U1023, left Bergen in Norway towards the end of March 1945 without specific orders, leaving him free to make on-the-spot decisions once he reached the south of Ireland. Nobody knew for certain what was going on, and circumstances were changing rapidly, and in any case, it was going to take a while before he reached his action area. He was driving an ordinary, old-fashioned Type VIIC-41 with slight modifications made later during the war, whence the '41' addition. The logbook of this last journey was destroyed before he surrendered and most of the following details were researched over a three-year period by Otto Krempl, who was on board during that last voyage. This material was later further enlarged by Günther Becks, who was a watch officer in the boat, and more information was added from notes by Heinrich Schroeteler.

* * *

The situation in Norway was already becoming critical by the time U1023 was being made ready in Bergen for what was to be our one and only operational mission. A deep diving test down to 184 metres confirmed our new boat was in no condition for withstanding such depths and a nearby depth charge could easily have sunk us. Serious quantities of water came squirting in through various 'buttonholes' and once back, nearer the surface, to dry out, the engineer officer announced there was no way we were going any deeper than 50 metres. The commander did not argue. We were pleased with him. He had joined us only a few days before we set out from Kiel, bringing with him ample schnorkeling experience. He knew what he was doing and was the sort of chap you could trust. He used a simple technique for running with diesel engines underwater. When using the schnorkel, we stopped every fifteen minutes or so to listen for any approaching sounds. The schnorkel was lowered once these had reached volume level three on the sound detector. Then we remained silent until the intruder had passed, and the volume had become less than three again. When schnorkeling, there seems to be no way anyone can avoid diesel engines from sucking air out of the interior once the head valve was shut by waves. The air intake pipe did not connect directly to the engine but allowed the engine room to be filled with fresh air and the diesels sucked the air they needed from this space. The closing of this head valve always resulted in most uncomfortable low pressure when it dipped below the surface of the water, but this was something we slowly got used to. It happened often enough for us not to take much notice of the pressure differences, but there were times when it got exceptionally uncomfortable and occasionally even painful. Then the entire crew collapsed due to the low pressure. Much later, after our surrender, when we had got accustomed to this torture, we even used it to annoy some offensive ex-enemy guards.

Female naval auxiliaries were an essential part of naval operations. They had a similar rank structure to the men, with similar uniforms but in a slightly different style. The lightning flash used by radio operators can be seen above the rank chevron on the right.

Two of them were throwing their weight around the engine room, pointing their guns at us, when someone unobtrusively closed the air vent while the diesels were generating electricity, creating the awful vacuum to torture everyone inside. Our men knew exactly how to react and how to adjust their ears, but the guards started to panic. They tried to get out but could not open the hatches. The lower pressure on the inside made it difficult to budge them – and the boat's own communication system had seen to it that all hatches were firmly locked shut. It may have been a stupid trick, but it worked and removed the obnoxious sods from the engine room. The people working there were always considerably worse off than the rest of us because they not only got a heavy dose of low pressure, but the fumes from the diesels had nowhere else to go, other than circulate around their space. Choking on exhaust fumes must have been pure hell.

Going back to the last war cruise, before these obnoxious characters came on board, we were on our way to Weymouth on England's south coast. Strangely, there was an almost total absence of depth charges. Not even one came close enough to say, 'that one was definitely aimed at us'. Asdic pings were also hardly heard and for much of the time we had the impression the English did not know we were intruding in their waters. It took more than three weeks to travel as far as south-west Ireland and from there the commander made for the Bristol Channel. Since no further orders were forthcoming, he continued to Land's End, sailed around the tip of Cornwall, and then headed east towards Portland. We had seen some action on the way, in addition to having practised a lot. Everything the old man could dream up to get us out of trouble was run through until we got the hang of it. It worked well, but Portland harbour was empty, so all we could do was run a lap of honour around the bay before leaving again. This took place on 4 May 1945, the same day as the German delegation led by Admiral von Friedeburg met Field Marshal Montgomery for signing the Instrument of Surrender. For some reason we had no knowledge of this. The radio was not terribly reliable and there were a number of interesting messages which did not get through. Perhaps one of the more exciting was a signal on 2 May from the U-boat Chief saying our commander, Heinrich Schroeteler, had been awarded the Knights Cross. We only heard about this later when we were already prisoners of war.

The crunch with this loss of radio contact came on 7 May, when we succeeded in sinking the Norwegian minesweeper *MYMS 382*. This turned out to be the last ship to be sunk by one of our old-fashioned types of U-boats. One of the small new electro boats of Type XXIII, U2336 (Kptlt. Emil Klusmeier), also with a broken radio, torpedoed two more ships an hour or so after we had fired ours. Following this, Schroeteler ejected the last acoustic T5 torpedo in deep water, to prevent the opposition from getting their hands on this new weapon.

It was 2 o'clock in the morning of 8 May, just past our lunch because we were on nightshift routine, when we received that by now famous order from the U-boat Chief, telling us the war was over. We were to surface, remain where we were and send a position report. We had now been submerged at our puny depth of less than 50 metres for several weeks. Schroeteler did not react to the order. Instead, he looked at it, giving us all time to think about our futures.

'We will continue schnorkeling towards Land's End,' was all he said at first. 'We are not handing this boat over to the Tommies with such a huge heap of rubbish,'

The pocket battleship (later reclassed as a heavy cruiser) *Admiral Scheer* after a bombing raid on Kiel shortly before the end of the war. (*Photo: Albert Nitzschke*)

he added. 'And we do not have to look like a load of criminals either.' Of course, through schnorkeling, we were unable to throw waste overboard and there was an awful load of rotting garbage onboard.

Everybody set about cleaning the interior and passing rubbish to the dustmen in the rear compartment, where it was ejected through the now empty torpedo tube. Then the commander told us all to shave, wash and put on some decent clothing. At the same time, he ordered naval items such as logs, coding machines and other secret gear to be taken to pieces to be made ready for throwing overboard. All of this had hardly been completed when some ships appeared to escort us back to Weymouth, near Portland Bill, where we had just come from. Once we had made fast there, a group of heavily armed German-speaking Poles came for an inspection and for creating some unpleasant exchanges. At a guess, these men had been sent to demoralize us, but we tried hard not to fall for their provocation.

Earlier, when the prize crew first came on board, they had been at sea for only two days, probably with a special order to find us. They looked tired and run down, with a definite air of bedragglement. Each man was carrying a machine pistol. We found their performance of pointing these at us amusing rather than a serious threat and wondered what they were trying to achieve. In contrast we looked clean and ready for anything and did not mind the arrogance they were pouring over us. We also noticed these men had come well armed but without food and we were not going to give them anything to eat. What was more, we still had a plentiful supply of everything and there was no need to economize on what could well be our last meal aboard U1023. The cook produced a wonderful meat stew with all the trimmings, even cream to go with tinned fruit for afters. Our guards stood in silence watching us eat this rather scrumptious meal. We took advantage of the situation by eating more than normal. There was no point in economizing. Among us, it had been agreed we would not offer these intruders any food unless they begged for it and somehow their arrogance prevented them from doing so. It was a while before their lieutenant commander asked whether his men could also have some food. Schroeteler put on quite some act: 'But of course. Did you not bring any food with you?'

It was not long before attitudes changed, and the Tommies saw we had better food than they had seen for some time. Things became a little easier after that, but we still ended up as prisoners of war.

NO SPECIAL DIFFICULTIES – U990 (Kptlt. Hubert Nordheimer)

There is one further interesting paper in the U-boat Museum from U990, with Kptlt. Hubert Nordheimer saying the boat had not encountered any special difficulties. This was four months before the boat was sunk by aircraft near Trondheim in Norway and provides a fascinating insight into the mind patterns of U-boat commanders. On 30 January 1944 there is an innocuous and easily overlooked entry in the log. At 0135 hours Nordheimer wrote: 'Port diesel broken down. Trying to make repairs but one cylinder has seized up and needs to be isolated for the engine to continue running on the remaining five. Such bad luck, just as I am only a few hours from the convoy I am severely handicapped with a maximum speed of 14.5 knots.'

Klaus Kuka, illuminating this incredible event in Ernst Pfefferle's *Kammeraden zur See*, wrote several bunks were empty, despite the crew not having slept properly for several days. Disregarding their tiredness, the technical division was at work finding their last strength for repairing the broken port diesel. One cylinder was cracked, and the engine valves were threatening to seize solid. To prevent this, earlier there were two men constantly lubricating the offending machinery, which was hot enough for oil to evaporate almost instantly, giving off a hideous smell with horrid smoke. Flesh would have burned, had the men touched the metal. Yet in the beginning, the main objective was not to lose time to reach an expected convoy, and this makeshift oiling procedure continued for some while. It was awful in the engine room, with men hardly able to breathe due to the poignant fumes. U990 continued until the following morning when the diesel protested by bursting into flames. The men in the engine room, looking most despondent, were now black, covered in a hideous oily layer. Despite their incredible effort of putting out the fire, they had not managed to get the boat any nearer to the convoy and the engineer officer decided it was necessary to exchange several valves. The men set about this cumbersome task in what had become exceedingly hostile conditions with a highly active radar detector, meaning every anti-aircraft gun had to be manned. Some of the engine cracks were wide enough for a match to pass through. Not ideal at the best of times.

Atlantic House, part of the 5th U-boat Flotilla Headquarters, after several bombs had landed nearby. The building also housed a medical unit, first aid detachments, several doctors and a camouflage unit. This flotilla under Karl-Heinz Moehle was especially dedicated to supplying everything boats needed for their first operational voyage, and thus many boats passed through it. This building was in Kiel near the waterfront inside the guarded naval base.

From the middle of the war onwards bombing damage became a serious problem, with many buildings destroyed. The Anglo-American air forces tended to concentrate on civilian housing rather than industrial and military targets, which meant there was comparatively little inconvenience to naval operations. The people who suffered most were those in isolated concentration and prison camps when their in-city secret supply and support systems were destroyed.

The cause of this trouble had started long ago and should have been dealt with before the boat put to sea, but the brief turn-round time in port did not always allow for making all the necessary repairs. Machinery is good when it is working and often produces considerable output in difficult situations, but there are times when it just gives up. It stops and cannot be made to go any further. Men on the other hand have a more flexible constitution with a different type of drive, meaning they can force themselves considerably further than their normal limitations. The momentous effort by the engineering division was worth it. Not only did U990 reach the anticipated convoy, but it sank a destroyer with its first torpedo, an acoustic one. The enormous sacrifices made by the men were quickly forgotten as the men looked forwards, towards further successes. From post-war records we know the torpedo from U990, aimed at Convoy JW56B, did not sink anything on 31 January 1944 but Nordheimer did sink the British destroyer HMS *Mahratta* on 25 February, while it was escorting Convoy JW57.

The report attached to the official log was concluded with the words: 'the voyage did not offer any special difficulties'.

THE SHORT LIFE OF U3010
(Oblt.z.S. Eberhard Ebert and later Fregkpt. Erich Topp)

U3010 was a new large ocean-going electro-boat of Type XXI. The following is based on an account written by Lt.z.S. Karl Hesse and sent to the German U-boat Museum by Hans Ney. It also contains information from Erich Topp.

* * *

In July 1944 a large proportion of the crew for U1201 was sent by train to the Deschimag AG Weser shipyard in Bremen, to take part in the assembly of this huge, prefabricated new electro-boat. Training courses and other activities were laid on as well, and after air raids, the men were also asked to help with rescue work in the city. Commissioned on 11 November 1944, the new U3010 did not get far. During its first voyage, on a brilliantly sunny day, the boat encountered an aircraft near Roter Sand Lighthouse, close to the spot where U31 (Kptlt. Hans Habekost) became the first U-boat to be sunk by a lone aircraft. This time, though, U3010 was hit not by the aircraft but by its own crew. Unable to close the correct vents and work the clutches in the right order, they caused one diesel engine to seize up, and the other one stopped working in sympathy. Instead of going on to Kiel, the boat had to be towed back for replacement engines, which took about four weeks and involved cutting a huge hole in the hull to get the damaged engines out and drop the new ones in.

Once again, the men set out along the river Weser to the Elbe estuary, where they cruised along the Kaiser-Wilhelm-Canal to Kiel. Since it was Christmas Eve, there was an appropriately decorated fir tree on the tiny bridge. U3010 had only just arrived in the naval harbour when two ships, the freighter *Hamburg* and the passenger ship *Deutschland*, arrived with refugees from the east. Like the Dunkirk evacuations, Germany was moving people out of the clasp of the advancing armies, only these numbers involved millions of civilians rather than the thousands of soldiers as at Dunkirk. Since some of U3010's crew had their homes in areas now under evacuation, men were given permission to help with the disembarkation, in the hope of also finding information about their families. All of them came back disheartened by the bleak news, without having met anyone who could provide specific details.

Following this, U3010 ended up in the far eastern Baltic for training and for the first-time lookouts spotted Allied aircraft in what had previously been a safe area, out of reach of British and American forces. The Russians were closing in fast, and Western bombers, flying from recently captured bases on the European continent, could now reach East Prussia. In March 1945 the first commander of U3010, Oblt.z.S. Eberhard Ebert, was replaced by Fregkpt. Erich Topp, who arrived with an order to take fifty Hitler Youth boys to the West. Accommodating so many was not easy, even in such a huge boat as this new type. To make matters worse, the boys were not among the most cooperative, making the crew feel pleased when they were set ashore in Travemünde. Whilst on passage, the boat

Access became a real problem even after minor air raids because rubble made it difficult to pass along roads. In this case it would be relatively easy to clear a path through the debris, but roads were often littered with huge chunks of masonry and heavy iron girders, meaning it took a while to clear. Since this rubble was tossed there by bomb explosions, it was often hard to walk over because the footings were nowhere near firm and an especially hard balancing act was called for when having to wobble over loose rubble.

had suffered more serious damage from running onto a mine, meaning it was necessary for the boat to go into a dry dock. This made it possible to see there was no way it was going to go any further in the immediate future. It did not take long before the men received the order to leave the boat where it was and make their way to Kiel to take over U2513. This journey of about 50 miles was completed on the back of lorries. It wasn't comfortable but the men got there fairly quickly. U3010 was then scuttled shortly before British troops arrived. The men who remained to do this, having found enough civilian clothing to make themselves look like foreign workers, filled their kitbags with provisions and made a determined effort to get home before becoming prisoners of war, but there were many with similar ideas and the density of British troops sweeping towards the Baltic was overwhelming. The majority were caught and taken to isolated fields where, despite being guarded by men with machine guns, some still disappeared to make their own way home, avoiding roadblocks that filtered many men into prisons-cum-concentration camps for several years after the fighting had stopped.

THE END OF U2533
(Oblt.z.S. Horst Günther)

The following is based on a report by Maschinen~gefreiter Alfred Philipp, with additional information from Horst Günther.

* * *

It was the end of April 1945 when more than thirty modern electric Type XXI boats were assembled to the east of the main channel in the approaches to Travemünde. Not much was happening, and each boat still had an almost complete crew on board. One day a ship came alongside and with the aid of a crane delivered one depth charge with instructions on how to scuttle the boat with it. The plan was to leave it in the central control room with its detonator set to explode at some shallow depth once the boat was sinking. Five men were detailed to remain in the boat to deal with this while the rest were taken off to join a group defending the U-boat School in Neustadt, not too far away.

> The order to scuttle came during the morning of 3 May 1945. By the time we sorted ourselves out, to be ready to start this sinking procedure, we saw other boats were already going down. A short while after they had vanished from sight, the depth charge

Personal luggage from U249 (Kptlt.d.R Uwe Kock) and U1023 (Kptlt. Heinrich Andreas Schroeteler) after their arrival in Loch Ryan (Scotland). U1023 was then used to tour British coastal towns so people could see the inside of a German U-boat. (d.R means der Reserve.)

detonations sent huge fountains of water high into the air. Unfortunately, many of the rubber dinghies with paddling men were still too close, meaning everybody got exceedingly wet and a few had to swim for it. In view of this danger, we decided not to risk our lives so late in a war which could not last much longer. We removed the detonator from the depth charge before flooding the tanks to sink our boat.

Our skeleton crew was just clear of the sinking site when a small motor minesweeper appeared with an admiral on board, who asked where we were going. All we answered was, 'Home.' He immediately cancelled this before ordering us to hand over our towing ropes, to be taken to a freighter further out at sea. This ship was already full of soldiers without hardly any space below and not much room on deck. I did not have any luggage and most of the others also came with nothing other than what they were wearing. It was difficult to find a spot where we could park ourselves. The ship had not gone terribly far when I saw several men with pistols threatening the captain. Sailors standing nearby said they had orders to take everybody to Norway to continue the war from there. It looked as if many men did not agree and wanted to force the captain to turn back, to remain in Germany. I was still digesting this debacle when several large fighter aircraft attacked with rockets, resulting in many dead and wounded on or near the bridge.

Another ship came alongside, but there was no longer any opportunity for removing the wounded or the dead. This ship eventually took several survivors, including myself, to Flensburg on the German-Danish border, which we reached the following day. We were in good company there. Although we did not know it at the time, the U-boat Chief and Supreme Commander in Chief of the Navy, Karl Dönitz, who became Hitler's successor, had set up his headquarters in the Sports Hall of the Naval Academy in Mürwik, not far from Flensburg. From there the German delegation drove south, to the outskirts of Hamburg, to meet a British escort for taking them to Field Marshal Montgomery's headquarters to sign the Instrument of Surrender. [Hamburg, in the meantime, had surrendered to prevent further bloodshed by declaring itself to be an 'open' city.]

Long before the war, the German Navy had given a standing order that an enemy was allowed to set foot on a warship only as a guest or as a prisoner. Ships were to be sunk instead of being surrendered. This order was emphasized again at the start of the war in September 1939. Since 1943 the action of scuttling ships was codenamed Regen~bogen (Rainbow), and the order was repeated in April 1945, before the Instrument of Surrender was signed. At that time millions of Germans were being evacuated from the east and although the German delegation asked for this to continue, the British forces could not agree. Rather than save people, thousands were forced back to harsh conditions and often prolonged deaths in the east. Human lives were very cheap at the time. To keep this flow of humanity moving, Grand Admiral Dönitz cancelled the scuttling order shortly before the Instrument of Surrender was signed, in the hope British forces would allow more refugees to come into what was becoming the Western Zone of Germany. The majority of men in the surviving ships did not agree, and a chaotic scuttling process did take place.

EASTER WEEKEND, 1945

U876 was a very-long-range Type IXD2, launched on the Leap Day of February 1944 at Deschimag AG Weser in Bremen and commissioned there by Kptlt. Rolf Bahn in May. This account is based on a report written in July 1945 by Gerhard Baumann, the second watch officer, and supplemented by information from Ursula von Friedeburg, Volkmar König, Korvkpt. Albert Nitzschke, Admiral a.D. Eberhard Godt, Hermann Patzke and several other veterans who were in Kiel at the end of the war.

* * *

The first members of U876's crew assembled in Bremen several months before the launch, to take part in the building instruction process. Arriving by train shortly after an air raid, they were horrified by the destruction between the main station and the shipyard. A good number volunteered to help with rescue and salvage work before immersing themselves in U-boat activities. (U-boat men were too valuable to be detailed for general air raid defence duties, where they could easily be injured, but they were allowed and even encouraged to help with humanitarian activities after the attack had stopped.) The British Prime Minister Winston Churchill stated U-boats were the one weapon which seriously worried him, yet despite his fear, he did very little to curtail their production. Not a single U-boat was even seriously damaged by bombs until almost the end of the war. As a result, during the first years of war, men reacted most lethargically to the many bomb warnings. They entered shelters not because they feared for their own lives but due to strict standing orders to do so as soon as sirens sounded. Now, in 1944, with the crew's arrival in Bremen, things were changing. Instead of concentrating on terror attacks against civilians, the Anglo-American air forces were also focused on heavy industrial and other naval targets.

Over the Easter weekend of 1945, U876 was lying at Deutsche Werke in Kiel, waiting as first in the queue for a move into dry dock. The men obviously knew Anglo-American forces were moving rapidly in from the west. Since a good number of the crew had come from the east, they were more concerned with the advancing Russian armies. The official news and word-of-mouth reports about the horrific treatment of soldiers and civilians in the east was most worrying. Not all experienced this vengeance: Inge Putzki, who was about 10 years old at this time, had nothing but praise for the Russians who helped her on more than one occasion. She also scorned some Germans for taking advantage of her status as an orphan by sexually abusing her.

The engineer officer of U876 was most depressed, constantly reproaching himself for not having brought his family with him to Bremen, and he was not the only one. There were others in similar positions. A few men had had both the foresight and the opportunity to bring their families to join them in the west, but others had not heard from home for a long time. Sadly, some of these men never heard from their families again and can only assume they died somehow on their trek to the west. The regular post service had broken down more than six months earlier, with only occasional dribbles of letters coming through. Many men did not know for certain how or where their loved ones died and never found out, even after the war, when the International Red Cross put in such a tremendous effort to help them. There were too many bodies and too few survivors. Retreating forces used frozen corpses for filling deep shell holes in roads. Life was horrific, often with only a little food and inadequate clothing for living out in the open without heating for days on end.

After lunch on Good Friday, with the entire shipyard working a Sunday routine, we got ready to travel over to the other side of the water, to the main naval base. Kiel had grown up on the western side of a huge saltwater inlet, similar to Norwegian fiords, while heavy shipyards were established on farm land on the opposite shore. By the time the German Nation was founded in 1871, there were three big yards there, each with its own housing for workers. The naval base, also with large apartment blocks nearby, was about 3km away, straight across the water from where U876 was moored. The Easter holiday of 1945 was enhanced by brilliant sunshine, powerful enough to suggest we were in for a good weekend, had these idyllic expectations not been interrupted by a loud air raid warning wailing from sirens high on roof tops. Recently, it had been reasonably quiet in the skies. Our own most efficient public radio broadcasts often told us the direction in which approaching aircraft were heading while they were still half an hour or more away from us and thus slowing or increasing our speed for hurrying into shelters.

The boat's galley hatch, which served as the front door in port, had not only been closed but also locked with depth charge clips to prevent it jumping open if rattled by nearby bombs. This made it necessary to climb out the long way via the top of the conning tower, not the easiest of undertakings. Much of the machinery, including some of the ladders, had been removed for remedial work and workmen had left serious quantities of tools obstructing the narrow route. There were ammunition boxes and, strangely enough, sacks of potatoes, all confirming we were no parade boat. Having climbed up to the top, we had to avoid the starboard side. The new coat of paint applied that morning was still tacky. Clambering down the port side we met our postman coming in the opposite direction with a pile of letters, many of them for the commander.

The post had been disappointing recently, with many letters not getting past the incendiary bombs dropped on them. This time, however, we acquired a rich haul, including several for me from home. Looking at the envelopes I got a real deep-down shock, enough to make my head spin out of balance. I noticed immediately that one of them was stamped at the main post office in Gotenhafen near Danzig [now Gdynia and Gdansk], a considerable distance west from where we lived. I was too nervous to read the vital information and had to calm down first. Gosh, my father, mother and younger siblings had got away from the Russians and reached our grandfather a good distance further west, where there were still reasonable ship and train connections with Hamburg. It is difficult to describe how I felt. It was just wonderful. Ecstatic. They got through with their naked lives and whatever they could carry in a tremendous effort that must have cost them dearly, but they were alive despite having become people who own nothing. They were now homeless refugees, but they had avoided the torture from the Russians. I was wondering whether there would ever be a future opportunity for us to return to our homeland where my parents had lived all our lives. I did not tell anybody my good news, except that I mentioned it quietly to the commander, who was stupid enough to pass the details on to our engineer officer. His family had got lost in the east without him knowing what was happening to them or where they were. Pretty awful for him.

Life was as mundane as it could be. The engineers were busy working full shifts, but many seamen did not have a lot to do other than play cards or chat and there were not a lot of new topics to talk about. There came an opportunity to get together with some female naval information helpers. Known as Marine~nachrichten~helferinnen, many wore small badges with a lightning flash, so they became known as Blitz~mädchen, meaning lightning or flash girls, and they were trained at the Marine~nachrichten~helferinnen~ausbildungs~abteilung – all one word and obviously an educational establishment with extra wide doors to hold the name shield. The first meeting with these women went quite well, although not entirely without strict formality, which enabled us to go home before midnight. Getting up the following day was a bit of an anti-climax. It was dull with low clouds, suggesting we were in for a drastic change in the weather.

Early that morning the radio service came on air with the wonderful news of three refugee ships being due to arrive in Kiel, causing our engineer officer to head off immediately, with the hope of perhaps finding his wife. He came back at 7 o'clock in the evening most despondent. He did find a few people who knew her, but no one could say where she was or what had happened to her. Talk about seeing a depressed, worried and miserable man. We could only guess what was going through his mind. It must have been awful. There was no way he could muster the energy to join in with our festivities and he took to drinking too much. These worries from home were often dampened by the work in hand, but it was Easter. We did not have anything to do. The increasing pressure of foreign armies encroaching from east and west always produced the question for us whether there was anything we could do to help stem the flood. The only contribution we could make was to get our boat ready and go to sea, to help fight this war. This weird concept of fighting to the very end without an option to surrender was hardly recognized by anyone at the time and it was only much later that people realized our resistance had been pointless. The propaganda of the time must have been good and possibly hit so amazingly hard because the public radio service had risen in incredible quality with helpful advice, news and accurate local information. Of course, in the U-boat we also listened to the successful and incredibly horrible black propaganda from British sources.

It was still Easter when I experienced the first serious bombing raid since Christmas of more than three years earlier, when I was still a cadet aboard the destroyer *Paul Jakobi*, then moored in Wilhelmshaven. This time I ended up with a friend inside the huge bunker at the shipyard by Deutsche Werke. It was massive: big enough to hold U-boats for fitting out. It had huge steel doors and ample space for people. Not much was going on when we got there. Among this incredible monotony, we debated whether it might not be better if we were to return to our boat, but then our minds were made up for us. All hell broke loose, with a deafening thunder giving us the impression this was going to be the end of the world. The noise and the shaking were indescribable and the results, once we got out to see them, were almost beyond belief. Large ships had foundered, other lay in flames and several U-boats had been converted to heaps of tangled iron. Our boat had a huge crane lying across it and was covered in rubble, making it look like some horror scene in the cinema. It was not only Deutsche Werke which had been hit. Howaldtswerft, next door, also looked most precarious from a distance and a multitude of fires with offensive smoke indicated the bombers had also, once again, plastered the high-density housing areas in the town, on the opposite side of the water. Our future and our surroundings looked grim. Work with U876 had been progressing quite well, with our own technical division dealing with a lot of the work, but now the shipyard was cut off, without electricity, water or means for creating compressed air. Although the administration jumped to it very quickly, making every effort to have debris removed and repairable machinery salvaged, there was not a great deal they could shift with such huge mountains of rubble blocking progress. The capacity of all shipyards was severely reduced as their specialized heavy machinery was damaged and they had to concentrate on repairing this, rather than working on submarines.

The only plus point amid all this severe damage was the fact that the huge U-boat bunker had saved our lives, making us determined to get in there for future air raids. This was not as easy as it sounds because the main naval base, with the facilities we needed, was on the other side of the water and many of the ferries had been sunk as well. These were hardly comfortable, but they did not take long to get across and, unlike the roads, the water had not been made impassable by huge mounds of masonry blocking traffic. Pedestrians could clamber over wobbly substrata along streets with great difficulty, but the fire brigade had got to the stage where they often had to abandon their valuable equipment in the worst-hit areas. Therefore, many fire engines took bicycles along to help the men escape by carrying them over rubble and then turn to pedalling once they found open roads. These amazing guys worked in some incredible hot spots, closer to the front line than many soldiers.

This serious damage made it necessary to introduce drastic changes in our repair plans. With so many boats damaged, the engineering leadership, still commanded by the man who helped to restart our U-boat programme in 1935, Konteradmiral (Ing.) Otto Thedsen, sent experts around to decide which boats might still get out to sea if they were to cannibalize working machinery from the more hopeless wrecks. The trouble here was only the very worst off were prepared to accept their boats had had it, and those in the badly hit boats were not always prepared to let others dismantle their machinery. Apparently, this got bad enough for competing crews to point guns at each other.

Luckily, being in the seaman division, I was not directly involved with this acquisition of spare parts as we approached our Second Black Day. The Anglo-Americans were probably of the opinion they had already won the war as they were pushing further east across Germany at an unbelievable speed. [These words, written in July 1945, provide an incredible insight into the minds of the people of that time. They were written as private notes by a man who did not want to forget the unbelievable experiences he had witnessed. They were not coloured with official propaganda, and he was not duty bound to support any regime.] During the afternoon of that Second Black Day,

I had crossed over to the other side of the water to visit flotilla headquarters. When an air raid warning sounded shortly after 9 o'clock in the evening, I went into the Scharnhorst Bunker by the 5th U-boat Flotilla, which was responsible for kitting out new boats going to the front for the first time. When I arrived, the bunker was already over full, bursting at the seams, with the ventilation system apparently off. The air was terribly stuffy. All seats were occupied, so there was no alternative to being squeezed into a tight corner standing up. This was at least better than having nothing to lean on. For a while it looked as if the approaching aircraft were making for another target, perhaps for Hamburg. We had remained hopeful inside the bunker for about 45 minutes before I heard the order to close the doors. The aircraft, having avoided several other lucrative targets, were now close enough to make us their obvious destination. The first detonations were muffled, a long way off, sounding as if they were aimed at the shipyards on the eastern shore, rather than at our naval base in the west. It was not long before they came closer, shaking the whole bunker while unleashing an incredible din while the air got stuffier and stuffier. Standing in my difficult position I could hardly breathe but had no alternative to remaining there in the horrid atmosphere until around 11pm, when the all-clear sounded. Breathing fresh air again was a real treat, although the surroundings looked dreadful with huge flames everywhere. Everything – iron ships, the water, houses – was burning, lighting up the dark sky with a weird flickering red illumination. A most incredible sight, had it not been so dreadful. This time it did appear as if the main target was the other side, leaving the naval base and its surroundings in comparative peace. Most houses had five floors with an attic at the top and cellars underneath. Those living nearer the top stored a variety of different heating coals in the attic and when this caught fire, it burned not only with incredible luminosity but also giving off a terrific heat, much hotter than burning timbers. It was a massive inferno. Many of the houses had been built before fire-retarding treatments were applied to timber and, to make matters worse, a good number of these apartment blocks also had internal wooden staircases. [Fire escapes were not yet mandatory in building regulations.] The fire brigade got over being trapped inside such possible death traps by hanging ladders in windows or on balconies on the outside of buildings and got up as quickly or even faster than a person climbing the stairs. With so many wildfires nearby, no one needed torches to see what was happening. The ceilings of many cellars had been reinforced with old railway tracks, turning them into admirable air raid shelters from where some escaped with their bare lives. There were enough corpses on the roads, making cycling impossible and indicating many had been overcome by the flames and intense smoke.

The following morning, when we crossed the water, we were met with a sorrowful sight. The command tower of the pocket battleship-cum-heavy cruiser *Admiral Scheer*, which had dominated the Naval Arsenal, was missing, making me wonder whether it had sailed during the night. When we got closer there was even more of a shock. The piers had gone as well, and the buildings were damaged. The whole area was dominated by heaps, no mountains would be a better term, of rubble, with masses of bomb craters making it look like some foreign landscape. *Admiral Scheer* had not left during the night. The ship was lying upside down on the bed of the dock basin.

I got even more of a shock when I saw our boat was still there, where it had been for some time, only now it was covered with rubble and debris, and nothing looked straight anymore. There were also casualties: some men of the skeleton crews had left their positions to escape but those who did, did not seem to have got very far. They were mown down by intense showers of splinters. All this looked awful and the stories of those who survived would have been hard to believe, had one not witnessed the utter destruction. Men killed half in and half out of hatches made it difficult for others to use the same exit and, of course, the killing was indiscriminate and untidy, not like carcasses one sees in butcher shops. These bodies were bleeding, and a lot of body parts detached themselves when one tried to move them. The workshop by the side of our boat was no longer there, or perhaps it would be better to say it had been converted to a heap of rubble, with a lot of it lying on top of our ship.

Despite the incredible destruction, we still set about cleaning up our U876. Removing the rubble was a good deal easier than dealing with what looked like dense layers of dust, and by the late afternoon it looked quite respectable again. As second watch officer, it was my duty to go back to the naval dockyard to report our damage and losses. This was not the easiest job because there were rather a lot of damaged boats in Kiel. Atlantic House, home of the 5th U-boat Flotilla, was in a manic state, over full with people, all having come for the same reason as myself. At least the building was still standing, although it had received quite a few knocks. Food was also in short supply under these conditions, and many of the messes were no longer functioning, either because there was no fuel to cook with, or the cooks were not available (a polite way of saying they were dead or injured) or there was no food. So, returning to our boat with still reasonable provisions on board, I was surprised it had been moved to lie next to the old cruiser *Emden*, one of the first new warships to have been built after the end of the First World War. I wondered who had thought of this ludicrous idea of mooring a submarine by its side. This new location did not look good at all. First, lying by the side of a juicy target like a cruiser did not feel safe. No one in an aircraft would notice its inferior armament and the airmen would not know it was obsolete. There was also another tall crane nearby. We had already had a smaller crane come crashing down on our decks and this big one could distort the superstructure. Did they have to put the boat in such a vulnerable position? At this critical stage, someone pointed out how the first naval casualties of the Second World War were caused by a British bomber crashing on top of *Emden* in Wilhelmshaven on the day after war had been declared. Now, would we become the last casualties of the war?

We all turned in that night with mixed feelings, without needing an alarm clock to wake us. A violent and exceedingly close detonation turfed us out of our bunks. Earlier in the war, we would have been accommodated in places with superior facilities but now our boat provided all we needed, and it felt safer than being on land. After all, we were in shallow water, protected by a thick iron pressure hull. Those on duty and awake confirmed there had been no air raid warning. At a guess one of the bombs which had fallen earlier with an exceptionally slow fuse went off all on its own. The guard on the outside told us he had not heard aircraft and there had been no warning before this terrific blast. One wonders why the Anglo-American air forces dropped so many dud bombs which kept disposal men fully occupied for many years after the war.

There was considerable debate about the suitability of our berth with so many juicy targets still standing to attract more bombs. In the end, after a lot of arguments, a tug turned up to move us out of what we thought was a danger area. Apart from several pieces of non-functioning machinery, we were in a not-too-bad condition and the cannibalization process of very badly damaged boats started again. In a way it was madness to think about going to war during this late stage, but we did not know the navy had almost run out of lubricating oil, fuel, torpedoes and everything else one needs to go to war. With the incessant hammering from above, we were prepared to do anything we could to ease the country's destruction. Our main problem was that although the 5th U-boat Flotilla was still working better than could be expected, there was an acute shortage of everything and many small items from cooking pots and crockery to binoculars were in short supply. We even considered borrowing items from the Hitler Youth. One has to admire these young lads, how determined they were in helping and dealing with quite incredible jobs. The shortage of everything made everybody think of somewhere other than official channels to acquire things from. Seriously damaged boats were detailed to pass everything they had to those who needed it, but you try telling that to the men inside those wrecks. They were still obstinate, with a strong determination to set out again, and they were not willing to hand over any of their valuable resources. It occurred to more than one person how there was rather a lot of oil and fuel inside the wrecks and the water was not terribly deep. You could get down to them with a heavy diver's belt and some submarine escape apparatus as air supply, but the navy was one step ahead of us with these thoughts. The wrecks had already been earmarked for official use and officialdom had made it illegal for us to search for our own fuel.

HOW WE BECAME PRISONERS OF WAR

What follows is based on an account by Karl Heinz Hartwig (watch officer in U2324), plus information from Ernst Pfefferle and men who were in Norway at the end of the war.

* * *

The space inside these tiny new electro U-boats was too small for loading torpedoes and the two they could carry had to be pushed in backwards through the exit doors. As compensation, the boats were fast. Fast enough underwater to outrun almost every surface hunter. The big problem arose when it was attacked by aircraft while on the surface, but it did not have to spend a great deal of time looking at the sky. It operated totally submerged, raising a schnorkel or air mast only when running the diesel engines to fill the batteries. U2324 patrolled the British east coast with a broken radio for much of April 1945. Therefore, when approaching the home base in Norway, the commander,

Kptlt. Konstantin von Rappard, had no knowledge of the Instrument of Surrender having been signed four days earlier. The return to port had been dictated by a shortage of fuel and provisions and the almost new batteries were also at an end. 'We spent a lot of time filling them but did not get much out of them again.' They had been put together with improvised war materials, where poor quality substitutes had to make do and technical help was now urgently required.

The crew had been submerged for a complete month in their exceedingly cramped quarters, not even surfacing for recharging the batteries, and engineers had dealt with a serious fire in the engine compartment while below the waves. Life had definitely not been easy and the fiord leading to Stavanger was approached with great caution at periscope depth. The men were fully aware there could be both aircraft and submarines waiting for them. Surfacing well inside the fiord, they were greeted with magnificent May sunshine, while a party-like atmosphere of coming home flooded in with the fresh air. There was other traffic about as well and it was not long before a patrol boat crew told the men the surrender of German troops in Norway was taking place that very day. British forces were expected any moment.

> Germany was dead. That could not be. There was no German state any longer. We were now slaves of foreign powers. This was unbelievable after all we had sacrificed. Every one of us had been looking forward to a happy peace and now we were all standing there with tears in our eyes. The English were on their way, so we had been told. Despite this chillingly awful situation everybody seemed to agree they were not going to get us. Should we sink our own boat? No. Once over the shock, we were filled with a powerful fury, and many talked about topping up with fuel and food before leaving again. Yes. That seemed to be the best logical solution, but where were we going to go from here?
>
> After having made fast in town, we were told Hitler had died in action while defending Berlin and Grand Admiral Dönitz, our U-boat Chief, was now Head of State. He had given new orders not to sink our own ships. The Allies threatened severe punishments for anyone who disobeyed. Not knowing exactly what to do left us in a weird vacuum of nothing happening, and we decided to keep working to prevent men from thinking about other depressing matters. We needed time and more news to assess the situation properly before making plans. There were several incidents where things came to a head, causing officers to grab their pistols, but nothing serious ever developed. At first, I thought living on would now be pointless and wondered whether we should not follow Hitler's example of fighting until the bitter end.
>
> Logical thinking was somehow difficult and after some relaxation in fresh air we thought differently. Despite this disaster, there were still many Germans left alive. We knew Russian soldiers had been told even unborn children were guilty of having created this war and should be punished. But from whichever angle you looked at this dreadful end of war problem, it was all mad. Mad, mad and even madder. We had to change our thoughts. There were many Germans – women, children, thousands, if not millions, of orphans and our parents and other old people – who were all dependent

on us. Nobody else was going to look after them. Who was going to help them if we weren't there? We had made our military promise to obey and to serve, and we had done that, but now we also had the additional responsibility of looking after those who survived Germany's worst nightmare. We all knew our proud country had been destroyed and we must step forward to help in rebuilding the ruins and our lives.

After a while we hoisted our flags for the last time and then burned them. This was also our last parade, shortly before English forces arrived and immediately stormed over to occupy our boat. They fell over it like a bunch of vultures, searching for the little food on board, but there was not a lot to be had. The port's provisions store had already been empty when we arrived. In any case, dealing with the navy's tinned food was not terribly easy. None of it had labels. Instead, the tins were embossed with numbers, and one needed to have the appropriate list to know what these meant. There were cases of boats far from home finding the tinned bread had the wrong number and contained condensed milk instead. I had burned the last logbooks and destroyed anything of value that had once belonged to the navy. It was a weird sort of existence. Some people milling around ignored us while many more treated us badly. Nothing at that time could be classed as fair and correct. Life had become a painful struggle. During the evenings, our men were forced to sweep the streets with guns constantly pointing at them. They were beaten with rifle butts and even jabbed with bayonets for the smallest hesitation. Humiliation and ill-treatment were now part of everyday life. Later, we learned how our highest leaders were forced to dance naked with female naval assistants in front of British film cameras. It was all awful. It would appear this ill-treatment was not part of British naval policy. Wilhelm Foehner, who left a detailed account of how he and U218 surrendered in Norway, made a point of saying the crews from HMS *Norfolk* and her accompanying destroyers treated the Germans with the greatest respect, looking upon them as seamen rather than enemies. He wrote that they were always fair and correct towards the Germans. After the war, a high-ranking British naval officer also wrote a long letter of apology to Ursula von Friedeburg, the widow of the Admiral who had been Chief of the U-boat administration division, saying the Royal Navy was just as horrified as the Germans when they learned about some of the atrocities committed by non-naval personnel.

The army of occupation had not been there for long when something most peculiar happened. The barracks in the naval base were being filled with women, many of them still delightful young girls, who had sympathized with our troops and had now come to marry them to return with us to Germany. Some must have lied about their age because they did not look old enough to marry. As a result, quite a few weddings took place in these horrific circumstances. These girls did not have a future in Norway without us being there to support them, and their situation in Germany was going to be even worse, but they did not know that and could not have guessed it. Germany was no longer a country of wine and honey: it could now offer them only hunger, deprivation and misery, and could not even provide them with a decent home. The space allowance for the homeless was just two square metres and children did not count – they had to be accommodated in the same space as their mother, if they had one still alive. Life in Germany was going to be hell, and it was awful to think how dreadfully these girls were being treated by their own families and neighbours.

Early on 27 May 1945 a flotilla of eight U-boats left Stavanger for England, sailing via Scapa Flow, where we spent one night. Scapa Flow: what an experience. This is where the Kaiser's high seas fleet was scuttled after the First World War to prevent the ships falling into Allied hands. When we arrived, we realized where we were, but we were too tired to think about mounting any similar protests. After leaving the Orkney Islands, U2324 endured a hefty storm where everybody went below except for myself and men from the prize crew. The boat had been rigged to prevent it from diving and there was not a lot to do until early one morning when we ran into Loch Ryan. By that time, we had got to know the prize crew. All of them were long-serving naval men, real seadogs, with whom we got on famously. They had been embarrassed by their own side looting from Germans, saying those characters were not real sailors but 'heroes' who did not contribute a great deal to their own side either. Now, when the war was over, our English friends came prepared to have a good time by bringing a good supply of delicacies, which they shared with us. It seemed weird. We were eating English food. Only a few weeks ago we would have been shooting at each other and now we were the best of friends. There were only a few exceptions when we were mistreated by sea-going men; for most of the time the Royal Navy treated us with respect and even reverence. One had to look out for desk warriors, and we met more of them when we arrived at Stranraer in Scotland. These awful characters had grown fat on the war, sucking the best they could get from their surroundings without doing anything seriously dangerous themselves.

Kptlt. Heinrich Schonder, a Knight of the Iron Cross, who went down with U200 in June 1943. The other two men are wearing lifejackets, which could be inflated by blowing into them. Some were also fitted with automatic inflation cylinders.

Chapter 13

Not Everybody Went to Sea

WORKING DURING THE WAR

A Second World War rule-of-thumb suggested about ten land-based support workers were required for every sailor at sea. Now, imagine the size of the force needed to keep U-boats in the Atlantic, and then remember there were other ships in the German Navy, and it was also necessary to defend the European coast from the Arctic to the eastern Mediterranean. This enormous wartime administration was created by trawling through the civil service for experienced officials to fill essential vacancies. As a result, Alfred Kroschel was called up as late as August 1940, at the ripe old age of 33, after Britain had refused to discuss several international peace initiatives. His son Wolfram left some interesting information in the German U-boat Museum, saying the few included photos of his father were originally part of an album his mother, Anna, had presented to him. They lived in Riesa, to the northwest of Dresden, and only a short distance further away from Meissen, home of the famous porcelain. This became the Russian Zone, or East Germany, after the war, where it was against the law to own photos of German soldiers in uniform. As a result, these valuable memories had to be destroyed or hidden away. Anna Kroschel died in 1961 and five years later Alfred himself was laid to rest in the same grave. After 1989, when the Russian yoke had been lifted and the Iron Curtain had been torn down, Wolfram decided to complete his mother's ambition of finishing that photo album for his father. In doing so, he produced a stunning piece of history.

Alfred Kroschel shortly after he had been conscripted into the navy.

Alfred Kroschel, who became a modest naval clerk, was remarkable because he was one of those unsung heroes one never hears about. Despite working in a mundane job, he was one of the few who officially became prisoners of war not once but twice during the same conflict. To be precise, he became a prisoner of war four times and when he

Alfred Kroschel after he had been promoted to Ober~maat (petty officer), enjoying his taste for cigars.

was eventually allowed to return home in November 1947, he had not seen his family for four years. This was an enormous sacrifice during the immediate post-war years when essential manpower to rebuild lives and homes would have made a considerable difference to ordinary people, struggling to survive under a cruel new order.

His strange new naval existence started for Alfred after he completed his initial military training. Basic survival instruction was given to all soldiers, no matter where they were destined for, and recruits generally wore a plain field grey uniform during this period. Specialized naval training was already under pressure, being unable to provide the necessary establishments to house the vast numbers being shunted through it. As a result, many men found themselves being moved to foreign countries, especially Holland and Belgium. Despite this search for suitable establishments, accommodation was not always ideal and transport to get there often left a lot to be desired as well. Alfred was lucky in being moved to Antwerp in a normal passenger train, but many men were moved in goods wagons, where they were lucky if they were also provided with a smoky stove and some coal during cold winters. In summer they just sweated in the heat. These military trains did not have priority over the existing railway system, which meant they were often shunted onto sidings to give way to more important timetabled traffic. Travelling was indeed a daunting experience for everyone.

After his naval training, Alfred found himself appointed to the role of official registrar within the headquarters of the 1st U-boat Flotilla in Kiel. He was sworn-in and told he was not allowed to talk about his work, nor disclose the information he was going to record. Any breach of confidentiality would not only put him in serious trouble with military authorities but could also influence his civil service pension after the war. This was nothing terribly new for him. Civilian registrars were also not allowed to disclose the information they

Harro Esmarch was important enough to have a small room-cum-office inside a concrete bunker, where he could work without interruption. Many war correspondents were given officer ranks, but the medal ribbons and his age suggest Esmarch earned his rank as Kapitän~leutnant.

An obviously posed picture with what looks like an administration petty officer (without swordknot) dealing with a considerable amount of money in the pay office.

recorded. Personal details for individuals or for next-of-kin were excluded when written on official forms. Alfred had hardly settled into his new position when, three months later, the entire outfit was moved to Brest in France. His work must have been appreciated. He was not only awarded the War Service Cross (Kriegs~verdienst~kreuz), but shortly before becoming a prisoner of war for the first time, he was promoted to warrant officer with swordknot. This serious advancement was not an entirely happy occasion. At around the same time he had to digest demoralizing news about his brother Friedrich, who had been listed as missing on the Eastern Front, where he had been fighting against Russian troops. Perhaps he was one of the lucky ones who died quickly, rather than being tortured by war to die a painfully slow end. So far, the authorities had been generous enough to allow Alfred regular home visits. Early in the war he was even seconded to his local church in Riesa to help with some voluntary work for four weeks, but all such luxuries had now come to a shattering halt. Compassion had to be thrown out of the window. He became a prisoner-of-war, to be kept in a cage behind barbed wire.

After D-Day, Brest was one of the first German Atlantic bases to be overrun by the advancing Allied armies and in September 1944 Alfred ended up as a prisoner of war with the Americans, who held on to him for only two months before shunting him into a prisoner exchange. This sounded good until Alfred realized the swap had been made with the city of Lorient. This major U-boat base had been surrounded by Allied armies, leaving no way out or in, and the overpowering Allies saw no reason for losing lives by

A medical warrant officer with swordknot. His rank can be determined by the elaborate shoulder strap, which is just visible.

attacking the heavily defended garrison. So, for the Germans it was a case of surviving in a besieged base, not only suffering attacks from the outside but also enduring shortages and deprivation within. Yet despite the difficulties, the Germans survived there for more than half a year, until the end of the war in May 1945. The suffering continued when the war ended and Alfred became a French prisoner of war. He was not repatriated with his family until later. [The first Instrument of Surrender was signed on 4 May 1945.] Returning home, he found himself under the harshest of hostile regimes in the Russian Zone, where humiliation was part of daily life and people did not have a great deal of freedom. He remained a prisoner of the East German regime until his death.

At around the same time, some two-and-a-half years after the end of the war, Friedrich Kiemle, who held a similar rank to Alfred, returned to his wife in Hamburg from incarceration first in Lorient and later elsewhere as a prisoner of war. The first question he was often asked when reporting for work was what rank he had held during the war. A warrant officer with swordknot was considered to high-ranking enough to be given the dirtiest of jobs within the post-war deprivation. If it was hard going for Friedrich in the British Zone, then Alfred, in the Russian Zone, must have had a terrible time.

Alfred and Friedrich were lucky inasmuch that they at least came home again. Kptlt. Wolfgang Hegewald, commander of U671, had lost his life in the English Channel, to the south of Beachy Head, between Eastbourne and Brighton. He had spent some of his last home leave in Hamburg with his fiancée, Ilse Zörnig, and went back to sea not knowing

The trouble with being stationed in a front-line, onshore workplace was the masses of funerals one was obliged to attend, and some men were called upon rather frequently to help. It was especially hard going when one knew the person inside the coffin.

he had made her pregnant. He never got to know his son. Wolfgang's mother did not consider Ilse a worthy daughter-in-law and did not provide much support. It had already been suggested Ilse should work for her as housemaid to learn how to look after a much superior future husband. Ilse did not accept and brought her son up on her own, but she did make use of the U-boats' legal powers for using her husband's name to become Mrs Hegewald and for the boy to have the same name as his father. The post-war years were difficult in Hamburg. There was hardly any living space, very little food, and shortages were everywhere. Yet they did survive. Sadly, Wolfgang killed himself a few years after I had got know him.

These days one can understand and come to terms with people like Hegewald being killed while doing their duty, but there were a significant number of others who were put to death by their own side for some insignificant wrongdoing. Heinrich Walle published a substantial article in *Auftauchen* (the journal of the German Submariners' Association (Verband Deutscher Ubootfahrer), no. 282, March/April 2020) about the execution of Oskar Kusch, who was shot by firing squad on 12 May 1944. He was not the only one. There were others and many more who suffered from what Ajax Bleichrodt (a Knight of the Iron Cross with Oakleaves and commander of U48, U67 and U109) called a total disregard of natural human failings. Men were punished for not having had the right experiences for their jobs, while any personal failings were often not even considered by those who controlled the 'master race'. Things were not much different in England, where children were punished by being beaten with canes because their teachers had not taught them properly.

Alfred Kroschel took this photograph in France, probably near Brest, where temporary graves proliferated in many available spaces.

By contrast, German festivities were considerably more formal with plenty of opportunities to practise saluting. This social occasion in Brest (France), which Alfred Kroschel attended, had a dramatic backdrop showing the Naval Memorial near Kiel with the inscription 'Always remember: Attack – Go to it – Sink It!'. It is interesting to note in both English and German this could mean sink the enemy or sink yourself. Often one found the lower ranks at one end of the room with an officers' table at the top end.

THE PoW LEAFLET

This is a translation of a leaflet handed to prisoners-of-war who had served in U-boats. This leaflet was written in German but has been translated back into English and therefore does not contain the original wording.

Leaflet for discharged German Prisoners of War
Official Notice
Issued by the Allied Military Authority

'We do not exterminate nations and we do not slaughter people.'
Winston Churchill, 18 January 1945

Germany has been destroyed and militarily, politically and socially beaten. The evidence for this is in front of your eyes. The armed forces no longer exist and there no longer is a German government. German families have been scattered by the wind. Your towns are in ruins. The railway system has been torn apart. Millions of your citizens are dead. Germans, you can thank the Führer for this gruesome greed. Millions have suffered because of his painful whip. To maintain decent living conditions in this world, the united nations* collected their strength to destroy the German tyranny. Some of you supported this German oppression while others allowed it to happen without protest and you are all guilty for everything that has happened. All of you will have to suffer for this. The pity and desperation that you now must carry into the future can only be blamed on you.

Germany will never conduct another war.

The defeat which Germany has suffered due to its own arrogance cannot ever be changed by military force. However, the political face of the world is going to change and the united military force, which has now won such a major victory over Germany, will prevent any German efforts to attempt another military attack. The German armaments industry has been destroyed and millions of German men have died. The united nations* will now still make a determined effort to be even more severe in destroying anything that has survived. Although the loss of life can be neutralized during the coming years by producing more children, the German industry will never again be allowed to create weapons for another war of aggression. Germany's position will never be changed with weapons by force. You can only hope that peaceful work will help to resurrect Germany again.

You will be discharged as prisoners of war to carry out essential work for maintaining life by creating food, clothing and accommodation. Germany has plundered the countries which it invaded and robbed those people of their means to survive. In Holland** thousands of people died of starvation. Now you Germans have got to deal with your own problems. The united nations* have no intention of allowing food for German consumption to be imported. All surpluses are going to be sent to

Europe's economy took a dramatic downward plunge once the war started, with many people finding themselves in dire financial situations. Some French bars, exemplified in the TV series *'Allo 'Allo!*, remained in business by having a high proportion of German guests and many soldiers enjoyed the superior hospitality these provided, together with excellent trimmings. In France it was easy to enjoy your tipple without being constantly reminded you were there to fight a war.

Kptlt. Wolfgang Hegewald, commander of U671, which was sunk in the English Channel to the south of Brighton. Six men were rescued by HMS *Wensleydale*.

the countries which Germany had occupied during the war. Your towns have been destroyed but much of your agricultural hinterland has been left without damage. The forced labour*** that was made to work in Germany is returning home to where it had come from. Therefore, there is now a desperate shortage of agricultural workers, and you are being discharged to help with this work. If you do not fulfil this objective with enthusiasm and energy, then your people are going to die from hunger during the coming winter.

Doing your duty

You must remain and work in the area where you are being sent to and anyone not complying with this will be severely dealt with by the military government. Anyone who does not work well and with diligence will be betraying Germany's future and will demonstrate that he is unworthy of the trust invested in him.

The united nations* do not wish to destroy Germany as a nation. Those who are guilty are going to be severely punished and the rest of the people will have to suffer by working hard in poor conditions. But with time Germany can be rebuilt so

Hermann Patzke of U377 came home from his prisoner-of-war camp in England with this magnificent picture painted by a friend. The reverse is even more interesting – it had been painted on a military canvas raincape.

that the nation will be able to, once again, contribute towards the progress made by civilization. This responsibility depends on you.

1. You will receive a Discharge Certificate and a Registration Form once you have registered.
2. You can keep your uniform, but you must give it a complete civilian character, which means you must remove all badges and military buttons. Items with a connection with the National Socialists have got to be handed in. You are allowed to keep medals, badges of honour and awards for long service, but you may not wear them.
3. A vehicle will take you to the main city in your area, where you must hand in your Registration Form to the Employment Exchange of the Military Government.
4. You will then be taken to the main centre of your local area, where you must report to the authorities to be given your ration cards.
5. Your local government will tell you where you must report for work.
6. People who are only provisionally discharged will not be allowed to return to their home area. They must work where the authorities direct them to. Anyone who leaves their work area without permission will be punished. You will also have to report regularly to the government of your work area.

Notes:

* This pamphlet was produced in May 1945, five months before the United Nations was founded on 28 October as an Intergovernmental Organization. Therefore, the phrase 'united nations' referred to in the leaflet does not warrant capital letters.

** Several visitors to the German U-boat Museum have pointed out that Germany continued to export food to Holland after the outbreak of the war, but the severe shortages there occurred because Britain prevented imports by sea. Ships making for Dutch ports were forced to discharge their cargo in the UK rather than in Holland.

*** Sefton Delmer, one of the leaders involved with black propaganda from the British Political Warfare Executive, wrote the following in his book *The Black Boomerang* (Secker & Warburg, London, 1962): 'I did not have any illusions that foreign workers in German-occupied countries would help the Allies with sabotage acts – contrary to the propaganda put out by my own department – I did not believe that the majority of foreign workers were "Press Ganged into Slave Labour". I looked upon them rather as willing collaborators, attracted to Germany by the good pay and good rations the astute Munitions Minister Speer was giving them.'

Several influential Germans have also pointed out the shortages of food in German prisoner-of-war and other concentration camps came about because the Anglo-American terror bombing campaign destroyed the framework which supplied food to these secret locations. Many of these camps were on the secret list, making it difficult or even impossible to help them once their supply chains had been destroyed by intensive terror bombing.

Many Germans do not agree with Winston Churchill's statement at the beginning of this leaflet, and many described how they had witnessed definite terror attacks aimed specifically at civilians in cities where there were no military or war supply targets.

RETURNING HOME BEFORE PORTS BECAME SERIOUS BOMBING TARGETS

Bands playing during arrivals and departures were later replaced by ambulances for taking off the wounded and when leaving many boats preferred to slip out quietly without advertising their intentions. The Korvetten~kapitän with the three broad sleeve rings is Hans Rösing, who became flag officer for U-boats West (France).

U-boat men could be cut off from any contact with the outside world for a long time, and so were always pleased when sacks of post were distributed on board. This is U71 probably in St Nazaire, although the boat also put into La Pallice on several occasions.

Several authors have claimed female auxiliaries were forced to attend welcoming parties for returning U-boats, but many veterans have said the opposite. Men and women were encouraged to take time off work for such occasions – always a welcome distraction from the daily humdrum life. Smelling men who had not washed properly for some time cannot have been too pleasant, even when they were celebrities. U-boat men had their own term for nurses, calling them 'carbolic girls' due to their strong smell of disinfectant. Many commanders took advantage of their status to kiss the welcoming girls, much to the disappointment of the men who paraded on deck. In the U-boat Museum and in Peter Tamm's collection there are more than a few photo albums with men having written comments like, 'What about us? Who will kiss us?' under such pictures.

A music band and a female naval auxiliary with the lightning flash badge greeting the 'Wild Moritz' after one of his supply missions. His nickname came from his full name of Georg von Wilamowitz-Moellendorf and he had already been a watch officer in four U-boats during the First World War, making him one of the oldest commanders.

Nurses with baskets of ripe strawberries greeting an incoming U-boat crew.

People were usually keen to get away from work for a short while to greet incoming boats and those on non-essential duties were encouraged to take time off for such occasions.

Chapter 14

Prisoners of War

THE END OF AN EXPERIENCED BOAT – U371

This account is based on a letter by Karl-Heinz Langohr of U371 and reports from Hermann Patzke of U377, Josef Ottersbach and Heinrich Mueller, who became prisoners of war in France shortly after D-Day and were subsequently taken to England.

* * *

U371 was a remarkable boat. It sailed on eighteen missions and attacked (and at least damaged) the same number of ships. When it was finally destroyed, Oblt.z.S. Horst-Arno Fenski had been in command for only one month, making him a relative newcomer with a quick end. 'We found ourselves surrounded by seven small warships with no alternative other than to surface and scuttle.' Fenski had been a watch officer in U752, commanded another successful boat, U410, for a year and was a Knight of the Iron Cross, but taking on so many hunters without air in the tanks and no electricity in the batteries gave him no alternative other than to save his crew.

> During the night of 4/5 May 1944, U371 had been lying on the bed of the Mediterranean for two days. Constantly bombarded with depth charges, suffering from an acute shortage of oxygen and with the batteries at an end, we had little choice. Yet giving up was most difficult as well. The muddy patch on which we had bottomed was now holding us fast, meaning the engineer officer and his team worked feverishly for more than thirty minutes before the boat started to rise. There was no way we could go on. We had neither electricity nor air. We had all been turned into motionless corpses that refused to die, and I did not regain my senses until I was in the water after the order 'Everybody out of the boat' had been given. The frightening thoughts, which had dominated our minds for some time, seemed to wash away as I found myself swimming under a brilliant starry sky. We knew we were in the Mediterranean, some 8 miles or so north of the African coast, near the edge of the Bay of Philippeville (now renamed Skikda) in northeast Algeria and it was not long before we were picked up.
>
> I ended up with some others in a French ship, to be taken ashore and imprisoned behind bamboo bars in a disused gun casemate of the old fort in Philippeville. The rest of the crew were taken by other ships to Algiers. The food we were given was awful, two slices of white bread with some fish soup, but this seems to have been the

same as was eaten by our French guards. They were not terribly happy. Groups of up to twenty often came to threaten us because they had lost almost forty of their comrades in our final battle. When we surfaced, a French ship started shooting at us while we were jumping overboard, infuriating Fenski, who then shot off the last acoustic torpedo. This was lying in its tube ready for discharge. The rabble of French- and Arabic-speaking men, whom we had almost got used to seeing regularly, was luckily under strict control of a French captain, who saved us from too much trouble with this bloodthirsty mob. We had been in the old fortress for about eight days when a well armed American escort arrived to take us away, but the French captain was most hesitant in handing us over without a direct order from his superiors. It seemed very much a case of the fort lying at the end of a long command chain, where those giving the orders were far enough away not to have any clues as to what was going on along the North African coast. Since the Americans seemed to have anticipated some trouble, they came well prepared and won the day by taking us to Algiers. The interrogation there lasted for five days and there was not a great deal to be said. The Ammies (Americans) knew more about our boat than us and all we had to do was to agree or disagree with them. Most of us did not say much. Even our refusal to answer their questions did not appear to upset them or bring reprisals.

Time is of little significance when you are locked in a cage, and I am not sure for how long we were there before being loaded into a Liberty Ship. This was not a terribly pleasant experience. We knew what was going on and thought the chances of reaching Gibraltar were pretty slim. Later we learned one of our pursuers was our sister boat U616 under Kptlt. Siegfried Koitschka. We were delighted he did not press home his attack. We had the impression the Ammies were somehow afraid of us, keeping us under constant armed guard. Looking back at this, it makes me wonder whether they had got to know about our intentions of capturing the ship on the high seas to take it, together with the guards, to one of our own French Biscay bases. Things never got so far, and our plans were more idle chatter than a serious plot. In any case, we revised our thoughts considerably when we heard about the D-Day invasion of Normandy.

On arrival in Norfolk [USA] we were disinfected the moment we stepped from the ship before being registered like criminals by having our fingerprints and photo taken. Following this, there came another thorough interrogation, but there was also a plus point: we were given complete sets of new clothing. Despite all this incredible officialdom, we were still guests of the United States Navy, where we were treated with respect and given good food. After a short stay in the reception camp, we were moved for two days in comfortable Pullman railway carriages to Camp McCain in Mississippi, where we no longer came under naval administration. Correct treatment was soon displaced by harsher army procedures, where it was terribly easy to end up being given only dry bread and water for thirty days with only one break in this diet once every six days, when a proper meal was served. There were some most prickly characters guarding us and almost every greeting by them started with a tight-fisted hard punch. Strangely enough, since the attack on Hitler during the autumn of 1944 we were prohibited from using the normal military salute. Instead, we had to use the Hitler salute with the outstretched arm. One of the awful punishments was to have to dig your own grave in the excruciating mid-American heat for ten hours or so. Then a match was dropped in, and the person had to fill the grave again. Pure sadism.

There was also work to be done such as mowing grass, cleaning dustbins and peeling potatoes; I ended up having to remove old worn-out soles from otherwise still good boots. This was quite a good job. My foreman was a helpful coloured man whom I pitied. He seemed to be worse off than us prisoners. He was not even allowed to drink from the same tap as white men, and I have no idea where or how he obtained a drink. We have been told often enough how Hitler supposedly refused to shake hands with [the athlete] Jesse Owens because he was black, but people usually forget to mention it was the Olympic Committee that prevented heads of state from congratulating athletes. Politicians were prohibited from taking any significant role in such a sporting occasion. What was more, we also learned the President of the United States refused to shake hands with his coloured athletes. None of them were invited to the White House with the white competitors.

We were forced to harvest peanuts and cotton, all back-breaking work in unusually hot and dry conditions for us Europeans. I ended up in three other camps; at one time working as a kitchen assistant where I managed to cheat the system by giving some extra food to old friends who had crossed my path again. This monotonous life went on and on until God knows what date. It was long after the end of the war when I was among some eight hundred men taken by ship along the American west coast, through the Panama Canal to hopefully be reunited with our families in Germany. We got as far as the Strait of Dover where we could see France on one side and the White Cliffs of Dover in England on the other. There the ship turned around to sail to Liverpool instead of going on to Germany. Arriving there was awful. We were shivering from the cold because there was nothing to burn for heating and, to make matters worse, we became aware of the civilian population living under similar conditions to us prisoners. They were desperately short of food and shivering as well. These were the poor victors of the war. I didn't see much of Liverpool, ending up in the small village of Killearn near Glasgow. This time I was all on my own, shunted to work on a farm without any barbed wire. No barbed wire was a magical experience. By this time, we all had got so used to it. It felt somewhat insecure to be without such restraints. The farmer and his family were very good, they allowed me to eat with them at the same table, they shared the little food they had, and we became best of friends. Of course, I worked hard for them as well.

It was the autumn of 1947 when my prisoner of war grading was reduced from black to grey and I was moved back to Germany, travelling by train to Harwich, from there by ferry to Hoek van Holland and then, again, by train to Germany where I was discharged. Although this process was controlled by German personnel, it was still pretty degrading. Anything of value was taken away from us, food was awful and the way we were treated was most depressing, but all this deprivation was forgotten once we got back home to our families.

Germany had changed considerably since the end of the war with millions of people living in the most cramped and horrifying conditions with little food or heating. What was more, millions of displaced people from the eastern provinces were also squeezed into the little available space as well. As a result, refugees became outcasts in the eyes of many. Most of us had no direct information about the suffering these displaced people had to endure, and the immediate post-war administration did not help in smoothing over the transition to the new order. Instead, the armies of occupation continued to destroy factories, harbour installations such as cranes, even high-water flood defences, and comparatively dry air raid shelters, where the homeless were sheltering, were still being destroyed after the war at an alarming rate. New plans with more promising possibilities were not injected into the economy until 1948, to prevent Western Germany opting to join the Communists in the east. At the same time, the use of what amounted to slave labour was replaced by a new and hopefully more stable currency.

RETURNING HOME AFTER THE WAR

What follows is based on notes made in 1947 by Josef Ottersbach of U778 (Kptlt. Ralf Jürs). Information from Helmut Wolff, contributed by Carl-Heinz Behnke, has also been used, along with anecdotes from other prisoners of war: Karl Prawitt, Volkmar Aussum, Heinrich Mueller and Karl Wahnig.

* * *

U778, a Type VIIC, had an interesting early history. The keel had been laid down in July 1942 at the naval dockyard in Wilhelmshaven, but the boat was not launched until 6 May 1944. The schnorkel was added even later, in January 1945, several months after the boat had been commissioned. Having left the 5th U-boat Flotilla in Kiel on 24 February 1945, the crew surrendered in Bergen, Norway, on 9 May 1945, after which U778 was one of the boats sunk by the Royal Navy during Operation Deadlight.

Movements of the crew of U778 after the war.

1945	
2 June	Left Bergen with a skeleton crew under supervision of the Royal Navy.
4 June	Arrived in the British anchorage Scapa Flow in the Orkney Islands.
6 June	Left Scapa Flow.
8 June	Arrived in Stranraer by Loch Ryan and left by train for London that same evening.
9 June	Arrived at Hampton Park in London.
14 June	Moved to Camp 196 South (Arbury Hall) near Nuneaton, Warwickshire.
22 June	Moved to Camp 196 North.
8 August	Moved to Camp 81 (Pingley Farm) at Brigg in Lincolnshire, near Scunthorpe.
1947	
12 June	Left Brigg to return to Germany.

On 12 June 1947, about two years after the end of the war, three other prisoners, myself and one English soldier as escort, were taken by Jeep to the railway station in Brigg, from where we travelled along a rather complicated route through London. We had a ride on the Underground before being taken by several trains to Bungay, west of Lowestoft, a journey lasting almost exactly 12 hours. A lorry was waiting for us at the station for transport to Camp 171, where our luggage was searched, but nothing was taken away from us. Following this we were given some tea while filling out a form with personal details before being marched off to get into the actual prisoner compound. I was most surprised to meet two old friends, Richard Dannehl and Erich Lehmann from my old U778, whom I had not seen for two years, and while looking around further came across several others whom I had known from the war. Many of the prisoners were ex-U-boat men but there were also others who had been brought to England after the end of the war.

The daily routine in this new camp was similar to what I had been used to. We were woken at 06.00 hours, and given half an hour to get dressed before assembling by the gate to march as a group to the dining hall. There we were given a ladle of porridge, some bread, a spoon of jam and some tea. Generally, the food was not bad and adequate in quantity, although compromises and rationing were still major issues outside the camp. There was a cinema and a library, we could play table tennis and had an adequate dose of lectures about how to behave in camp and what life was like back home. Each hut provided at least four people each day for general work in the camp and I had the luck to be detailed for cleaning the kitchen, where there were ample opportunities for appropriating left-over food. By this time, I had become friendly with Egon Janne from U907 (Oblt.z.S. Servais Cabolet), who had also surrendered with us in Bergen. Unexpectedly, several personal items, such as watch, photos, rings and a suitcase, which had been taken from me earlier, were now returned and we were provided with showers and hot water where we could also wash our clothes. Apart from this, there was not much else to do other than to lie in the warm sun and dream of better times. We discovered there was a small shop which issued a variety of items, but you had pay with money and we did not have any. Luckily a U-boat engineer officer, Oblt.z.S.(Ing.) Hans Kreuzburg, gave me enough to buy some cake, coffee, cocoa, paper for rolling your own cigarettes, eleven razor blades, some shoe cream, shampoo and forty cigarettes. Following this, the camp also issued us with various clothing items which we no longer had in our possession. There were more lectures, concerts, football matches and my fairly lazy life was only interrupted by having to be in the kitchen for cleaning from 09.00 to 10.30, which was not bad because there were often interesting leftovers and some more interesting foods which had not yet become leftovers, but we used our initiative to make sure these goodies should not go mouldy before being used.

On 25 June 1947 we had to report with all our luggage for another one of those irksome searches. Once again, I passed through without difficulties and nothing was taken away. Early the following day, we were provided with a powerful bean soup and given some food for the journey. Then there came yet another one of those searches.

God knows what the Tommies were looking for. The journey took us to Hull, where over a thousand assembled prisoners boarded one of the wartime victory steamers. The ship was basic in facilities, but each man was provided with a place to sleep and adequate blankets. Treatment aboard was not bad. Food was limited but varied. This was quite surprising since we knew there were considerable acute shortages for the ordinary working people in England. The civilian population was not provided with enough food, making it necessary for almost all to grow as much as they could on small allotment plots, which appeared to be everywhere where we passed. Many of these allotments had identical small, curved-roof huts made from corrugated iron, which had been air raid shelters in back gardens during the war. There were hardly any restrictions aboard the ship, leaving us free to wander on deck or just to lie in our own bunk with the blankets provided.

Being at sea again in a proper ship felt weird. It was even weirder to see the old *Elbe One* lightship guiding us into the river where a German pilot cutter from Cuxhaven came alongside. There was an ocean terminal for large passenger liners there, but our ship did not moor on its own. The tug *Alte Liebe*, named after the famous pier, came out to pull us alongside the quay. At the time, I did not know how difficult this was, especially when the powerful tide could play havoc with those who did not know its quirks. Stepping ashore on German soil added to the weird feeling deep inside me. On the one hand we were eager to get home but, on the other, many of us were apprehensive about what was going to happen next. It was only later, when talking to others who had not been prisoners in England, that we discovered those who happened to have been near home at the end of the war were considerably worse off than us in England. A train took us through Hamburg to another prisoner of war camp at Munsterlager, where we arrived shortly before 21.00 hours. Unfortunately, a large group of prisoners from the Russian Zone arrived shortly before us and it took a long time before we could all be processed. We were provided with food and other than delays there were hardly any humiliations or nasty practices. The general release process ran relatively smoothly, despite having to collect a multitude of papers. Progress through this transit camp was most irksome. Many of us were now eager to get on, but bureaucracy remained as a constant companion.

Again, things were not easy, as everything was heavily rationed but the men hardly starved. A few, who had come from Belgium and Holland, reported they had suffered considerable shortages. They had only a little food and they lived in the soft mud on which their tents or makeshift shelters had been pitched. Their food often came as one huge piece and had to be cut by the men themselves. They drew lots for the order in which a person could select which piece to take. The person doing the cutting always had to take the last piece, to make sure there was no favouritism, and each portion was of equal size. On the other end of the same scale, the men also heard from prisoners how an entire camp in England was punished by not being given any tea. Instead, the inmates had to drink coffee made from proper roasted beans. During those years coffee was the national drink for many throughout Germany and having to do without it was a common complaint from many.

Now, where this luxury came as a punishment, the men tried hard to offend the guards, to be given more coffee.

So far, the transport had been quite reasonable but now, for the journey to Köln (Cologne), the men were cramped into goods wagons. Again, they could hardly complain, as civilians travelling along similar routes travelled squashed together, standing in open coal wagons without a roof over their heads. These trains had come from the mining districts of the Ruhr, obviously bringing coal to the cities, and went back empty. People were allowed to travel inside them. Long after the war photos of these trains were published with captions saying they contained Jews on their way to concentration camps. People making these false claims also could not distinguish between refugees and 'hamsters' – people taking their belongings into the countryside in the hope of exchanging them for food on farms.

> For the last three hours or so we travelled with the additional luxury of having our goods wagons attached to a passenger train, which arrived in Köln-Deutz at seven o'clock in the evening. It was a wonderful feeling to see the twin spired cathedral from a long way off and even more thrilling to board a tram to take me home. It

Being at sea meant being squashed close to others and cut off from the world, without any news of what was happening at home. Once back in base there was nothing better than getting away from people and reading the newspapers, even if they were a few weeks old.

One of the officers from U17 performing the duck dance after having fallen into the water.

really was weird. I got back home without anyone knowing I was arriving, exactly five years to the day after I had left to go to war. In all this kerfuffle of going home, I lost touch with Egon Janne, who had given such incredible support during those difficult prisoner of war years and it was another forty years before we met again.

For much of the time as prisoners of war in England, Josef Ottersbach and many other Germans worked on farms. For their efforts they were paid 5 or 6 shillings per week in camp money, which had no value in outside shops. There were 12 pennies (abbreviated 'd') in a shilling and the price of 2/6 meant 2 shillings and 6 pence. There were 2 ha'pence (half-pennies) in a penny, and at that time farthings, or quarters of a penny, were still legal tender. There were 20 shillings in a pound.

Most of the following prices are in pennies.

Hair oil	2/9
Talcum powder	2/6
Toothbrush	1/6
Toothpaste	1/6
Skin cream	1/2
Shaving brush	9d
Shaving soap	7½d
Flints	6d
Sewing needles - one packet	5d
Writing paper (pad)	5d
Combs	4–10d
Envelope	4d
Shampoo	4d
Tin of shoe cream	4d
Vaseline	4d
Sewing thread	3½d
Shoelaces	3d
10 Razor blades	2½d
Wick	2d
Box of matches	1½d
Cigarette paper for rolling your own	1½d
Crayon	1½d
Pins (one packet)	1½d
Pencil	1d

For shoe repairs, it was necessary to visit a local cobbler, who charged 3/6 for replacing worn out soles but only 1/3 for replacing the heels only.

Chapter 15

Letters, News and the Radio

THE DREADED NEWS NO ONE WANTED

Thousands of people received a letter similar to this one. Many must have been copied from a standard template. The field post number M 42961 refers to the Headquarters of the 9th U-boat Flotilla in Brest (France) and this letter deals with the loss of U377 (Oblt.z.S. Gerhard Kluth).

* * *

Commanding Officer
Headquarters of M.42 961

Command Headquarters, 22 February 1944

Frau Hanni Mallmann,
Hamburg 22
Imstedt 29

Dear Mrs Mallmann,
The reason for writing to you today is most painful. For some time, we have been having serious fears about the boat on which your husband was serving. After the passing of a predetermined period of time, it is now certain the boat will not return. For this reason, the U-boat Command declared the boat to have been lost. As so often happens in this U-boat war, we have no idea what could have happened because each boat was totally alone at sea, without much contact to the outside world and we have no details. We do know the boat was operating in the North Atlantic, but we know nothing about what could have happened.

Dear Mrs Mallmann, I know this is the beginning of a long period of anxious waiting for you. Please be convinced that we will do everything we can to find out what has happened to our comrades, and everything will be done to keep you informed.

We are constantly in touch with the Red Cross and other military offices who might supply further information, and they will inform us of any news. In view of this, I would like to ask you most sincerely to trust us and not to make life more difficult for yourself with worry. Even if you don't hear much from us, we will not forget you. There is always the possibility that prisoner of war news will reach you quicker than any official channels, so if you do hear anything please get in touch with us right away. Of course, you will also be immediately informed if we get any more news.

Your husband's personal belongings, still in our base, will be looked after by an officer here and passed on to you in due course. To deal with this for a whole crew will involve some considerable work, so please be patient.

Any questions of any type which you may have should from now on be directed only to Command Post of Fieldpost Number M 42961. Of course, we are available to help you with any advice as far as we can.

While I am waiting for good news, I send you my best wishes.

Heil Hitler!

Yours sincerely

Heinrich Lehmann-Willenbrock (Signed by hand)

NOTICE FOR THE NEXT-OF-KIN OF MISSING SOLDIERS

This printed leaflet was sent to the next-of-kin of missing soldiers during spring 1944.

Notice for the Next-of-Kin of Missing Soldiers

Not only are our opponents using every opportunity to break the resilience and resistance of German people without regard to the suffering and worries they cause, but they are also making every effort to pull those people into their service.

This is done in various ways. Rumours are spread about soldiers having become prisoners of war and then women receive anonymous letters about their loved ones having been heard on the radio. Duplicated notes are sent as well with details and times of enemy broadcasts which these women should listen to.

These efforts have obviously been especially designed to create frightening confusion, to make people angry, to turn them against their own authorities. The broadcasts give the impression the general knowledge percolating through the community is far superior to what is known by our authorities and these broadcasts also suggest our own officialdom is not concerned about what is happening to our own soldiers.

Our offices are eager to learn what is going on and every effort is being made to obtain information about missing people. Constant efforts are being made to keep in touch with reliable international authorities, which pass on such information. Our own officials make every effort to pass on any news to the next-of-kin.

Authentic information about missing soldiers can be obtained from two sources:

1. Appropriate Command Centres dealing with reliable information about the death or capture of soldiers.
2. From letters written by missing soldiers in prisoner-of-war camps, where the next-of-kin can be certain the words were written by the person they know.

All other news, wherever it is coming from, is doubtful and can be seriously misleading. The next-of-kin of missing soldiers are therefore urgently urged to pass anything from other third parties on to the appropriate authority which is dealing with their missing

> soldier. This includes letters, notes and conversations, with names and addresses of where they have come from.
>
> This way the appropriate offices can check all information and reduce the suffering and anguish which our enemies are spreading in our communities. By doing this you will be providing the greatest service to our lost soldiers, and you are helping to stop the people in our communities who are working against us.

THE TELEGRAM

M42961 was the 9th U-boat Flotilla in Brest (France) and Werner Schünemann was the engineer officer of U606 under Oblt.z.S. Hans-Heinrich Döhler, who did not survive the sinking. In this account, the German umlaut has been written with an 'e' instead of the two dots over the letter, thus Schuenemann.

> Deutsche Reichspost Telegramm
> From the Field
>
> GEORG SCHUENEMANN LEOST MUENSTERWESTF
> JUST NOW THE RED CROSS REPORTED YOUR SON WERNER IS AN AMERICAN PRISONER MORE DETAILS TO FOLLOW IN A LETTER
> BEST WISHES CHIEF M42961

FOREIGN BROADCASTS

The following is an extract from Wolfgang Hirschfeld's (radio operator in U109) secret log, dated April 1942.

> During the evening, we are now listening to the BBC in the German language. It is strictly prohibited to listen to such broadcasts but in U-boats we can laugh about such orders. I am convinced the U-boat Chief, Admiral Dönitz, is also aware of this. The lies which the English are using to create uncertainty among us are childish. The most amusing is the so-called Secret Transmitter Number One. Once we are tuned in, even the commander of the U-boat comes to the radio room to listen. The transmission always starts with the same words, 'Attention. Attention. This is Gustav Siegfried One. The Chief is speaking.' He speaks with a distinct voice, like an old SA [Storm Trooper] leader. Then he complains about party officials and curses the SS. He never attacks or offends the Führer. Today he told us stories about how the Lord Mayor of Bremen extracts good looking Polish women from the fish factory to sexually abuse them in his cellar and the broadcast always ends in the same way by saying, 'Fellow citizens, do not allow this to happen anymore. Defend yourselves against the evil in our society.' The Chief insists he is broadcasting from a mobile radio station on

> the mainland, but I have friends in the B-Dienst (Radio Monitoring Service) who have confirmed radio direction finders have traced the source to southern England.

U-boat commander Thilo Bode of U858, who had been watch officer aboard U505 long before it was captured by American forces, became the English correspondent for *Süddeutsche Zeitung* in London after the war, when he started a study to find out what influence this British black propaganda had on German people. From notices in the German Submariners' Association magazine *Schaltung Küste*, I knew this study was being carried out in association with Munich University. Many years later, when I happened to be in that city, I made a point of cold calling on the University to find this material. A helpful librarian appeared to be keener than me in finding it and took me to a huge card index where we found a multitude of references. From there, the librarian then took me into a store full of papers. It was rather disappointing to find all these records from the card index were missing and I returned empty handed to my hotel. Thinking Thilo Bode had died, I was surprised to meet someone who knew him and discovered we had a mutual friend, who had since died. Thus, I managed to speak to him on the telephone. He told me the authorities had tried to interrupt his study – not the Germans, but the British seemed intent on withdrawing these details from the public gaze. Apparently not all the freedom which was poured over Europe by the D-Day invasion was as free as I had imagined.

For anyone searching for further information, there were several major British radio stations broadcasting black propaganda in German. The most significant ones were *Soldaten~sender Calais* and *Radio Atlantik*, which were laced with juicy misleading messages. For example, the radar foxer referred to as Aphrodite was known to have been highly ineffective and did not confuse Allied operators for long, but the radio made it seem as if this was highly effective and worried the Royal Navy. The recording studios were in a purpose-built building on the Woburn Abbey Estate in Milton Bryan, which is now used as a Scouts camp site headquarters. The radio transmitter, the so-called Radio Aspidistra, was located at King's Standing in the Ashdown Forest near Crowborough; it is now being used as training centre by the Sussex Police.

There are two books of special interest here, although both disappeared a long while ago. One is *The Black Boomerang* by Sefton Delmer (Secker & Warburg, London, 1962) and the other is *The Black Game* by Ellic Howe (Michael Joseph, London, 1982).

The two men on the right are wearing heavy rain gear while the man on the left is dressed for slightly less fierce weather with a coat and sou'wester.

A photo from a personal photo album on display at the International Maritime Museum in Hamburg.

Chapter 16

A Brief Chronology of Mid-war Events: Stepping, Sliding and then Cascading into Total Destruction

1940

winter–summer

Looking at European rather than British sources, it becomes apparent there were several international peace initiatives during the first ten months of the war. Britain's refusal to take part in any of these then led to a global conflict. It would be good to find further details of these initiatives, and why the elected British Government was keen on negotiating for peace but such plans were rejected by the small but powerful War Lobby.

1941

10 May The 'secret capture' of portable secrets from U110 by the Royal Navy. By this time Britain had several working Enigma machines and we do not know for certain what was captured from U110. A study dealing with the influence of coding material would be welcome, especially as Britain already had more than one coding machine.

27 May The battleship *Bismarck* was sunk. (Her consort, the heavy cruiser *Prinz Eugen*, put into the German base of Brest (France).)

June Nine of *Prinz Eugen* and *Bismarck*'s supply ships were sunk.
22 June Operation Barbarossa, the German attack on Russia. German military Intelligence discovered the joint Allied plan for Russia to invade and control western Europe as far as the North Sea. As a result, not knowing that both Britain and the United States were aware of this, Germany tried to enlist British help to prevent it. At the same time, Germany felt forced to launch a concerted military campaign for nipping the offensive in the bud.

July High frequency radio direction finders (H/F D/F, 'Huff Duff') went through their first sea trials and were installed in large numbers from October onwards. These direction finders could determine the direction from which even short radio signals were coming. U-boats searching for targets maintained radio silence and then sent a signal when they started an attack. Many radio operators had several signals waiting to be transmitted at the first opportunity after breaking radio silence. H/F D/F told the convoy when a U-boat approach was beginning and the direction it was coming from. U-boat attacks were never coordinated and each boat usually attacked on its own, with others remaining clear to prevent one from sinking another. By the end of 1941 Britain had the perfect submarine-

July 1941 continued

killing combination. First, radio intercepts made it possible to direct merchant ships away from U-boats or, at least, they could avoid the full force of any attack. Once an attack was starting, the convoy was able to determine the exact starting time and the direction it was coming from. As a result, the defences could be placed in the most effective area for radar to 'see' the approaching submarine. Once the attacking U-boat had been forced to dive, the defenders used Asdic to determine the correct position to drop depth charges. The results were shattering. At first Britain did not have enough submarine chasers to hunt their quarry to destruction. Instead, commanders were told to put U-boats down and then return to their protective position around the convoy to prevent other U-boats from bursting through gaps in the defences. The submerged speed of a U-boat was much too slow for keeping up with even the slowest convoys.

15 November The first purpose-built supply U-boat (U459 under Korvkpt. Georg von Wilamowitz-Moellendorf), necessary for far-off operations, was commissioned. So far, other large U-boats and surface ships had been used to help with the supply situation. Small, solid-bottomed boats for ferrying bulky items between submarines at sea and special cranes for lifting torpedoes were hardly ever supplied. A similar disadvantage occurred with the huge U-boat bunkers. These provided good cover in ports, but U-boats were not provided with adequate protection for getting in and out of these powerful bastions. As a result, a significant number of U-boats were lost in their home waters.

7 December Japanese forces attacked the United States naval base at Pearl Harbor early on this Sunday. Shortly afterwards, Germany and Italy declared war on the USA. The Intelligence information that made this attack possible was found by a boarding party from the German auxiliary cruiser *Atlantis* (Kpt.z.S. Bernhard Rogge) on 11 November of the previous year aboard the British freighter *Automedon*. Since this led directly to the Pearl Harbor attack, and the United States' entry into the war, this must rank as one of the key events of the time. Yet only a few historians have recognized this momentous event, and it seems only one book gives a detailed account: Eiji Seki, *Mrs Ferguson's Tea-set, Japan and the Second World War* (Global Oriental Ltd, Folkestone, 2007). From January 1942 onwards, many U-boats crossed the Atlantic with help from supply U-boats to operate in American coastal waters. At first, they were faced with little or no opposition, and as a result many ships, mainly petroleum tankers, were sunk. There is considerable evidence to suggest the attack on Pearl Harbor did not come as a surprise to the American High Command.

21 December Swordfish aircraft from the British escort carrier *Audacity* kept U-boats away from Convoy HX76 but eventually, on this day, U751 (Kptlt. Gerhard Bigalk) sank the *Audacity* during a fierce battle. Karl Dönitz, Commander-in-Chief for U-boats, declared: 'The risk of being sunk is greater than the possible success. The presence of aircraft makes wolfpack tactics impossible.' Escort carriers were hastily converted merchant ships with their superstructure removed and replaced by a flight deck. The first carriers did not have lifts and kept their aircraft in the open, where they were also serviced, often in appalling weather.

1942

1 February The new four-wheel Atlantic U-boat Enigma machine was made operational. This switch from the three-wheel version to the new four-wheel Enigma code machine made it impossible for Bletchley Park in England to decode operational radio signals. The blackout lasted until the end of the year, when one of these new devices was captured from U559 (Kptlt. Hans Heidtmann). Land-based and coastal naval units continued to use the three-wheel code writer.

6 July This day saw the first Leigh Light successes. U502 (Kptlt. Jürgen von Rosenstiel) became the first U-boat to be sunk by an aircraft using a Leigh Light. This was Wellington 'H' of 172 Squadron RAF piloted by the American W.B. Howell. There were no survivors from U502. Leigh Lights were searchlights fitted to aircraft; they were switched on when the aircraft was too close for radar contact, making it possible for the airmen to see their target during dark nights.

30 October One of the new four-wheel Enigma machines was captured from U559 (Kptlt. Hans Heidtmann) in the eastern Mediterranean. Lieutenant Anthony Fasson and Able Seaman Colin Grazier entered the sinking U-boat, while 15-year-old Galley Assistant Tommy Brown swam over from HMS *Petard* to help them. A small boat from HMS *Pakenham* came alongside to pick up this most valuable material. As a result of this incredible effort, Bletchley Park in England broke into the new four-wheel U-boat radio code, named Shark in England and Triton in Germany. Fasson and Grazier went down with U559, while Tommy Brown survived only to die a short time later in a house fire. Forty-three of U559's crew were rescued, while seven died. This must rank as one of the most significant events of the war.

End of the year Around this time there was another drastic change in U-boat operation areas. The majority of Atlantic U-boats vacated the eastern seaboard of the United States in favour of operating in the 'air gap' in mid-Atlantic, which could not yet be reached by land-based aircraft. Some long-distance boats operated in the Caribbean, on the Atlantic side of Gibraltar, in South American waters or in African waters, where there was less opposition. It did not take long before land-based aircraft reached the 'air gap' in the mid-Atlantic. (A good number of land-based aircraft were returning from patrols with unused armament, even where there had been engagements. Thus, their armaments were reduced, enabling the fitting of extra fuel tanks to give aircraft a longer range, allowing them to reach the 'air gap'.)

End of the year A new type of anti-convoy torpedo became operational towards the end of 1942. The first version was called Feder~apparat Torpedo, or FAT. Those who did not know its intricacies called it Flächen~absuchenden Torpedo (Spring Apparatus and Surface Searching). The Allies named it 'Curly'. It was aimed in a similar way to earlier torpedoes but travelled in a straight line for only a preadjusted distance before curling, looping or zigzagging within the convoy to hopefully hit some other ship if it missed its aimed-at target. Earlier torpedoes continued running on in a straight line beyond the merchant ships. This torpedo was later further developed into the Lagen~unabhängigen Torpedo (LUT) or Independent of Position Torpedo, which did not need to be precisely aimed at a specific target but just shot towards it.

1943

8 January The biggest convoy battle of the war started when the slow convoy SC122 with fifty-four ships was caught up by the faster HX229 with forty ships and they ran into the Jaguar Patrol Line. The significant point about this biggest convoy battle was that there had been around a hundred U-boats at sea for every day for six months before this massive clash took place. This shows U-boats were somehow kept away from targets at a time when the radio code could not be understood, and this significant point has been missed by many historians. A detailed study into how this was done would be most interesting.

30 January The Battle of Stalingrad ended when what remained of the German Army in Russia surrendered. This has often been cited as the turning point of the Second World War.

April There was a significant Atlantic convoy crossing early in April 1943 when the 'Crisis Convoy' HX231 crossed the Atlantic from Canada to the UK, while the escorts under Commander Peter Gretton drove away almost all the attacking U-boats to cross with minimal losses.

Black May May 1943 was significant because more than forty U-boats were sunk in that one month. Average monthly sinkings before this were less than twenty per month, and only six in January 1943.

23 May U752 (Kptlt. Karl-Ernst Schoeter) became the first U-boat to be sunk with rockets fired from a Swordfish aircraft piloted by Sub-Lieutenant H. Horrocks and a Martlet aircraft piloted by Sub-Lieutenant W.G. Bowles, both flown off HMS *Archer*. These anti-submarine rockets had been in use for only three weeks. (The commander of U752 should not be confused with Kptlt. Karl-Heinz Schröter, who commanded U1195 and U763, or with Horst von Schroeter of U123 and U2506.)

3 July U628 (Kptlt. Heinrich Hasenschar) probably became the first U-boat to be sunk with an ahead-throwing mortar of Type Hedgehog that had been fired from an aircraft piloted by Wing Commander Peter Cundy. These weapons exploded only on impact and, unlike depth charges, did not interrupt sonar operations. A single explosion was likely to sink a U-boat, killing all the crew in the process. An American version, called Mousetrap, also came into service. This weapon meant it was no longer necessary for the hunter to pass over the target when the U-boat had the opportunity of moving out of the attack zone at high speed.

10 August U84 (Kptlt. Horst Uphoff) became the first U-boat to be sunk by an acoustic torpedo of Type Fido, launched by Lieutenant William Felter, who had flown off the aircraft carrier USS *Core*.

3 September The Allies made a successful landing in Italy. The Italian leader, Benito Mussolini, had been killed a few months earlier on 25 July. Italian forces surrendered on 8 September.

September The Leuthen and Rossbach Patrol Lines were pitched against convoys. These boats were armed with new acoustic torpedoes of Type Zaun~könig (Wren) or T5, while each boat had also been fitted with heavier anti-aircraft guns. The plan was for U-boats to remain on the surface for a shoot-out with attacking aircraft. This became a significant and expensive defeat for Germany. Unknown to the Germans, only one in ten of these torpedoes actually worked.

16 October U470 (Oblt.z.S. Günther Grave) became one of the first boats to be sunk with the aid of sonar or sonobuoys, dropped from an aircraft flown by the Australian Wes Loney.

1944

13 March U575 (Oblt.z.S. Wolfgang Boehmer) became the second U-boat with a schnorkel to be sunk. The boat was detected by H/F D/F and then sonobuoys were used to find its position. Rockets fired from aircraft played an important role in the sinking. Schnorkels fitted to U-boats came into widespread use from May 1944 onwards.

6 June D-Day – the Allied invasion of Normandy.

6 August U736 (Oblt.z.S. Reinhard Reff) became the first U-boat to be sunk with an ahead-throwing mortar of Type Squid, launched from HMS *Loch Killin* (Lieutenant Commander S. Darling) after the range to the target had been located with Type 147B radar.

1945

4 May The Instrument of Surrender was signed by the German delegation at Field Marshal Montgomery's headquarters on the Lüneburger Heath to the south of Hamburg at 18.30 hours. It was later displayed in the Imperial War Museum in London.

Glossary

~ Long German compound nouns have been broken up by inserting a flowing hyphen or tilde (~) to make it easier for people with limited knowledge of the language. Words shown with a tilde in this book appear as one word in German.

GERMAN RANKS AND THEIR EQUIVALENTS

Commissioned officers:

Kapitän zur See (Kpt.z.S.)	Captain
Fregatten~kapitän (Fregkpt.)	Captain (junior)
Korvetten~kapitän (Korvkpt.)	Commander
Kapitän~leutnant (Kptlt.)	Lieutenant Commander
Ober~leutnant zur See (Oblt.z.S.)	Lieutenant (senior)
Leutnant zur See (Lt.z.S.)	Lieutenant (junior)

Warrant officers with swordknot (Portepee):

Ober~boots~mann	Chief Boatswain
Boots~mann	Boatswain

The now-famous swordknot, worn on swords and daggers. Tying these was difficult enough for the navy to lay on special instruction sessions.

Later in the war there was a more senior rank of Stabs~ober~boots~mann, where 'Boots' was often replaced by the man's trade. These men were also referred to by the general military term Feldwebel (Sergeant).

Petty officers without swordknot (Portepee):

Ober~maat	Chief Petty Officer
–maat	Petty Officer (where the man's trade was inserted instead of the dash).

Seamen:

Matrosen~haupt~gefreiter	Leading Seaman with 4.5 years of service
Matrosen~ober~gefreiter	Leading Seaman
Matrosen~gefreiter	Able Seaman
Matrose	Seaman

Kapitän (without 'zur See') was a Master Mariner or Captain in the merchant navy, or a person qualified to drive canal and river transport along the extensive inland waterways.

Alberich Skin: A rubber covering for U-boats to absorb Asdic impulses. A similar coating was also applied to schnorkel heads to help absorb radar impulses.

Asdic: An acoustic device for detecting submerged objects. Later known as sonar.

D-Day: The Allied invasion of the European continent in Normandy on 6 June 1944.

English: It was not until sometime after the war that the terms 'British' and 'UK' came into common European use. During the war everything from Britain came under the name English, and it is not uncommon to find descriptions such as 'English soldiers from Scotland wearing kilts'. This wartime flavour has been preserved throughout this book.

Hedgehog: An ahead-throwing mortar whose charges exploded only on impact with something solid.

H/F D/F: High frequency direction finder, known as Huff Duff, capable of detecting even short German signals and used for the defence of convoys. Mounted on escorts and some merchant ships. U-boats often observed radio silence until starting their attack, when details were sent back to base and to alert other boats in the area, thus H/F D/F indicated the start of an attack and at the same time told the convoy the direction it was coming from.

Ing. = Ingenieur: Engineer.

Kiel: Germany's main Baltic naval base.

Kriegsmarine: The German Navy from 1935 to 1945. The Navy usually referred to itself just as 'Marine', not 'Kriegsmarine'.

Leigh Light: A powerful searchlight attached to aircraft for locating U-boats at night, often after they had been detected by radar.

LI: Leitender Ingenieur = engineer officer. Not to be confused with a leading engineer, who tended to be a petty officer rather than a commissioned officer.

Mousetrap: An American version of Hedgehog but with the propelling explosive inside the projectile rather than in the thrower's frame.

Ober~steuer~mann: Small boats would have had a Steuer~mann but the lowest position in U-boats was always Ober~steuer~mann. Kriegsmarine dictionaries translate this into English as 'mate' or 'lieutenant' in French. In U-boats he was always a warrant officer with swordknot. Colloquially he was also called the Steuer~kerl, meaning Steuer~bloke or Steuer~chap. The man steering the rudders was called Ruder~gänger or Helmsman.

Schnorkel: An air pipe allowing diesel engines to run inside a submerged submarine. Called Schnorchel in German and Snort or Snorkel in America.

SMS: Seine Majestäts Schiff = HMS in English; used until the end of the First World War.

Sonobuoy or Sonarbuoy: A floating buoy which transmitted submerged noises to aircraft flying overhead.

Squid: A larger version of the Hedgehog fitted to the stern rather than the bows of ships. It hurled larger charges ahead of the ship and was controlled by an advanced firing system.

Wik: sandy bay.

Wilhelmshaven: Germany's main North Sea naval base.

WO: Wach~offizier = watch officer. Instead of a First Officer, small boats had watch officers. In U-boats there were usually three with the number of their position given first.

Translations in this book and in my previous publications derive from two German Naval Dictionaries both produced by the Supreme Naval Command for military circulation and printed by Bernard & Graefe Verlag in Berlin before the war. The translations in these dictionaries are sometimes different from modern naval terms.

Men who returned home long after the war found nature had made a concerted effort to hide the starkness of the ruins and some Nissen huts were surrounded by colourful gardens. Many were used for growing vegetables rather than flowers. Surprisingly enough, nature turned the bomb sites into havens for wildlife with a multitude of self-seeded plants everywhere, even high up in the ruins.

Appendix

A CORRECTION – THE BATTLE OF BRITAIN FABRICATION

After Lionel Leventhal of Arms & Armour Press had published my second book, *The German Navy in World War Two*, in 1979, I was told by several Germans that my details for the planned invasion of England were not correct. As a result, I spent a considerable time hunting for the original German papers but never found anything concrete about the by now famous Battle of Britain. It may be famous in Britain because much of the material was written in England for public consumption. It is not mentioned in German records, nor in British wartime accounts, and several early British books published during the war were changed after 1945 to include the term. One must assume this hype was nothing more than an illusion from the British War Lobby to drive on a population that was not too excited about launching into another war. So where did the plans which I helped to publicize in 1979 come from, at a time when the events were still deeply shrouded by the British Official Secrets Act?

It was towards the end of October 1939, shortly after U47 (Kptlt. Günther Prien) returned from sinking HMS *Royal Oak* in the British anchorage at Scapa Flow in the Orkney Islands, when it occurred to Grand Admiral Raeder, the Head of the German Navy, that one day he might be faced with an order to tackle an invasion of Britain. This was a subject he had not thought about until this period. Even after the war had been raging for two months, such an idea still seemed absurd, making him feel he would be ridiculed if he mentioned such thoughts to his staff. In view of this, he set up an almost private and highly secret group to investigate this question if the Navy were forced into such an impossible scenario by the Army or Air Force. There was already considerable friction between the navy and the air force. Two admirals, Otto Schniewind and Kurt Fricke, were given this task early in November 1939 with strict instructions not to discuss their findings with others. Schniewind, who joined the Navy in 1907, had been Chief of the Operations Department within the Naval War Staff and was Chief of Staff of this so-called See~kriegs~leitung. Fricke, who joined the Imperial Navy in 1910, was one step behind him in this promotion process. Both were, obviously, experienced men, having seen action during the First World War.

In his Memoirs, Raeder wrote:

> At first glance, the jump across the Channel, whose opposite shore could easily be seen from France in good weather, would seem far less dangerous than the Norwegian landings. But any experienced naval leader would know that just the opposite was

Günther Reeder (U7 and U214) with the navigator or Ober~steuer~mann Meinke from U214, who also acted as third watch officer. He is wearing a hat with a plain peak, while commissioned officers had a golden scallop as seen here. U-boats did not have a lower-ranking Steuer~mann, and the man steering the boat was called the Ruder~gänger (helmsman).

Communication with another ship at sea required a signalman to use either semaphore or morse. The grid to the right of the man is an air intake for the engine room. This shows U203 under Kptlt. Rolf Mützelburg, a Knight of the Iron Cross with Oakleaves, who died accidentally when his head hit the saddle tanks along the side of the boat after he had dived off the conning tower for a swim.

> true. A long and careful preparation was absolutely necessary. Such a landing would be extremely difficult, attended with the gravest risks, and such an operation should be regarded only as a last resort in case England could not be induced to negotiate for peace by any other means. A U-boat campaign would in all cases be far more practical.'

The report handed to Raeder by Schniewind and Fricke made the following points:

1. An invasion of England would require absolute mastery of both the sky and sea. So far, only part of the British fleet had been thrown into action at any one time and an invasion would certainly result in every available warship being brought into the sea crossing areas.

2. Such an invasion could not come as a surprise. Therefore, the opposition would take action to block the continental Channel ports the moment an invasion force started to form. There are only a few open landing beaches in southern England with deep water. Much of the coast consists of vertical cliffs made from chalk or soft sandstone, most precarious for climbing up, and the Thames Estuary and the Essex coast consists of a terrific sticky mud at low tide where it is easy to get stuck by sinking in. Since the shores of the English Channel are unsuitable for landing a large number of ships, it might be better to look for alternative landing areas with firm sand further north. [It may be interesting to add this was 'the secret' in the novel *Riddle of the Sands* by Erskine Childers (1903). Sadly, the film is nowhere near as good as the book.]
3. Preparing shipping for an invasive crossing would be exceedingly harmful to Germany's internal economy where a lot of heavy traffic used the extensive waterways. Therefore, it would be impractical to withdraw barges and tugs from these inland waters. In any case, many of these barges were highly unsuitable for crossing the open sea and could complete such a journey on only a few days each year when the weather and sea state were suitable. Such suitable occasions could not be predicted far in advance.
4. For an invasion fleet to cross the Channel it would be necessary to first remove large sections of the German mine barrier guarding the continental coast and then rearrange two such barriers on both sides of the invasion routes. Although this sounds simple, it is an immense task and the planning could not foresee any interruption by the large number of minelaying aircraft in England, which could play havoc with an invasion force, especially as it would be impossible to hide the preparations from English eyes. [The barges assembled in France and Belgium were collected from the German waterways because they were too dilapidated. Many of them did not have engines and therefore needed to be towed, and all of them could only get across the Channel in the most favourable weather, but they still became a powerful propaganda aid for the English War Lobby. Surely British Naval Intelligence must have recognized this?]
5. The secondary invasive move of bringing supplies across the Channel would be almost impossible to fulfil without harbours and their unloading installations. Those in existence would certainly be wrecked by English forces before Germany could reach them.

The vulnerability of this barge assembly in continental ports was emphasized early in September 1940 when British aircraft destroyed eighty tightly packed barges in one attack. At around the same time, attacks by minelaying aircraft became a worrying threat while Germany was creating a high water through-route along the French coast. These British activities made it clear the routes along the French coast would have to be swept clear of mines before anything of value ran along them. The original plan was to sail close

Harald Gelhaus commanding the training boat U143, a small coastal Type IID. The tops of these conning towers were exceedingly cramped, with hardly enough space for four lookouts with their duty officer, and it became even more awkward when the commander was up there as well. There was not even room for a sighting compass in the top left-hand corner. This folding version had to be raised above the wall and rotated at right angles before it could be used. There is a voice pipe down to the central control room behind the white cap. U143 was part of the 22nd U-boat Training Flotilla, whose escape from East Prussia is mentioned in Chapter 11. By that time Gelhaus had already earned himself a Knight's Cross while commanding the larger U107. After this he was moved to a land-based position.

to the coast at high tide, where shipping could be protected by land-based, rather than seagoing, heavy guns.

During the summer of 1940, when the war between Britain, France and Germany had been raging for almost a year, there were people in many countries who felt this ridiculous conflict was too detrimental for everybody. As a result, there were several international peace initiatives, but Britain refused to enter any negotiations. The word 'surrender' did not feature in these initiatives. No one was asked to surrender. It was a term used by the

British War Lobby to spur on their own population. There is enough evidence of there having been more people in Britain keen on ending the war rather than enriching it, but all these processes for peace failed. The British War Lobby was determined to continue with the war, expecting both Russian and American support. The last overtures for ending the war came on 19 July 1940 when an appeal for peace was broadcast. This was rejected an hour or so later by a civilian without any elected office in the British Government, but who was fluent in German. His name, Sefton Delmer, was hardly known, and he had never broadcast before, but the quick response would suggest the reply had to be made quickly to prevent any input from Parliament entering into peace negotiations. In his book (see below), I did not find any details about who authorized Delmer to reject this last peace initiative. Bearing in mind the Ultimatum to Germany to withdraw forces from Poland was hurriedly made mainly by a few men led by the Foreign Secretary Lord Halifax, it would seem the British War Lobby was powered by just a few exceedingly rich industrialists.

William Shirer, originally a journalist for the *Chicago Tribune* and reporter for the International News Service, also was the author of several classic books, including *The Rise and Fall of the Third Reich* (Secker & Warburg, London, 1960). He wrote how German leaders were shattered to find Britain had turned down another opportunity for peace and for building Europe rather than destroying it. Sefton Delmer, in his book *The Black Boomerang* (Secker & Warburg, London, 1962) admitted that making such a monumental decision without first consulting the government and the people caused widespread anger in Parliament. Perhaps this was one of the saddest periods in the history of mankind. It may have made the 'free' rich richer, but many millions died needlessly and often in horrendous conditions.

The museum boat U995 at Laboe near Kiel.

Index